THE MATHESON MONOGRAPHS

The principal objective of the Matheson Trust is to promote the study of comparative religion from the point of view of the underlying harmony of the great religious and philosophical traditions of the world. This objective is being pursued through such means as audio-visual media, the support and sponsorship of lecture series and conferences, the creation of a website, collaboration with film production companies and publishing companies as well as the Trust's own series of publications.

The Matheson Monographs will cover a wide range of themes within the field of comparative religion: scriptural exegesis in different religious traditions; the modalities of spiritual and contemplative life; in-depth mystical studies of particular religious traditions; broad comparative analyses taking in a series of religious forms; studies of traditional arts, crafts and cosmological sciences; and contemporary scholarly expositions of religious philosophy and metaphysics. The monographs will also comprise translations of both classical and contemporary texts as well as transcriptions of lectures by, and interviews with, spiritual and scholarly authorities from different religious and philosophical traditions.

SACRED ROYALTY

SACRED ROYALTY

From the Pharaoh to the
Most Christian King

Jean Hani

Translated by Gustavo Polit

THE MATHESON TRUST
For the Study of Comparative Religion

Originally published as:
La Royautée sacrée:
du pharaon au roi très chrétien
by Guy Trédaniel, Editeur, Paris, 1984.

This first English edition © The Matheson Trust, 2011

The Matheson Trust
PO Box 336
56 Gloucester Road
London SW7 4UB, UK

www.themathesontrust.org

ISBN: 978 1 908092 05 2 paper

British Library Cataloguing-in-Publication Data.
A catalogue record for this book is
available from the British Library

Cover: Portrait of Richard II, Westminster Abbey:
Wooden panel-painting, the earliest known portrait of
an English monarch, dating from the 1390s.

CONTENTS

INTRODUCTION

Several years ago, when we published our study *Les Métiers de Dieu*[1] as an introduction to a spirituality of the active life, we left out of our exposition the priesthood and the royalty, the loftiest reflections of the divine activities *ad extra*, which by their very importance exceeded the framework we proposed to ourselves, and we wrote that we awaited another occasion to speak of the problem of social organisation in order to set forth the bases of a sacred politics, several aspects of which we had quickly sketched in the conclusion of the book.

This occasion is presented to us by the spectacle offered today of the breaking up of our civil societies; a decomposition the beginnings of which date back distantly, to be sure, but which is accelerating dangerously. The extent is such that these societies seem to be afflicted by a galloping consumption, to counter which thinkers—theoreticians and inventors of systems of every kind—seek remedies in vain, since the source of the evil is situated at the level of the modern intelligence, which, in this domain as in others, operates according to ineffective governing principles that very few are prepared to renounce.

Thus, the most urgent task at the present time is the reformation of the intelligence. As others have said before more eloquently, it is a matter of reconstituting an intellectual elite in the true sense of the word; that is, capable of rejoining the spiritual principles of the Great Tradition which the West progressively betrayed five centuries ago, ever since the age of the celebrated Renaissance, which in reality was in many respects a true death.

---

1. An English version is available as *Divine Craftsmanship: Preliminaries to a Spirituality of Work* by Jean Hani, translated by John Champoux and Robert Procter, San Rafael, CA: Sophia Perennis, 2008.

The reconstitution of this intellectual elite must function not only in the higher spheres of religion—which, too, is in a sorry state—and philosophy in the true sense of the term, but in all domains that depend upon them, in particular that which immediately follows in order of precedence, for it governs the entire outward life of man: the social and political domain.

The problems posed within this area are difficult to broach today, for politics is an article of distrust, even contempt, on the part of our contemporaries who still retain sound ideas; an attitude which we easily understand when it is a question of political life as enacted before our eyes, and which offers us the scarcely uplifting spectacle of decadent regimes and heads of state who are often no more than wretches, dangerous megalomaniacs, or even agents of subversion—people who have scaled the heights of power and take advantage of a populace ironically declared to be sovereign, but which in reality is powerless in the face of peculations of every kind and stupefied by propaganda, like a crowd immersed in the burlesque of a carnival. The temptation is great, therefore, to lose interest in the political situation and retire within one's own ivory tower. But this is a position that must be surmounted, no matter how distasteful; for one who still has sound judgment and ideas, to abstain is to resign. Of course, we do not necessarily refer to an active engagement in civic life, which may not be one's vocation, and in our times is not without hazards. It seems to us that all men who are pained by an awareness of the present state of affairs can and must, if one may say so, seek the truth within the political domain also, and, having found it, teach others; for in the situation in which we find ourselves, this is the only way that things can change: by the minds of others changing for the better and recovering the right path.

It is to these men that this book is addressed in order to help them recover political truth to the extent we are able, because the first work of charity is that of the truth, on this plane as well as on all others. To tell the political truth, to repeat it gradually, is at a given moment perhaps the only thing possible, but it is of capital importance, for this truth, at first proceeding step by step, will end by shining forth with powerful brilliance and sweeping away all established errors.

This political truth is not to be invented; it has long existed, or rather, it has always existed. It has not varied, at least not in its foundations, but only in its modalities, for it is not the fruit of human opinions, but, on the contrary, springs from superhuman principles revealed to man by metaphysics and by religion. Immutable throughout the course of time, it is universal in its extension; it is found in one form or another in all peoples and at all times, "from the Pharaoh to the Most Christian King"[2], passing through India, China, Africa, etc; only the modern world, child of the modern West, is ignorant of it or fights it. This truth is part of that sacred and universal tradition to which we refer in all our studies, for it is also the sole irrecusable reference for whoever wishes to find the truth that transcends opinions.

This political truth is what is incarnated in sacred royalty, namely, in the religious conception of the temporal power, the only one capable of organising a fully normal society, that is, a civil society that, while assuring the necessary material well-being, serves the final destiny of man, which is spiritual, since this type of political power is subject to the impulsions of the Divine Spirit, the source of every norm of life in all domains.

A politics always depends upon a philosophy and, as Thucydides rightly saw, when principles get incarnated in a lasting institution, it will develop all their consequences. Bad politics is nothing other than bad philosophy erecting its principles into maxims of public law, so as in the end to lead the society to catastrophe. But it is not enough to say that, in order to have a good politics, it is necessary to have a good philosophy; it is necessary to specify further—since many of our contemporaries have forgotten this—that philosophy is not really good unless it depends upon metaphysics and is in perfect agreement with Revelation. Moreover, a philosophy so defined can be really and totally efficacious at the level of political action only if the rulers govern with their eyes fixed on the divine law, and with Divine

---

2. "The Most Christian King", *le roi très-chrétien*, was the traditional title of the king of France. See below p. 191.

aid, which requires that they be integrated in a spiritual organism that places Divine aid at their disposal. It is precisely this organism which is termed sacred royalty; sacred because, for the government of a given country, it participates in that Power which by its Providence governs the entire universe. And this participation is rendered effective by the rite conferred in the name of the Divine Power: the coronation or royal initiation.

No doubt, some will not fail to object that this lofty conception of government of a spiritual nature has not been able to prevent, at all times and in all places, the appearance of scarcely respectable princes, either owing to their incompetence or their weakness, or even because of their scandals or crimes, and whose memory history has documented. This could make one think that sacred royalty is no more capable of assuring the common good than any other political regime. To this we would reply first of all, that one must not exaggerate the number of bad princes, nor accord too much importance to history regarding this point: as happens in novels, it likes to bring to light the dramatic. In addition, since it makes use of the chronicles of the past, it is necessarily influenced by them. Now, for the most part, chronicles record only the crises, famines, terrors, etc.; in short, the calamities of the life of the age in question, and without further thought, passionately designate as responsible those who in reality were not. Thus, the number and importance of things that went badly, and those responsible, are considerably increased, while what is good, as well as good men, are left somewhat in the shadows. Moreover, let us not forget that history has often been deliberately denatured, whether owing to rivalries between individuals, groups or peoples, or for ideological reasons. In this respect, for two centuries the French have been presented with a history for the most part readily falsified in view of a precise ideology which more or less systematically calumniates man and his deeds at every opportunity. Having said that, we do not, of course, deny the existence of decadent or blameworthy princes, but only that this is not an argument against the systems of government of which they were detainers. Those who fulfil the loftiest functions, including the holiest, are not always the best. But one must not find in these weaknesses of *men* arguments against the *institutions*.

If an institution is good, there is no reason to condemn it for the simple reason that at a given moment a ruler has been unworthy of it; for it is evident that in such a case the fault clearly comes not from the institution, but from the man, and precisely because he has not been faithful to the institution. And the impartial observer, when he considers with serenity the history of humanity, will have to acknowledge that all great things—we mean to say all truly great things, not the artificial greatness of many of the feats of modern "progress"—and all lasting things have been accomplished by people living under the kind of regime of which we are speaking. In any case—and this, we believe, is an observation worth noting—the institution of sacred royalty had, among others, the capital advantage that, through its intrinsic qualities, owing to the fact that it is founded on the nature of things, it offered society a solid framework that precisely allowed it to overcome, without irreparable harm, the misdeeds of a bad reign, and which for it was a guarantee for the future.

Let no one tell us, however, that it is impossible to turn back the clock, that the political regime of sacred royalty is past, and inconceivable in our world; in short, that it is an altogether obsolete conception. We think, on the contrary, that it is very timely, because only that is truly timely which is eternal. In relation to humanity, sacred royalty is in essence universal and eternal, for the simple reason that it is founded on universal and eternal principles. Certainly, we do not have in mind a pure and simple restoration of what has been, in the exact form that it had in times past—for nothing is ever repeated exactly in all its modalities—but of becoming aware of that which ought normally to exist, and which will necessarily return, whatever the form it may take, once the present decomposition has reached the end of its final stage. And that date is perhaps not as distant as might be thought. Meanwhile, for those who pursue it, the study of the models of the past will in any case have the advantage of allowing them to reason about the political problem in the light of sacred Tradition, and thus, as we have said above, of contributing to an intellectual restoration, the necessary prelude to a restoration of the institutions.

CHAPTER I

SACRED ROYALTY

"It is necessary that the princes deign to recognise that the monarchy is at root a republic ... a republic with an hereditary president"; these words of Thiers[1] may apply to a good number of present-day kings that still remain in the great nations, but they could not apply in any way to true royalty. However, they allow us to situate sacred royalty *a contrario* inasmuch as they attest to the degradation of the authentic royal function. The true king differs radically from the constitutional king as well as from the republican magistrate—to which he is assimilated in a sense—by the nature and origin of his authority and function, and modern conceptions regarding these have nothing to do with the reality we propose to examine. Regardless of differences in detail in this or that country, the principles of these conceptions are very well summarised in the exposition of one of the "fathers" of modern theories of power in the eighteenth century: speaking of "political authority", Diderot writes, "No man has received from nature the right to rule others," which is certainly true if one speaks of political power. The consequence of this proposition, which must be acknowledged, is that the right to rule—which does exist—has to come from a superior being; but Diderot does not take this consequence into account. He considers paternal authority only for a moment in order to discard it from the social and political sphere: "If nature has established some authority, it is paternal power; but paternal power has its limits and, in the state of nature, it ends as soon as the children are able to direct themselves." Does the power then come from God? No, because, he continues, "the power of God is always immediate

---

1. Discourse to the National Assembly on 8 June, 1871.

1

in the creature" and "God is a jealous master ... who never loses his rights and never communicates them." A sophistry, a ridiculous proposition, a falsehood which no philosophy worthy of the name could admit.

"All other authority (than the paternal)," the author continues, "comes from a source other than nature. If this be well examined, it will always be traced back to one of these two sources: either the force and the violence of the one who has taken possession of it, or the consent of those who are subject to him through a contract, made or assumed, between them and the one to whom they have conferred authority," because "the prince has received from his own subjects the authority which he has over them."[2]

This theory—which is not Diderot's, for it is that of almost all the "philosophers" of the century, and which comes to them directly from the English "free thinkers" and the works of Locke, but which originates earlier, as we shall see—is the basis of all the political constitutions and all the political philosophies of the modern world. It is the work of thinkers wandering in Aristophanic "clouds", and has nothing to do, not only with the teachings of sacred science, which is obvious, but also with the most serious results of ethnology concerning different civilisations; results which contradict Diderot's three propositions on violence, the social contract, and the delegation of authority. It is false to assume that power is a conquest of violence, as when Voltaire also said: "The first king was a lucky soldier." Chesterton rightly pointed out that the saying concerning the strongest who, with great struggle, arrogated authority to himself, is not foolish only if the mystical element and the admiration aroused by the sovereign are not taken into account.[3] The saying takes into account only the origin of violent regimes, tyrannies imposed by usurpers, who always and everywhere have been carefully distinguished from legitimate rulers. It is true that many kingdoms were founded by "victorious warriors", but their victory served only to *designate* them for power, and not to

---

2. Diderot, *s.v.*, "Political Authority," in *The Encyclopedia*.

3. G.K. Chesterton, *The Everlasting Man*, 1927, p. 67.

found this power, which has always been conferred in the name of something superior to material force and of a spiritual order, which is what Chesterton designates, inaccurately, by the word "mystical", and which would be better termed "sacred". The same remark applies to the social pact, the existence of which is undeniable, but the role of which under normal conditions consists merely in the *election*, the acceptance by the people of the ruler who will exercise power, but it does not consist in *investing* him with power. For in normal societies, power and authority do not come from the people, who, therefore, are quite unable to delegate it to the ruler. One had to await the deviations of the modern West to encounter such a statement, against which the entire universal tradition rises up. For tradition, authority has a supra-human source, which is its only possible justification. Let us note in passing that Christianity is in perfect agreement with this universal tradition, basing itself on the words of Christ, who told Pilate: "Thou couldst have no power at all against me, except it were given thee from above: therefore he that delivered me unto thee hath the greater sin" (John 19:11). This implies nothing less the divine origin of the imperial power of Rome. Despite all its errors, ethnology has the merit of showing how the source of political power in societies termed "primitive" involves a non-political element—which the ethnologists identify with magic. This identification is altogether inaccurate: in the first place, because they do not know in a precise manner what magic is, since it is confused with witchcraft, in which they see, at most, merely inventions, imposture and gestures without real efficacy; secondly, because, according to them, these inventions and shams are no more than means for an ambitious person to justify the violence that they assume he has imposed upon the group—which brings us back to the concepts of modern philosophers and sociologists—or at best, for creating the force which he has to impose on the group, which ultimately amounts to the same thing. The theory of the majority of ethnologists is weighed down with two errors: materialism and evolutionism. The first prevents them from acknowledging the truth and the nature of magical operations (as well as those of religion, let it be said

3

in passing); the second, which moreover is related to the first, makes them put forth as a principle, as an indisputable dogma, that men were savages to begin with, that they lived in hordes like animals—for humanity, according to them, descends from the apes—hordes in the midst of which, they assume strong men gradually began to appear, who imposed themselves by violence. This point of view, however, has been severely criticised by an ethnologist who has not allowed himself to become penetrated by the aforementioned philosophical double error. "The power of the ruler," writes Servier, "is a cultural fact which varies from one civilisation to another.... It is absurd to wish to view this as the necessary stage, after the horde, of all social evolution.... It is vain to seek, in any civilisation whatsoever, the traces of an evolution of social structures going from the family to the clan, then to the city, to the nation and to empires. In humanity we find human groups which are perfectly organised and generally endowed with complex structures that are impossible to class and distribute over the length of an evolutionary scale."[4]

Having said this, what is true in the results of ethnological research generally attests to a non-political, or non-sociological element, as at least the secondary basis of political power. Only this element is not magic, but it is rather *religion*, which is what Chesterton was saying when speaking of "mysticism". Of course, we do not claim that there has not been magic, including its degenerate form, witchcraft, in the exercise of power in primitive societies and in all traditional societies, but this was only secondarily so. For contrary to what many ethnologists and historians of religions still think, magic did not come before religion, so that religion emerged from it. Rather, magic is some-

---

4. J. Servier, *L'homme et l'Invisible,* Paris, 1964, pp. 317 & 318. It is a pleasure for us to render homage here to J. Servier, who, from the beginning of his scientific activity at the French University, had the courage to fight the tyrannical and stupid "dogmas" inherited from the 18th and 19th centuries, which rendered ethnological researches sterile. The day that French science frees itself from the materialist quicksand, it will acknowledge all that he has done for it.

thing altogether different from religion; it co-existed with it, and was practiced on a different level.

It is this religious—or, more exactly, sacred—element that is the foundation of power in every normal society. Power comes from the Divinity, but, sociologically speaking, it comes through the mediation of paternity. The natural archetype of socio-political power is paternal authority, because the archetype of civil society, as Aristotle clearly saw, is the family. Just as society is an extension of the family in the form of a community, and not, as the moderns teach, a collection of individuals, so too the ruler, the king, exercises a power which is an extension within the group of the paternal function, which is of divine origin through the mediation of nature; the earthly father is the image, the reflection, of God the celestial Father, because "all paternity descends from the Father of lights" (Eph. 3:15 & Jas. 1:17).

It is from this source that royalty in its normal form—sacred royalty—proceeds; it is paternity, a paternity raised to the second power, sacred by nature, but whose sacredness is confirmed by means of rites.

* * *

But before entering upon its study, it is important to make clear what we mean by sacred royalty. Ethnology and the history of religions employ the expression in a very precise sense, inherited from the analysis made by Frazer in his famous work, *The Magical Origin of Kings*. Whatever subsequent modifications may have been made to Frazer's conception, what is essential in it continues to be the guiding pattern of official scholars in their investigations. In order to define the "sacred king", the "divine king", they start from a kind of "portrait-type" of the sacred king, whose characteristic features are the following: 1) he is a god incarnate, 2) he is capable of influencing the life of his people in a beneficent manner, 3) more particularly, he is a maker of rain and good weather, 4) his powers are dependent upon his strength, his physical vigour, and that is why 5) his reign is limited, since after a fixed period, or upon approaching old age, he is killed, in fact or symbolically, and his divinity, along with temporal sovereignty, passes to a younger and more vigorous man. Having taken this scheme from Frazer, they apply it to all cases, so that in order to be considered a "divine king", the prince under investigation must fit the prototype, failing which he will not be considered a "sacred king," and will be eliminated from the group of princes deemed worthy of entering the Frazerian pantheon of "divine kings".

Although it is fundamentally true, we reject this abusive definition inasmuch as it applies fully only to rulers of societies that are termed "primitive," and even then not to all. We who do not study royalty from the point of view of the ethnologists, nor from that of the history of religions, but rather from the standpoint of the universal sacred Tradition, consider sacred every king whose authority comes expressly from divinity and who exercises his power under the guarantee of the appropriate rites which authenticate such divine delegation, whatever may be the particular features of this divine character of the sacred royalty. These particularities, which vary from one tradition to another, such as the power to make rain, or to cure, etc., obviously spring from the divine quality where they do exist, but they may also not exist in this or that culture, which does not mean that the divine quality of the sovereignty is absent. As for the fact of killing the aged king, far from being a specific feature of sacred royalty, it is simply a fact of decadent cultures in which it constitutes the degenerate form of rites which we shall define later on, for they are found in various royalties pertaining to very developed cultures with a high degree of civilisation.

Let us add, in order to bring these preliminaries to an end, that we also do not agree with the position of those who reserve the quality of "sacred king" to those princes who are "priest-kings" and whose person combines royal and priestly powers. This conception is not unfounded, for assuredly there is no sharp distinction between the two powers, and even in traditional societies in which there exists a constituted priesthood along with the prince, the latter always retains a certain priestly character; however, this can be considerably reduced, without that signifying that the prince has ceased to be a "divine" or "sacred" king.

Thus, we shall keep to a very broad definition, in accordance with traditional teaching, and say that all royalty is sacred when it is acknowledged that a mandate from heaven is exercised, which is confirmed by an act of the spiritual authority and the appropriate rites.

The universality of this conception of royalty throughout different cultures and ages already represents—prior to all theological and metaphysical justification in favour of its regularity—a capital testimony, which will now claim our attention.

SACRED ROYALTIES ACROSS SPACE & TIME

Although the divine character of royalty is constant in all traditional cultures, it does not, however, always present itself in an absolutely identical form. Broadly speaking, we may distinguish two conceptions made up of two series of ideas, which moreover are linked and mingled in varying degrees. The prince appears now as similar to those numerous beings endowed with divine gifts which are called *numina*, gods or "spirits", a kind of visible god, a divine emanation or incarnation, a god-man or a man-god; but in another respect, as an agent of the Divinity, the depository and executor of His Will, inferior to Him, elected by Him, yes, but also judged by Him. We may term the first conception *divine royalty*, and the second *royalty by divine grace*. But, once again, the distinction is not sharp, and strictly speaking, each of the two conceptions can be defined only by the predominance of one content without excluding the other. That is why, in any case, the sacral power can be considered, as a first approximation at least, to be a degree intermediate between God and man, but whose constant is clearly its divine character.

ASHANTI · Of the first conception, we find examples in Africa as well as in the Middle and Far East. Thus, with the Ashanti, a people occupying the central region of the Gold Coast and constituting a large part of the Akan race, the king is the incarnation of Nyame, the supreme god, who is the King *in divinis* as creator and Providence. It is considered that he is the supreme lord of the society of men, living among them and helping them

7

throughout the course of their lives, for "all men are sons of Nyame." "Nyame is the King," declare the Ashanti. But the presence of Nyame among his children is brought about through the mediation of the prince, and while he is on the throne the prince participates directly in the royalty of Nyame, and his person is sacred. He wears the *adaebo*, a triangular chest-piece symbolising divine and universal authority, and he sits on the *sampini*, a dais of three steps. Both symbols signify that the sovereignty of Nyame and of the king extend through the three zones of the universe, a tripartite structure encountered almost everywhere, including the Western tradition. The king must not merely distinguish himself by his physical integrity, but also, and above all, by his virtues, for he is a blessing for his people if his soul is pure. He then "shines" by means of these virtues and is assimilated to *Awia*, the Sun, hence the choice of the colour gold for many of his accessories: his throne, which encloses both the spirit of the previous kings and the spirit of his entire people, is golden; and also his crown, his ring, his bracelets and his sandals. He thus appears as the earthly figure of the "king of glory," Nyame. The king of the Ashanti is therefore the human support of the manifestation of the supreme god, and that is why his soul must be pure. In addition, in order to maintain this purity or, if need be, to restore it, the rite called *kra-guare*, the "purification of the soul," is practiced on the birthday of the king and on feast days. This rite allows the king to make still closer his intimate union with Nyame, which is the condition for participating in his power. The *kra-guare* falls into the well-known category of altogether analogous rites practiced in almost all sacred royalties.

SHILLUK · Among the Shilluk, of the region of the White Nile, the king is assimilated to Nyakang, the founding god of Shilluk royalty. When a king dies, a sanctuary identical to that of Nyakang is constructed over his tomb, thereby showing the assimilation of the king to Nyakang. The sanctuary of Nyakang is constituted by a *temenos* in which several huts are raised, one of which is the holy place. The newly elected king is lodged there for a month in order to communicate with Nyakang and assimilate his substance.

EGYPT · But in Africa,[5] it is Egypt that offers us the perfect example of sacred royalty, and it does so within the framework of a vast empire with a particularly evolved and refined civilisation.

In Egypt, royalty is not as in other great lands a political institution legitimised by the gods; it is an integral part of the rulership of the world by the gods. This is what the myth of the divine dynasties expresses symbolically, according to which Egypt was first governed by gods who, having decided to return to heaven, first founded the historical royalty which was to govern in their stead.

The pharaoh is in himself of a divine nature, and it is this divine nature that is the foundation of his power. This fundamental datum is made explicit in different theological developments. Broadly speaking, there were two main conceptions. According to the first, it is considered that the supreme god is present *in* the king, that he inhabits him in the way in which he is present in a statue for worship or in a sacred animal. The king is the incarnation of God, an incarnation produced at the moment of his enthronement and, at the death of the prince, this presence passes to his successor. This presence is expressed in the title of the king, formed by five elements, the first of which is termed the *Name of Horus*, Horus the solar god. Thus, to designate the sovereign it is ordinarily said "The *Horus So-and-So*," so that the name of the god is followed by the fifth element of the entitlement, which is the proper name of the king.[6] The *Name of Horus* is inscribed on a "shield" on which there is hawk, the sacred

---

5. It is worth insisting on the "African" character of Egyptian civilisation. By studying it along with those of the Near East, Greece and Rome, the books on ancient history have lost sight of this, as is well demonstrated by S. Sauneron in his study, *Les prêtres de l'ancienne Égypte*, Paris, 1957.

6. Here, for example, is the titulary of a prince of the 13th Dynasty:
The Horus has unified the Two Lands
Lasting Splendour
Soul of the Gods
Ra shines with life
Sobek is happy [Sebekhotep]
This last title, Sebekhotep, is the true name of the king.

animal which is the support of the king. The king is also called "The Horus who is in the Palace".

According to another theological conception, the pharaoh is "the son of God," and his power comes to him from the fact that he has been engendered by the god of heaven; he is the "son of Ra," and this designation corresponds to a second element in his title which is inscribed on his coat of arms. The king is the "living image" on earth of his father (*ikon zosa*, in the Greek of the Rosetta Stone). This divine filiation of the pharaoh is expounded in texts recounting the birth of the sovereigns and which are accompanied by reliefs presenting the scenes corresponding to the different moments of the event. We possess those of the history of Amenophis III, of Ramses II, of Nectanebus and Hatshepsut (in Dayr al-Bahri). Almost all of them follow a practically identical scheme, which is as follows: In a celestial assembly, Amon-Ra announces to all the gods the next birth of a new king. Thoth pronounces the name of the queen who will be his mother. Amon, *with the features of the reigning king*, goes to the sleeping queen, who awakens upon perceiving the perfume of the god and smiles at His Majesty. Amon-Ra tells her the name of the future king and the god unites with the queen. Khnum, the ram-god, fashions the body of the child on his potter's wheel; Heket breathes life into the clay figurine. Khnum and Heket conduct the pregnant queen toward the place of birth. The birth of the child king then takes place, and he is suckled by the goddess Hathor.

To grasp the spirit in which these types of mythical narrative were understood, it suffices to recall that in India there exists a "rite for the procreation of a child," according to which the husband, upon uniting with the woman, pronounces this formula: "I am Heaven, thou art Earth"; thereby, man and woman are identified, during the act of procreation, respectively with Purusha and Prakrti, namely, the two divine principles of universal Creation. This way of acting corresponds to the conviction that the individuals are accomplishing an act that in great measure surpasses them: they are merely human "supports" of the divine activity that acts through the universal Energy and Life. It is thus that one has to understand the meaning of the Egyptian narrative referring to the birth of the new king: there too, the human father, who is really the reigning pharaoh, is merely a "passage," serving only as the intermediary of the divine power. The human mother conceives spiritually; she is, as it were, *Mut-em-Ua*, "Mut in the Barque," that is, the Mother, Femininity.

This divine ancestry makes of the pharaoh a solar being, since his true father is Ra, the Sun. For this reason he wears in his diadem the *ureus*, the serpent of Ra, which spits the fire that devours his enemies, the dark powers. For this reason also, the royal palace is named *akhet*, "the Horizon," a word written with the figure of a mountain with two summits between which the sun rises;[7] and finally, this is why the appearance of the king in full pomp on his throne is called *hi*, a word designating the sunrise, and in particular, the sunrise on the primordial hill on the first day of Creation.

The pharaonic monarchy is hereditary, and it is the divine filiation which founds this heritage. Later, the ceremony of coronation confirms and manifests this heritage. Its purpose is to present the divine election of the king as the work of the gods.

The ceremony begins with the enthronement of the young king, who appears above the throne before the Great; he is proclaimed and receives homage. There then takes place a representation that shows the council of the god in whose midst Ra salutes the new king whom he has elected as the heir.

Scenes of the consecration of Pharaoh Amenophis III: he can be seen, from left to right, receiving through the "water of all life" the lustration from the hands of Horus and Seth, then taken by Atum and Khons to Amun-Ra, who crowns him, while Thot inscribes "his years".

---

7. It is noteworthy that the word also designates the temple, for example in Abidos.

11

Next comes the conferring of the royal names by the priests, followed by the conferring of the power by the gods, that is, by the priests who act *in persona deorum* and who generally wear the masks of the gods. The king is brought into the sanctuary where the god salutes him as Horus. After that, he receives from the priest *Inmutef* a lustration which fills him with divine power. He then proceeds to the coronation: the prince receives the two crowns, white and red, corresponding to the two Lands (Upper and Lower Egypt), and the diadem bearing the *uraeus* from the hands of Horus and Seth, and sometimes also Thoth (that is, from the priests who act in their name). The placing of the crowns and the diadem is of particular importance, for the crown is more than an emblem: like the throne,[8] it is charged with *barakah*, and signifies that the sovereign leaves his individual thought and character in order to receive the thought and character of the god at the same time that he receives his power. In addition, the prince receives the other royal insignia: the mitre, the whip, and the mace.

After the rite of the "union of the two Lands" under the symbols of the papyrus and the iris, there takes place the "inscription in the annals": Thoth and Seshat inscribe the names of the kin on sheets from the *ished* tree. Then follows the erecting of the *djed* pillar, symbol of the principle of stability, of the continuity of life: the purpose of the rite, of course, is to stabilise the royal power in harmony with the stability of the world, represented by the four planes that cross the pillar horizontally and which correspond to the four elements. There is another rite of stabilisation which reinforces the erection of the *djed* pillar: the king fires arrows towards the four cardinal directions in order to reinforce his authority to the ends of the earth and to annihilate his enemies; he also frees four birds who will announce his access to the throne. The erecting of the *djed* and the firing of the arrows are rites which are also carried out during the commemorative

---

8. The throne of the pharaoh is cubic in form, and adorned with two lions walking and surmounted with a baldaquin, which is to say that it presents, as do all traditional thrones, a very important cosmic symbolism, which we shall study.

feats of the divine dynasties; what is renewed above all is the triumph of Horus. But it is always a matter of assuring the stability of the kingdom and the order of the world: the texts which are then read recall the creation of power *in principio* by the reign of the solar god. The erecting of the *djed* takes place also during the *Sed Festival*, which is a feast day of the king's regeneration, a regeneration of which we have spoken earlier.[9]

Since the pharaonic royalty is the most perfect example of divine royalty—including the worship of the sovereign with priests designated for such a function—it is worth having a conception that is as exact as possible of this divinity of the sovereign: the precisions given by this case will apply, *mutatis mutandis*, to the other analogous cases we shall consider.

We would certainly be deluding ourselves if we were to consider that the pharaoh was god purely and simply, like Horus or Ra—that he *was* Horus or Ra. In reality, the Egyptians always maintained the distinction between the man and the god in the king. We have seen that the king was called the Horus So-and-So, with his name coming after that of the god; this double designation shows the tension between the two natures in the prince. He is the incarnation of the god, but he is always distinct from the god. Besides, Heliopolitan theology made it quite clear that the king, as "son," was inferior to his father, and that his power came to him as something lent to him. The reigning king was no more than a symbol: he incarnates the divine principle, the creative Word, for which he serves as the support of its manifestation. The true king is Horus, the Horic principle. To the king are attributed the title and qualities of that which he symbolises, so that the prince constitutes, as it were, a living theological metonymy. And the worship that is rendered to him, the adoration, the gestures of prayer, are not addressed to the man, but to his *ka*, that is, to the divine personality with which he has been invested;[10] and G. Posener says excellently, "it is not

---

9. At the *Sed Feast* a very special rite of rebirth is also practiced, the *tikenu*, or passage through the skin of a sacrificed animal; a rite that we shall encounter again in the *diksa* of India.

10. The texts of the royal temple of Dahshur specify that the priests are

13

the man that is venerated, but the Power which is clothed with a figure."[11]

The same observations apply to the Ashanti king, of whom we have spoken before; he is identified with Nyame, the god (inasmuch as he has been endowed with his power), and at the same time, he is the subject of Nyame, whose wrath he fears.

In this way, one may grasp the radical difference which separates this traditional divine royalty, which is a supra-human institution, from the "worship of sovereigns" which flourished in the Hellenistic and Roman epochs, during the course of which there were despots who deified themselves, owing to the servility of their subjects, the most surprising example of which is that of Demetrios, one of the Diadochi, and the history of his apotheosis seems to push back the limits of the degradation as well as the stupidity of men. In the year 290, by decree of the Athenians, in fact, he was honoured as the "only (sic) god because—the Athenians said—the rest of the gods are either too remote, or have no ears, or do not concern themselves with us; you, however, we see, you are there, not in wood or stone, but really; we love thee, grant us peace, o beloved."[12] It is true that the Diadochi did no more than follow the example of the founder of their dynasties, Alexander, who accepted, if not encouraged, being worshiped.[13] And what can be said of the last representatives of this "cult of sovereigns", the emperors Domitian, Aurelian, Caligula, Elagabalus, and Diocletian, who had themselves called *dominus* and *deus*, and obligated their subjects, on pain of death, to venerate them as such publicly. In reality this "cult of sovereigns" was a poorly hidden "personality cult", as it is termed today, and an unbridled worship of man; and in most cases, man given over to

---

"priests of the living *ka* of the king", and not priests of the king.

11. G. Posener, *De la divinité du pharaon*, Paris, 1969, p. 102.

12. Athenaeus 6.252.

13. The Ptolemies of Egypt did not refrain from deifying themselves, using the pharaonic tradition, but, of course, denaturing it as well. By way of example, there is this inscription in honour of Ptolemy XIII at the temple of Isis at Philae: "to the Lord, king and god" (Dittenberg, OGI, 1868).

his worst instincts. It was the complete degeneration of "sacred royalty," and even a total inversion of the sacred. For in this case, it is not the divine power that descends upon man to invest him with a superior personality; it is man who decides, by his own will, to put himself—or more exactly, to try to put himself—in God's place. This does not mean, however, that the imperial institution was not a sacred royalty. We shall speak of this again later.

Heavenly and solar descent as the foundation of the king's divinity was not confined to Egypt. In reality, it is the constitutive part of most royal theologies. Such is the case amongst the Mongol peoples in Central Asia and in the Far East.

Among the Paleo-Turkic people of Mongolia and Siberia, the *kagan*, "emperor," comes from Heaven, which is the supreme God, *Tangri*. In a letter written in 584, a *kagan* presents himself as "born from Heaven, wise and holy son of Heaven". Celestial descent can present itself in a mythic form similar to those encountered in certain totemist peoples; thus, in a text taken from the official Annals of the kingdom, one can read that "the origin of Genghis Khan is Borta Cino (the wolf), come from Heaven."

TIBET · In ancient Tibet as well, the origin of royalty—which held power before the government of the country took on a theocratic form—is identified with a heavenly descent. The king who ascended to the throne constituted a new epiphany of the Celestial Ancestor, the first king, an archetypal king, as it were, who reappeared in the new king in the manner of an *avatara*. The funerary stele of a Prince Krisron bore a genealogy which began with Odespurgyal who "descended from heaven to become the prince of men". The divine ancestor is renewed in the new king, since, as the chronicles say, he is simultaneously present on two parallel planes, the earthly and the heavenly. And the kings are the successive manifestations of the "heavenly Kri" or "heavenly king" who descended first in the founding Ancestor of the dynasty, who then transmits the *barakah* to all. The divine character of the king is attested in one of his principal insignias, the helmet (*dburmog*), which is not a warrior attribute but the symbol of royal power that comes to the king from his divine essence. Another insignia is the cord (*rmutag*), symbol of the luminous "cord" that emerges from the head of the king and joins him to heaven; it was said that at their death the princes rose back to heaven through this cord, which the shamans employ to make the souls of the dead arrive in heaven. Moreover, the kings, like shamans, could go up to heaven at will in order to converse with the divinities there.[14]

JAPAN · Japan offers us an example, unique in our day, of a divine monarchy and true theocracy which has been perpetuated up to our time without interruption for more than 2,600 years. We have before our eyes an institution which is astonishingly similar, in its basis if not in its details, to that of ancient Egypt, and which in the twentieth century can give us an idea of what the pharaonic royalty was.

As with Egypt, the Japanese archipelago, according to tradition, was governed first by the gods (*kami*). The primordial couple *Izanagi* and *Izanami* (corresponding to *Purusha* and *Prakrti*, the universal Essence and Substance) engendered a certain number of gods, among them *Amaterasu-omikami*, goddess of the Sun, and her brother *Susanoo-no-mikoto*. The latter received the governance of the earth, while the goddess received that of heaven. But since he had governed his domain badly, the heavenly *kami* took possession of the earth and Ninigi-no-Mikoto, the grandson of the goddess, was sent there. Finally, he gave the power to a great-grandson of Amaterasu, Jimmu-tenno, who was the first human emperor of Japan, and in 660 BC founded the still reigning dynasty. We have before us a line of authentically "divine" rulers, although having passed over to the human state. The emperor of Japan bears the title of *Tenno*,[15] namely, "celestial sovereign": he is also termed *Ten-shin*, "son of Heaven". "He is

---

14. According to other Tibetan traditions, the descent from heaven to earth of the king is accomplished by the intermediary of the cosmic *mountain* marking the centre of the world. The *mountain*, like the *cord*, is a symbol of the *Axis Mundi*.

15. The word *mikado* properly designates the imperial palace, but is often employed to designate the emperor himself, according to a custom that occurs elsewhere: in ancient Egypt, *pharaoh*, the usual designation of the king, signified in the first place "the great palace" (*per aa*); likewise it was also called "The Holy Seat".

considered a living *kami*," a contemporary Japanese author, Ku-mitake Kume, informs us, "loved and venerated by the nation more than anything else on earth." He is also called *Aki-tsu-mi-kami*, "divinity in human form", and "god manifested";[16] according to Chikao Fujisawa, he is also *Sumera-mikoto*, "the sacred Word capable of provoking spiritual union"; also, "the power which gathers the nation in all spheres"; and finally, *Naka-ima*, "the incarnation of the eternal present".

Nonetheless, here as elsewhere, the line of descent does not suffice to establish definitively the imperial divine status. The sovereign is converted into *Aki-tsu-mi-kami*, "human god", only after the consecration, so that once again this appears as indispensable to "make the king".

The consecration comprises several rites. The first is the *senso*, the accession to the throne which is brought about by the bestowal of the "Three Treasures" (*Shansu no Shinki*), which are the insignia of power: the Mirror, the Sword, and the Necklace of Jewels. These are objects of a divine origin, either made or found by *kami*. According to the myth, these three treasures were given to Prince Ninigi when he was sent to earth by Amaterasu, who told him: "Illumine the entire world with the brilliance of the mirror; reign over the earth by the marvelous power of dominion of these jewels; triumph over those who do not submit by brandishing this divine Sword." The chief insignia is the Mirror, about which Amaterasu also says, in one of the holy books of Shinto, the *Kojiki*: "Consider this mirror exactly as if it were Our August Spirit, and revere it as if it were We whom you revere." This Mirror, which is deposited in the great temple at Ise, is the sacrosanct object of Shinto, for in it resides the solar goddess. A copy of it was made and is deposited in a temple of the Imperial Palace.

The symbolism of the Three Treasures has been expounded in different ways, of which the most plausible one, following the Zen thinkers, sees in them the images of the three imperial virtues, knowledge (in the Mirror), bravery (in the Sword), and

---

16. Let it be recalled that the same title was used by some Ptolemies, also proclaimed "manifest gods" (*theoi epiphaneis*).

Left: The Japanese emperor wearing the *akebono*, dawn-coloured garment, following the taking of the oath. He holds in his right hand the *shaku* (sceptre); *Right*: Enthronement of the emperor, who wears the *koonozengo* and the *ryuei-no-kammuri* coiffure.

benevolence (in the Jewels), with the following cosmic correspondences: the Body of the Sun, the Essence of the Moon, and the substance of the Stars. The bestowal of the Three Treasures upon the new emperor is the principal rite of consecration, for it is this that transmits the spiritual influence.

After the *senso* comes the *sokui-rei* or enthronement. In one of the temples of the Palace, the *Shinshin-den*, the emperor sits on the Throne, the *Taka-mikura*, "Lofty and august seat", in the form of a palanquin, painted with black lacquer and decorated with a phoenix and a *kirin*, a mythical animal, and also with flowers of eight petals and beneficent clouds in five colours. On its hexagonal roofing are fixed seven mirrors, of which the central one is situated over the head of the emperor and directed towards him.

The third rite is the *daijo-sai*. It is preceded by a purification (*chinkon-sai*) intended to pacify the spirit of the emperor and assure his life and health. For the *daijo-sai* the prince is seated in the temple of the *kami*, the *Shinden*, in the Palace. He wears his priestly dress, for he is the high priest of Shinto. The *daijo-sai* is a rite of communion with the Divinity: the Tenno "savours the rice" with his divine Ancestor Amaterasu. Through this rite, he is capable of "incarnating the spirit" of the goddess and attains the state of *Ama-tsi-hi-tsugi*, that is, he acquires the "spiritual light" of *Ama-tsu-hi-tsugi*, the "heavenly successor of *Toyo-uke-no kami*", and he becomes *Aki-tsu-mi-kami*, "god in human form". Then, dressed in his priestly garments of raw silk, he enters the inner chamber of a sacred pavilion, the *Yuki-den*, where he finds the Divine Couch (*shinza*) upon which the Ancestor Jimmu-tenno received the command to preserve the Divine Mirror. Inside the sacred pavilion he accomplishes a series of rites throughout the night until dawn. The sovereign offers his deified ancestors foods which he shares with them: first, rice, cultivated near the Palace according to minutely detailed rites for its tilling, planting and harvesting, and accomplished by the representatives of the emperor. The cooking is accomplished over a fire lit by rubbing, with *hinoki* wood from the imperial forest.

The last part of the coronation, the *shimpo*, consists in the emperor sending offerings to the temple at Ise, the residence of Amaterasu. Afterward a feast is celebrated, a sacred banquet which the prince shares with his subjects.

Throughout all the ceremonies of the coronation, according to a traditional text, it is considered that the sovereign is "wrapped" in the personality of all his predecessors, and finally, in that of *Ameno-minaka-nuchi*, "Lord of the true centre of Heaven," the supreme divinity of Shinto.

CHINA · As with the Japanese *tenno*, the emperor of China was the "Son of Heaven" (*tien-tsu*), with the sun as his emblem. He participated in the divine nature by birth. The supreme god—Heaven, in China—deposited in him the "celestial mandate" (*tien-ming*) to rule. This mandate is the fruit of a *barakah* possessed by the founding Ancestor of a dynasty, as we have seen before in the case of Tibet. The origin of every dynasty is a hero miraculously born of the works of Heaven. Thus the myths relate that the ancestor of the Yin kings was conceived by his mother after she swallowed a swallow's egg (the bird which is considered the "messenger of the gods," and here the bearer of the divine "seed"); the ancestor of the Kings of Chou was conceived by his mother after she had walked in the "footprints" of "giant steps", that is, the steps of the god of Heaven. This fecundation by fitting into the steps of a divine giant is to be found in the Chinese legends, and in addition in those of many other traditions. Other marvellous features point to the supernatural character of the initial ruler of a dynasty; thus, the five primordial rulers of China possessed the supreme gift of Efficacy (*ling*) characteristic of divine beings (*chen*): Huang-ti, for example, possessed Efficacy from his birth, and could speak before he was three months old.

The superhuman greatness of the imperial institution appears clearly in a passage from Lao Tzu: "The Way (*Tao*) is great; Heaven (*Tien*) is great; Earth (*Ti*) is great; the King (*wang*) too is great. In the Middle, then, there are four things, but of these only the King is visible."[17] To understand this text and the profound meaning of the imperial institution, the Taoist doctrine, codified particularly by Lao Tzu, must be recalled briefly, specifying that this properly metaphysical doctrine has at all times inspired the concept of royalty in China, parallel to the exoteric doctrine codified at a certain point in time by Confucius, but equally ancient, since both doctrines are simply two faces of one and the same Chinese Tradition—contrary to the attitude of most Sinologists, who conceive their studies solely from the historical point of view, and distinguish periods in which the royal doctrine supposedly was Taoist and others in which supposedly it was Confucian. No doubt certain princely lines and certain emperors adhered more particularly to one or the other doctrine; but this in no way changes the fact that the real conception rests fundamentally on the Taoist metaphysical doctrine, and moreover, it could not be otherwise, in China as elsewhere, for reasons which will appear further on.

Taoism takes its name from the word *Tao*, translated as "The Way," but which in fact designates the supreme Reality. It designates at one and the same time the superior Non-Being or Beyond-Being (*Wu-ki*) and pure Being or Unity, termed the "Great

---

17. *Tao Te Ching* 25.

Extreme" (*tai-ki*) and the "Great Unity" (*tai-i*).[18] The polarisation of Being generates the universal Essence, termed "Heaven" (*Tien*), and the universal Substance, termed "Earth" (*Ti*). The Great Unity, Heaven and Earth form the first and fundamental triad, the origin of universal Manifestation which is produced between the Essence and the Substance; symbolically, between Heaven and Earth:

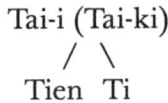

$$Tai\text{-}i\ (Tai\text{-}ki)$$
$$/\ \ \backslash$$
$$Tien\ \ Ti$$

Man is part of manifestation, the total extension of which is comprised between the two poles of Essence and Substance, Heaven and Earth. But at the same time, man is the centre of this manifestation and he synthesises it: we speak, of course, of man in his primordial and fundamental nature, which the Chinese tradition terms "true man", and which in Christian language corresponds to man before the Fall. Man is placed between Heaven and Earth, and he is the result of their reciprocal influences, but by his central position he is situated on the Axis, the *Axis Mundi*, around which the entire Manifestation is extended. This Axis measures the distance between Heaven and Earth, the extension of the cosmos, and indicates the hierarchy of the states of manifested Existence. The summit of this Axis touches *Tai-i*, and it is by this Axis that Heaven and Earth communicate and are relayed to Unity. The "true man", who is normal man, is situated therefore at the central point at which the powers of Heaven and those of Earth, which the Chinese tradition terms respectively *Yang* and *Yin*, are united, and where they are in perfect equilibrium. The "true man" is the one in whom *act* is equal to *potency*, and in whom the celestial nature dominates the earthly. Therefore, in his world he fulfils the role of "motionless mover", imitating the "non-acting" (*wu wei*) activity of Heaven. Hence it is he who normally should be the "king of creation", a function

---

18. More specifically, the "Nameless *Tao*", corresponding to *Wu-ki*, and the "Named *Tao*", which corresponds to *Tai-i*.

which was entrusted to him by God, and which he exercised normally before the Fall, according to the Book of Genesis.

This position of the "true man" is expressed in the Chinese Tradition by a triad: Heaven (*Tien*), Earth (*Ti*), Man (*Jen*), with Man being placed between the two extremes so as to show his central position. In addition, this triad is expressed in the character 王 in which the upper horizontal stroke represents Heaven, the lower one, Earth, and the middle one, Man. Moreover, the middle stroke is crossed by a vertical stroke, which is the expression of the Axis uniting Heaven and Earth, and which together form a cross. This character expresses the nature of the "true man" and shows him as "son of Heaven and Earth" occupying the central point situated on the *Axis Mundi*. Now, this character transcribes the word *wang*, designating the "King", the Emperor, which means that the king is identified with the "true man". Of course, it is not the individual as such that exercises the royal function, but the superior personality with which he is invested, and which is linked to the royal function, and which in a sense is bestowed upon him at the same time as the "heavenly mandate". In the next chapter we shall see in what this function consists and how it corresponds to the nature and role of the "true man" (*chen-jen*) and, at a superior degree, to the nature and role of the "transcendent man". Now, the "transcendent man" is termed *chun-jen*, an expression in which the word *chun* is that which characterises divine being, which the Judeo-Christian tradition expresses in saying that before the Fall man was made "in the image of God". By this it can be seen, therefore, why and how the sovereign as such can be said to be of a divine nature, which again, moreover, is expressed by his title of "son of Heaven", a formula in which the mention of Earth is omitted in order to emphasise his "divine" character and to distinguish him from the ordinary man, who is "son of Heaven and Earth". This does not mean that this latter formula is not applied to the emperor; quite the contrary, for among the prerogatives of his function is that of realising the integration of all the subjects in the general harmony of the Universe.

This is what the symbolism of the imperial instruments and buildings demonstrate particularly; they all translate into graphic form the nature of the "true man" and of the "transcendent man".

Thus, the dress of the ancient emperors was round above (the collar) and square below, signifying that in the "true man" represented by the prince, his head reaches Heaven, while his feet rest on Earth, so that the very person of the sovereign constituted, as it were, an image of the Axis uniting the two poles of Manifestation. In addition, in this dress were represented the sun, the moon, the constellations and lightning (see plate p.24): another manner of indicating that, as we said above, the personality of the prince as "true man" is a synthesis of the Universe.

The same intention, during the era of the Tsin Dynasty, governed the decoration of the imperial palace, in order to make it a veritable summary of the world. Thus, the palace of Huang-ti presented reductions of the Milky Way and the Arch of Triumph which crosses it; in the palace of the emperor Wu there were animals from the four kingdoms; there were lakes, the shores of which represented distant lands and the "Isles of the Immortals"; there were genies of bronze on high columns and, for the emperor, a tower with a double spiral walkway, from the top of which one could gaze out into the vastness. It was yet another way of signifying that the prince was the "master of the world". But the most profound symbolism of the imperial residence was the central edifice, the *Ming-tang* or "Temple of Light", the form and role of which we will consider when studying the royal function in the next chapter. Let us say simply for the time being that this building had a square base and a round roof; the same structure governed the chariot of the Emperor, composed of a square box connected to a vertical mast topped by a circular canopy (see plate p.25). Thus, dress, chariot and palace by their fundamental structure, analogous to the character *wang*, expressed the nature of the sovereign as incarnating the function of "True Man" and "Transcendent Man", "son of Heaven and Earth", fixed in the "Invariable Middle" (symbolised by the central cross of the character *wang*), and ultimately identified with the Axis of the World.

EMPEREUR DE LA CHINE
en habit de ceremonie. en habit ordinaire.

The emperor donning the *mangpas* interspersed with nine dragons and the attributes of universal power (J.B. du Halde, *Description de la Chine*, The Hague, 1786).

The emperor on his everyday, non-ceremonial chariot (J. de Moyriac, *Histoire générale de la Chine*, 1787).

The character of "divine royalty" is not as marked in all traditions, and what can be seen is an approach by degrees towards another conception, that of "royalty by divine grace". This is what occurs in the Indo-European zone, in India and Iran, for example.

INDIA · In India the king is considered to be a *deva*. In the Hindu tradition this word, which is the same as the Latin *divus* and the Greek *di(w)os*, designates an intermediate god or a genie. The sovereign is the *deva raja*, the "divine king". According to the *Laws of Manu*, the king was created "at the beginning" from particles taken from the Eight Devas called the "Guardians of the World" (*lokapala*) and in charge of ruling the eight cardinal points; the essence of these Devas constitutes the "royal majesty" (*pratapa*) and, according to the commentary of Kulluka, express the role of the king.[19] The same doctrine is expressed in another way when it tells us that royalty emerged from the god Indra, who is the archetype of the king, as Agni is the archetype of the spiritual head; or also, that the kings bear within themselves a part of the essence of Vishnu.[20] The object of the coronation ceremony (*rajasuya*) is to transform the human individual, granting him this divine personality. In accordance with all ancient rites, the *rajasuya* consisted in a reiteration of the creation, since, in virtue of the fundamental analogy between the macrocosm and the microcosm, any particular creation—in this case, that of a king—has to reproduce the natural process of the world's creation. In the first phase of the *rajasuya*, the candidate undergoes a regression to the embryonic state in order to "lose" his individuality, which will be substituted by the supra-human personality. In the cosmic order, this phase corresponds to the period of maturation of the universe or to that of the harvests. There follows a symbolical gestation of one year intended to achieve the formation of the new body of the candidate, a "divine" body. This symbolic body is obtained, either by the mystical marriage of the prince with the caste of the *brahmins* (*brahmana*), or with the people, a marriage which will cause him to be born from their

---

19. *Manusmriti* 7.1 ff.

20. *Mahabharata* 12.59.127 ff.

respective wombs, either by the rite of the union of the two masculine waters with the feminine waters, or even by that of gold (= fire) with silver (= water). Afterward there takes place a series of rites by which the king acquires sovereignty over the "three worlds" (*tribhuvana*), incarnates the cosmos, and becomes the cosmocrator. First, the king raises his arms vertically, a gesture that symbolises the raising of the *Axis Mundi*, with which the king is going to identify. Then the king is anointed: standing on his throne, with his arms still raised, he then appears as the Axis of the World fixed to the Earth's navel—the centre of the world, symbolised by the throne—and touching heaven. The model of the royal anointing is the anointing of Varuna and Indra, the gods of sovereignty. The king is consecrated by reference to the consecration of Varuna and Indra as kings. The formulae of consecration say that the king is anointed with the unguent thanks to which Indra, when he was anointed, won victories and conquered the world. After that, the king receives an aspersion of

The affusion of Prince Mahajanaka (Ajanta fresco, 6th century AD). The analogy between the Hindu and the pharaonic rite is particularly striking.

27

water symbolising the waters which descend from heaven along the Axis (= the king) to bless the earth. Finally the king takes the Three steps of Vishnu, giant steps by which the god conquered the world; by this rite the king is identified with Vishnu, he extends his power to the entire earth, the entirety of the world, for he ascends symbolically to the zenith.[21] This course subdues the evil influences and allows life to develop naturally; through it, moreover, the king attains to heaven, becomes a *deva* and enters in communion with *Prajapati*, "Master of creatures". A *rajasuya* of this type was still celebrated in 1956, upon the accession to the throne by the king of Nepal.

During the historical period, the *rajasuya* ceremony was accomplished only twice during a reign. But it is altogether probable that in earlier times it was practiced more often, even annually, for without doubt it reproduces the fundamental pattern found almost everywhere, and has the role of reanimating, as it were by its repetition, the divine life in the person of the sovereign.

For the sovereign is not personally "divine". In India, it is royalty that is divine, not the king as individual. He is revered as a god only because his *state* and his *role* are divine. At the same time the king is also subject to *Dharma*, the divine law governing the world, which is the principle of royalty.[22] The king is not Indra, nor is he Vishnu: Indra and Vishnu are *in the king*,[23] in order to serve the people.[24] It is the same in Thailand: the Khmer king is a *deva* as in India, and takes the name "living Buddha"; but this expression has to be understood: he is not an incarnation of the Buddha; he is merely the support of a ritual act that places him—him and his kingdom—in communication with the unseen Buddha. The king offers his person as a support to receive as a reflection of divinity so that it may radiate in his kingdom. The

---

21. Here is the formula for conferring sovereign power to the king (the rite of *Vajapeya*): "Thou art the walk of Vishnu, thou art the step of Vishnu, thou art the stride of Vishnu."

22. *Brihadaranyaka Upanishad* 1.44.

23. Rangaswami Aiyangar, *Rajadharma*, 1941, p. 108.

24. *Mahabharata* 1.19.

Indian royal throne, with animal motifs on the back
(drawing after a carving at the Guimet Museum).

making of a statue of the king as a Buddha should not be viewed
as an apotheosis, as P. Mus said, but as a *devotio*: he gives himself
to the Buddha, and his human body becomes the earthly "trace"
of its divine model; the royal person becomes the support of a
reflection of the Buddha.[25]

It will be noted that in both cases that have been evoked, that
of India and that of Thailand, there has been no mention of a
divine *filiation* of the prince; royalty here appears more clearly
as a divine *gift*, a royalty *by divine grace*. However, too great an

---

25. P. Mus, *Barabudur*, passim. See G. Coédès, "Le culte de la royauté
divinisée," in *Conferenze*, t.I, Rome, 1951.

importance should not be given to this observation, for the mention of a divine filiation of the king can also coexist with the idea of a donation of power through grace. There is no need to be surprised at this: at root, whatever may be the form taken by the doctrine of royal power, it is in the final analysis always *by grace* that the prince receives this power. Divine filiation, like the genealogies that trace the royal line back to a god, all have a symbolical value, something which modern scholars have often not understood: they have the function of expressing in mythic language—which is proper to the sacred—the superhuman source of divine power.[26] In both conceptions of royalty that we have mentioned—*divine royalty* and *royalty by divine grace*—everything is a matter of proportions in the expression of the two constitutive elements of royal status: on the one hand, the sacral character or status of the man who exercises it, and on the other, the mode of realisation of this status. In the end the resulting difference is rather small in either case.

IRAN · This coexistence of two conceptions appears clearly in ancient Iran. In fact, there is nothing clearer than this declaration of Darius in his *Behistun Inscription*: "By the grace of Ahuramazda I am king; Ahuramazda gave me the kingdom." Nonetheless, the person of the prince has a strongly marked divine character; for example, in the ceremonial of the "adoration" of the king the *proskynese* was customary, as in Egypt. Thus, Themistocles, desiring to see the Great King, is told by Artaban: "Among the many fair laws that we have here, the fairest is that which commands reverencing the king and prostrating oneself before him as before *the image of the god who governs the world*."[27] It is the same expression—"the image of the god"—that was em-

---

26. When we speak of "symbolic value", we do not employ the word "symbolic" in the sense too often given to it in the profane world in order to oppose it to words like "real", "concrete" etc. What is "symbolic", far from being unreal, is on the contrary much more real than something simply "concrete", for the symbol, which points to the bond uniting the visible thing to a superior invisible reality, confers on the visible thing a greater reality.

27. Plutarch, *Themistocles* 27.

ployed to designate the pharaoh in that most characteristic form of *divine royalty*.

And here again, in Iran, we meet with a mythical genealogy. The king is holy because he descends from the gods. He is the brother of the Sun and the Moon and his true abode is in the stars; certain kings were regarded as Sun-Kings, others as Moon-Kings. In a letter to the Emperor Constantius, Shapur II titles himself thus: "I, Shapur, king of kings, companion of the stars, brother of the Sun and the Moon."[28] The royal mantle and the tiara, moreover, were adorned with stars and with solar and lunar signs.[29] As Brother of the Sun and of the Moon, the Iranian king, by his very nature, had an affinity with fire: he descended from heaven like lightning in a column of fire. It is told that when Mithridates was still a child, a bolt of lightning burned his swaddling-clothes without touching his body, and that a trace of celestial fire remained on his face and that he hid it with his hair. When he was a man, a lightning bolt once again fell near him, striking the building while he slept, passing through the quiver that hung over his head, incinerating the arrows.[30] The igneous nature of the king was symbolised by the *nimbus* of fire surrounding his head, the *xvarnah*, which was also a symbol of good fortune. This is why the king could not be looked at without danger: during the Sassanid epoch, while seated on the throne, he veiled his face so that the "solar brilliance" emanating from him would not harm those present. Curiously, a vestige of this belief persisted to our times at the court of the Shah: when entering to see the sovereign, one covered one's face with one's hands, crying, "*misuyam*", "I am consumed". This idea that the king, descendant of the solar God, had a shining face is common to India and to Iran. In the Mahabharata, king Yudhishthira also covered his face with his clothing, so that the world would not be consumed by the fire which he radiated; and the *Laws of*

---

28. Ammianus Marcellinus, 17.5.1.

29. Arsaces, founder of the royal dynasty of the Parthians, was considered a divine person, (Amm. Marcell., l.c.). In addition, the divine origin of the Arsacid king is mentioned by Xenophon, *Cyropaedia*, 7.2.24.

30. Plutarch, *Quaest. Conv.* 1.6.2. Cf. Athenaeus 5.512D.

Manu also say that the radiance of the king is that of the sun and burns the eyes like the sun.

The divine character of the king of Iran is also reflected in an important feature of the court etiquette: like the divinity, the king is practically inaccessible during the age of the Achaeminid dynasty and that of the Parthians. To penetrate into the interior court of the palace without permission was a crime punishable by death, as we see in the *Book of Esther* (Chap. 4) and in Xenophon,[31] and Herodotus tells us that no one could enter into the presence of the king except for a few who are specially privileged: all communication between the sovereign and his subjects was done through messengers.[32] At banquets, some of the guests ate outside the royal apartments; the others ate with the king, but not at the same table. In reality there were two halls, one leading to the other; the king could see his guests through a curtain in front of his door, but he remained invisible to them.[33]

The principle of the celestial descent of the Iranian king caused the appearance of a series of narratives concerning Cyrus and Mithridates Eupator, whose case was also related back to Zarathustra. According to these narratives, the king is the incarnation of Mithra, the principal adviser to Ahuramazda; as in the case of Mithra, the king was born in a cave, from a star that descended to it, just as a bolt of lightning falls from the sky. Many prophecies circulated through the centuries immediately preceding the birth of Christ and at the beginning of the Christian era: they spoke of the "Great King", that is to say Mithra, whose reincarnation—the new *avatara*, to employ the technical Hindu term—was awaited because he was to bring salvation to all humanity. It was believed that these prophecies would be realised in the person of certain sovereigns, especially Mithridates Eupator, of whom we spoke above. It was related that at his birth a star was seen shining with such brilliance that it seemed

---

31. Xenophon, *Cyropaedia* 7.5.41.

32. Herodotus, 199.

33. Heraclitus of Cumae, in Athenaeus 4.25.145.

to eclipse all the others, and that the same phenomenon was reproduced during his coronation. Likewise with Hushetar; the night he was born, a sign was seen in the sky: a star falling from heaven to signal the newborn.

If we allude to these narratives and to the prophecies that are their origin, it is because they refer to a particular aspect of royalty, to the theme of the *King of the World* and of the *Saviour King* of which we shall speak later.

BABYLONIA · The situation of royalty as we have described it in the Indo-Iranian zone is almost identical to the ancient empires of the Near East, in Sumer as with the Assyro-Babylonians.

The sovereign sometimes seems to be assimilated to a divinity. The celebrated Hammurabi is glorified in the *El-Amarna* Letters as the sun which rises over the land day after day; he is called "Sun-god of Babel"; an Assyrian inscription is addressed to him in these terms: "Thou art the image of Marduk, master of the world." Hammurabi also bore the title of "son of god", "son of Sin" (the Moon), "son of Dagon", "son of Marduk". But there is no need to attribute to the titles the full consequences that seem to impose themselves at first sight. In fact, a prince such as Gudea, for example, is in reality titled "son of Ninsun"; however, it is also said that he is "the shepherd considered by Ninsun in her heart, rewarded by Igalimma with the principality and the sublime sceptre...." Certain names of kings bear the determinative of the divinity, for example Naram Sin, in Akkad, or also those of the third dynasty of Ur; Sargon I was titled "king of the land", "he who rules the four kingdoms", the divine title of Anu, of Enlil and of Shamash (the Sun), and the Assyrian kings took the title of Shar Kishati, "king of the universe". Despite everything, the fundamental character of royalty is not divine as in other cultures, and all these divine titles have to be situated together with the texts that very clearly indicate that royalty is the object of an election on the part of the divinity. Above, we have seen the text that referred to Gudea. Similarly, Eannatum, the king of Lagash, is "he whose name was pronounced by Enlil, given strength by Ningursu, considered by Nanshe in her heart, nourished with the sacred milk of Ninhursaga, granted a name by Inanna." Ashurnasirpal II is "called by Ishtar", who "entrusted

Ashurbanipal on his ceremonial chariot (fragment of a relief at the Louvre). As in China, the chariot is covered by a canopy. The king is wearing a tiara.

him with the sceptre of righteousness"; and Asarhaddon, speaking of himself: "In the joy of their hearts, the gods, lifting their eyes upon me, had chosen me legitimately to be king."

The ceremony of enthronement confirms this impression. The new king comes to the temple and, according to an expressive formula, "grasps the hands of the god": this gesture is one of homage and, in return, the god transmits the power which he alone disposes, giving the prince the sceptre and the crown and proclaiming his name, showing that it is once again the god who is the author of the election. In placing the crown on the head of the chosen one, the Assyrian priest says: "May Asur and Nin-lil, *the lords of thy diadem,* place the diadem on thy head for a hundred years ... may thy priest and the priest of thy sons find favour before Asur. With the sceptre of righteousness make immense thy country. May Asur grant thee swift satisfaction, righteousness and peace."

In fact, the exact conception of royalty of the Assyro-Babylonians is perfectly summarised by the tradition according to which, they say, at the beginning of time, and then again after the Flood, "royalty descended from heaven". *Royalty*, not the *king*; it is the *function* that is *divine*, not the titulary.

GREECE & ROME · Alongside the splendours displayed by the oriental monarchies, the kings in ancient Greece and Rome pale in comparison, not only because, during the most brilliant epoch of classical civilisation, the title of king was no longer anything more than a survival, and the titulary confined to the most restricted religious functions, of which we shall speak later, but also because, even in the archaic epoch, during which the king fully exercised his functions, he never occupied in these countries the eminent place that we have seen in Egypt, India or other places. Nevertheless, in Greece as well as in Rome, royalty appears with the same fundamental characteristics by which it is known everywhere: it possesses an undeniable sacral character.

In Crete, Minos, whose name designates less a fabled hero than a function—as in Egypt, the word pharaoh—is the son of Zeus, and every nine years he withdraws into the sacred cave of Ida to render accounts to the father of his administration, and to receive instructions and a renewed power for a new period. In Homeric society the king is qualified as "divine" (*theios, di(w)os*), "son of god" (*diogenes*), "suckling of Zeus" (*diotrephes*). Agamemnon and Menelaus descend from Zeus through Tantalus, Pelops and Atreus. The king holds his dignity (*time*) from Zeus;[34] his power is a "sacred power" (*hieron menos*),[35] for the king incarnates the divine power of which the symbol is the sceptre: that of Agamemnon is the work of Hephaestus and it is

---

34. *Iliad*, 196.

35. *Odyssey*, 7.167 and passim.

Zeus himself who gave it to him to reign.[36] The kings of Athens all descended, by way of legendary genealogies, from divinities. In Ilia, the kings descend from Zeus, in Corinth, from Apollo.[37] In Sparta as well, where there were two kings, they all descended from Zeus.

What is remarkable in Greece is that the affirmation of the divine source of royal power was concreted around the Hearth (*Hestia*); the importance of the cult of the Hearth, in the family as well as in the City, is well known. The public *Hestia* was the sacred centre of the city, as can be seen already in Homer.[38] The first role of the kings, to which we shall return later, was to celebrate the cult of the Hearth, which, as Aristotle affirms, was the true source of royal power.[39] Thus, Battus, the founder of Cyrene, was the first king of that city, because, having founded it, he had lighted the public Hearth; likewise for the royal family of the Codrides in Ionia.[40] This is easily explained if we recall that the hearth has the value of the *omphalos*; it is a centre, and like all centres ritually constituted, it is symbolically assimilated to the Centre of the World, which the Pythagoreans represented as a hearth, the cosmic *Hestia*, the hearth of the Universal Fire, the source of all things.[41] As an *omphalos*, the hearth, and especially the public *Hestia*, was the point of intersection of the earth with the World Axis, which according to all traditions is the way by which Heaven communicates with the here-below and conversely.[42] This appears clearly in Hellenic homes, where an opening was made in the roof through which the smoke es-

---

36. *Iliad* 2.100 ff; 9.38. Cf. 18.478 ff.

37. Pausanias 5.1.2.3.

38. For example, *Odyssey* 8.40 ff.

39. Aristotle, *Politics* 7.5.11.

40. *Ibid.*, Herodotus 1.146.

41. The cosmic character of the hearth-altar has at times been emphasised by the presence of bands or ribbons arranged in a cross according to the four cardinal directions, as with the Buryats.

42. We have seen this in connection with the Chinese tradition, cf. pp. 19-23.

caped. The hearth stone was an altar stone and a sacrificial stone on which the fire burned the offerings and made them "rise" toward Heaven, whence, in return, the blessings "descended".[43] Thus, it was altogether normal, in a tradition in which the ritual hearth played the chief role in the hallowing of the city, that the "heavenly mandate" should come to the sovereign in this way. Something analogous took place in ancient Ireland, where the famous Stone of Fall, brought by the divine ancestors Tuatha De Danann, played the part of an *omphalos*, serving to enthrone the king of Ireland by the sound which could be heard coming from the stone.

In Rome, although the cult of the Hearth was part of the royal prerogatives, it does not appear that it was considered to be the source of power. We know more or less how the election and investiture of the king took place. When a prince died, an interrex was named with the mission of designating the future king. In this designation, moreover, he only played an intermediary role, for it was Heaven which in reality designated the chosen one: this designation took place through the auspices. Once the new king was known, the augurs proceeded to his enthronement, the aim of which, as always and everywhere, was to publicly manifest the will of the gods and the investiture of their chosen one. The chosen sat on a seat of stone, facing South. An augur, wearing *infulae* and holding his staff, was at his left; with his *lituus* he traced certain lines in the sky, made a prayer and put his hand on the king's head, so that the gods might manifest with a visible sign—a lightning flash or a flock of birds—that they accepted the king. Once the sign was perceived, the king, now converted into a sacred, "divine", personage, assumed his functions. This very simple ritual was employed, for example, by Numa.[44]

This sacred character of the Roman kings is confirmed by legends referring to it: Romulus is the son of the god Mars, who was united to Rhea Sylvia; he did not die, but was taken to heaven and joined to the god Quirinus (this story means that the royal,

---

43. We have developed these different symbolisms in our studies *Le symbolisme du temple chrétien* and *La divine Liturgie* (Ed. de la Maisnie).

44. Livy 1.18.6 ff. Cf. Virgil, *Aeneid* 7.174.

divine principle, after having descended from heaven is reab-
sorbed there upon the disappearance of a prince, and returns to
descend upon his successor). In Numa, the "divine" character is
expressed in the legend of his secret visits to the nymph Egeria:
what is probably in question is a hierogamy, a rite that, in a sex-
ual form, places man in relation with a divine power manifested
in a feminine entity. This type of hierogamy is often encountered in sacred royalties. Another case, in ancient Italy, is that of
Rex nemorensis, the "King of the forests": that was the name of
the priest of Diana in Nemi, who doubtless had as his wife the
sylvan Diana, *Regina nemorum*. This, surely, is a survival of an
ancient royal rite. And it is to a hierogamy of this genre that the
incest of Oedipus should be related, this incest being merely a
late moralistic misinterpretation of the primitive royal rite in the
version of the oedipal myth we possess, and which obviously is
not the original one; what was quite certainly in question was
a hierogamy with a mother goddess, doubtless the *Terra Mater*.

A final confirmation of the "divine" character of Roman royalty is given to us by the ceremony of the *triumph*, in which the
royalty is so to speak perpetuated, at least in part; for the ritual
of the triumph, in the opinion of most experts, is modelled on a
royal ritual. The one triumphant was disguised as Jupiter-king:
his face covered with vermillion (exactly as the statue of Jupiter
Capitolinus on festival days), dressed in a purple tunic embroi-
dered with gold, a laurel wreath on his forehead, another in his
right hand; with the sceptre with an eagle at the end in his left
hand, he advanced, mounted on a quadriga, while a slave held a
crown of gold in the form of oak leaves over his head; and thus
he went to the Capitol where he celebrated a sacrifice. This ritual
of triumph deserves our attention, for it will play an important
part, as we shall see, in that species of monarchic restoration that
was the Empire.

GERMANIC LANDS · The sacral quality of royal power is also
well documented in the entire zone of Germanic civilisation. The
Scandinavian kings had as their mythic ancestor Odin (called
Wodan or Wotan among the Germans properly so-called), and
also Yngvi Frey, the god of the seasons, like the princes of Uppsala, who reigned in Norway until the Middle Ages: their royal

house was called Ynglingar, and next to their name they bore the name Yngri. The "royal nobles" of the Gothic Amali, from whom they chose their king, traced their ancestry also from Odin, under the name of Gapt. The Merovingians, for their part, according to the tradition of the Salian Franks, have as their ancestor Mero Vech, who was supposedly the son of Chlogio's Queen, after she was raped by a marine monster while bathing.

Even in the Germanic area a certain form of de facto "apotheosis" and a cult of the deceased kings is met with. Thus, the saga of King Gudmund of Sweden tells us that the people made sacrifices to him, naming him their god. The same occurred with the kings of Norway, Olaf Geirstadal and Halfdar the Black. This attitude of the Nordic peoples explains the legends that were formed regarding the survival of several princes, beginning with Charlemagne, who, they say, did not die, but was taken up—like Romulus, as we have seen—and is living in the Untersberg, near Salzburg. The last king of the Amali dynasty, Theodoric the Great, is supposed to have had the same destiny: raised up on his horse while still living, he wandered mysteriously over the world under the guise of a *wilder Jaeger* and would appear on certain occasions. It was also told that at the moment that Emperor Frederick II was dying (in 1250), a man in Sicily saw an army of horsemen and, in their midst, the Emperor, heading towards Etna (Etna was a "mountain of the dead" in which King Arthur had already been situated after his disappearance).

A closely related, although different, belief was the conviction that a deceased prince lived again in one of his descendants: Olaf the Holy, king of Norway (d. in 1030), passed as being the reincarnation of a king of the Ynglingar family, five generations previous, and who, in Geirstad, was the object of a tumultuous cult because he was considered a "divine" being.

Should these facts lead us to think that the kings of the Germanic tradition were divine beings "in their own right", as were the pharaohs of Egypt? Certainly not. The god did not descend into the Germanic king; what they are convinced of is that *a part* of the divine being lives in the king, that the king is, from on high, united to the divinity and the *divine power*. In summary, we are once again faced with the same conception as in the Indian or

Assyro-Babylonian traditions and so many others, namely, that the royal dignity and its power descend from the divinity upon the person of the king, but that the king remains its servant.

This well-marked sacral character of Germanic royalty may initially surprise when it is also known that, for historians, this royalty is supposedly a "democratic" royalty, since it was elective and the prince was designated by the people's assembly. The matter deserves to be examined, for it will allow us to specify what the traditional doctrine of power is—to which we have alluded at the beginning of this chapter—and what distinguishes between the *choice* of the one who exercises the authority and his *investiture*.

Let us first of all point out that the Germanic monarchy was not entirely elective, for it combined the elective system with the hereditary system, since one could not become king unless he belonged to the noble class. But it is certain, however, that even the son of a king could not become king unless he were *elected* by the assembly of the people. This assembly, called the *thing,* was constituted by arms-bearing freemen. Nevertheless, the Germanic royalty was not a "democratic" monarchy, as are modern monarchies, because the *investiture* of power really came from the divine world. In fact, the *thing* was not an ordinary, *profane* assembly, but a sacred assembly. We know from Tacitus that it was opened by a priest who summoned those attending as a "holy race", "sons of Heimdall"; that is to say, that all present were considered as participating in the divinity, since their origin was the race of the Aesir; likewise, the amphictyony of the Suevi, which opened with a sacrifice and in which the god was considered to be present.[45] It is probable that the *thing* took place under the auspices of *Mars-Thingsus*, an avatar of the Indo-European god of the sky, *Tiwaz,* blending the characters of the warrior god and the god-master of the world, guarantor of the universal order. Thus the *thing* was a sacral assembly, the purpose of which was—in investing the king *in the name of the divinity* in which he participated *ritually* (through the sacrifice)—to

---

45. Tacitus, *Germania* 39.

guarantee the order of the social life by entrusting it to the chosen prince. Thus sacralised, the people could elect the king and transmit the sacral dignity to him.

The same ways could be observed by the Celts: the king was elected and invested amongst them by the nobility, in representation of the military caste, but always under the supervision of the Druids, bearers of the spiritual authority.

It will be necessary to remember this particularity of the political institutions of the Northern peoples when we study French royalty, for something analogous is found in it regarding the relationship between the king and the people, and which seems to come from Nordic institutions by way of the Franks.

* * *

Here we shall stop this review of sacred royalties across space and time, for although it is true that a much greater number could be examined than we have, it is no less certain that such an examination, besides ending by being tiresome, would give us no further essential element regarding the matter. Even if one were to include in such a review the case of less important and less structured societies than those which have served us as examples, societies which have no "royalty" properly speaking, but rather a "chiefdom", one would arrive at the same results and, there as well, one would note that the conception and organisation of power are founded on a spiritual basis, and that the power is always considered to come from On High.

CHAPTER II

THE ROYAL FUNCTION

In the preceding chapter we have seen that the "mandate from heaven" allows the holder of power to exercise his function *legitimately*; but in addition, it allows him to exercise it *really* and *completely*. We shall now examine in what manner.

The royal function—one could, moreover, say political power in general—is to maintain, or if necessary, to re-establish, the social order which, when it is what it ought to be, lives in unity and harmony, peace, justice, and material and spiritual prosperity. This ideal of order and justice is, socially, the deepest aspiration of all men. But when their minds have not been deformed by bad prophets, they sense instinctively that the principle of unity that order must realise clearly cannot reside in the *multitude* of individuals, but in an *alterity*, which they seek and with which they endeavour to establish favourable relationships as with a transcendent reality. It is a common faith in this reality which is the principle of unity and of order, of peace, prosperity and justice, because authority is not an effective force for unity except by reference to a transcendent reality. The community is an entity unified and maintained by a power of spiritual cohesion. But just as this transcendent reality is *one*, so too its visible aspect in the social body must be *one*: this visible face of transcendence is the king. The king is to the kingdom what God is to the world: he is the Law of the world present in his kingdom, and it is through him that God, the only true master, exercises his power over men. It is in the king, inasmuch as he is the visible face of the ruling divinity, that men are united and form a community capable of helping them realise their destiny.

The royal function is very well defined and analysed in the commentary of the *Laws of Manu* left to us by Kulluka. Of

course, the subject is the Hindu king, but the terms of this work
have a sufficiently universal bearing so as to be applicable to any
sovereign, by means of some easily accomplished transpositions.

According to this document, his function makes the king the
shepherd, the protector of his people against aggression by his
justice, and by his power against calamities; in addition, the more
the king is a good king, the greater is his protective power. Eight
devas define and specify this royal task: the Sun, the Moon, Fire,
Wind, Yama, Kubera, Varuna, and Indra. Like the *Sun*, the king
scatters the dark beings, the enemies, overcomes his rivals in
splendor, and knows everything through his spies; he possesses
the light, the energy and the principle of a supernatural power
which enable him to accomplish great exploits. But the king is
also called *somya*, "like the *Moon*", that is to say, placid and gentle, hence gifted with a quality that tempers the "solar" power.
The king must please his subjects, by protecting them in accordance with *dharma*, by giving them gifts, and by multiplying religious feast days. But this goodwill does not exclude rigour: as
Yama, the god of death and punishment, the prince must control
his subjects; he is their judge. That is why, as *Yama*, he must carry
the sceptre upright, ready to strike at need. As *Fire* (*Agni*), who
fills the universe and purifies it, the king exterminates evil doers;
Agni is also the one who carries offerings to the gods, and in the
same way the king must accomplish certain sacrifices relating to
his role as mediator. *Kubera*, "Lord of the North", is the god of
wealth associated with *Riddhi*, "Prosperity"; he is generous and
is the god of fecundity; like him, the king must be wealthy, not
in the first place for himself, but for his people, and yet for himself as well. However, there is an aspect regarding this which will
seem surprising to the modern mentality, which worships egalitarianism, yet which is natural and plays an important role: the
wealth of the king is the *sign* of the divine Wealth—"the Rich" is
one of the 99 Divine Names in Islam—namely, the inexhaustible
fecundity of God, of which the king is in some wise the steward
of his people. We will have occasion to return to this point when
we speak of royal *pageantry*. *Varuna* personifies the static aspect
of power; he is the god of *dharma*, the Law, which the king must
follow and defend on earth; he is the protector of the Truth and

the Law, and the master of the laws of nature. *Indra*, for his part, represents the dynamic aspect of power: he regulates vitality in the world, the vegetation; he is also the god of war, the destroyer of evil forces, slayer of demons, the god of battles. Following his example, the king assures the prosperity of the land by respecting *dharma* and by regulating the powers of fertility. The king's bow is identified with the *vajra*, the "lightning bolt" of Indra; the feast of Indra, the source of prosperity, is one of the king's duties. Finally, the god of the *Wind* personifies freedom, for it goes wherever it pleases; it too is a destroyer of demons and producer of wealth. Following his example the king is the "Extender", who extends his kingdom through his conquests. This role of the wind rejoins that of *Vishnu*, another great royal God, as we have mentioned before. It is told that the first king, *Prithu*, was the favourite of *Vishnu*. He was crowned by the god, who "entered into his body", and that is why all kings receive the domination of *Vishnu* over the world; the name of *Prithu* signifies "the vast", and he is the source of prosperity for the earth, which is *Prithivi*, "the Vast".[1] This aspect of royalty is linked to the *Ashvamedha* sacrifice, to which we shall return.

This commentary of Kulluka constitutes as it were a "table of contents" which we shall analyse.

The first thing that strikes the reader of this text—and it is its presiding idea—is that the social order, which is maintained by the king, depends on the cosmic order; this stems from the fact that the royal qualities and duties are directly placed in relationship with the divinities symbolised by the elements of nature or the principles of its Law, of *dharma*, such as *Varuna* and *Indra* amongst others, and who preside over the two complementary principles of stability and movement, the static and the dynamic. Now, this dependence of the social order on the order of nature is the primary basis of the traditional doctrine of power at all times and in all places.

Here, for example, is a hymn composed for the enthronement of the pharaoh Merenptah, in which the moral order, the social

---

1. Translator's note: the terms are respectively masculine and feminine.

order, justice and material prosperity, are placed together in parallel fashion and intimately connected:

> Let the whole land rejoice, the favourable time hath arrived;
> A lord of all the lands hath been assigned;
> All ye righteous ones, come and see!
> Truth hath overcome the lie;
> The sinners have fallen on their faces,
> The greedy have been sent away.
> The water hath halted and hath ceased falling,
> The Nile carries the swollen waters;
> The days are long, the nights have their hours,
> The months come as they ought;
> The gods are content, their hearts are glad;
> Life passes in laughter and in wonder.

The same inspiration is to be found in the royal hymn of Solomon, Psalm 72:

> Give the king thy judgments, O God, and thy righteousness
>   unto the king's son.
> He shall judge thy people with righteousness, and thy poor with
>   judgment.
> The mountains shall bring peace to the people and little hills, by
>   righteousness.... He shall spare the poor and needy, and
>   shall save the souls of the needy...
> There shall be an handful of corn in the earth upon the top of
>   the mountains;
> The fruit thereof shall shake like Lebanon ...

Thus, order and prosperity go hand in hand, and both depend upon the respect for that which in India is termed *Dharma*, the Law. *Dharma*, of course, is the religious, moral, juridical, and customary law governing a people; but this law is not, as in modern and lay societies, the product of human considerations largely subject to the contingencies of time and place (when it does not go *against* the natural and divine law); it is an impersonal authority, sacred and eternal, the reflection on the social plane of the divine Law that regulates the order of the universe

Egypt, too, possessed an acute awareness of this universal Law, which there was termed *Maat*. The word is often translated as "justice", but this is only one aspect of *Maat*, unless the term "justice" be given the extended meaning which it has in the Bible, and which expresses submission to God in all things. "Do the thing of *Maat* for the king, for the *Maat* is what the king loves; say the thing of *Maat* for the King, for what the king loves is the *Maat*," say a number of funerary inscriptions. *Maat* is the right state of nature and society, as it has been fixed by the creative act. In all things it is necessary to mantain or restore this state of *Maat*, instituted by God at the beginning and which must be conserved and guaranteed by the king. It is said of Tutankhamen that he "hath driven away the disorder of the Two Lands (Egypt) and *Maat* hath been firmly installed; he hath made of lies an abomination and the land is as it was at the beginning." Indeed, *Maat* is what characterises the primordial state, as another inscription at Thebes proclaims: "*Maat* descended to the earth during their age (that of the gods) and made an alliance with the gods.... *Maat* came from heaven during their age and associated with those who lived upon the earth." The presence of *Maat* in the land depends upon its union with the king, for it is through the channel of the king that the *Maat* continues to descend, on condition, however, that the king himself be united to *Maat*. Thus, the queen Hatshepsut wrote: "I offered to Amon the *Maat* which he loved, for I know that it is from it that he liveth. She too is my bread and I drink of her dew. Am I not one with him?"

In China *Tao* is a conception altogether analogous to *Maat* and, like it, is a difficult word to translate, for its meaning varies with its context, and it expresses synthetically many important ideas. It is usually translated as the "Way", but fundamentally the term which best renders its essential content is "Order". We have already said that the "Way of Heaven" (*tien-tao*) means the "Order of Heaven", the "Celestial Order", and we have pointed out the relationship which unites the king (*wang*) to the *Tao*.[2] *Tao*, the order of the world, the cosmic order generated symbolically by Heaven, that is to say, Divinity, is also the rule of the king, which is expressed by saying that the *wang-tao*, the order of the king, is analogically identified with the *tien tao*, the celestial order. The "Royal Way" (*wang-tao*) more specifically designates the vertical axis, the *Axis Mundi*, with which the king is identified inasmuch as he possesses the "mandate of heaven" (*tien-ming*) and in which he is the "Son of Heaven" (*tien-tse*).[3] The prince and the *Tao* are macro-cosmically united along this vertical line, and are microcosmically united by virtue of the analogical relationships which link man to the cosmos. Ideally, the prince, rising by successive degrees of consciousness to the higher reality, ends by attaining the "Way", the *Tao* which rules the phenomenal universe. Such is the Taoist teaching: "In the kingdom," we read, "there are four parts of majesty, and one of them pertains to the king. The ways of men depend on those of the earth, the ways of the earth upon those of Heaven, the ways of Heaven upon those of the *Tao*, and the way of the *Tao* upon the universal order."[4] Another text, of Ssu Ma Chien, alluding to the imperial chariot, identifies it with the Great Bear (another way of evoking the *Axis Mundi*), and he describes the function of the sovereign thus: in his chariot "he moves in the Centre; he rules the four Quarters; he divides *Yin* and *Yang*, (that is, the initial polarisation of the universal Energy); he determines the four seasons; he balances the five elements; he unfolds the divisions of time; he fixes the various calculations." The king here appears in the role of a *Cosmocrator*, of a Master of the world; in reality, he is so at the level of his kingdom, his function being that of regulating its life by imitating the order of the universe. Worthy of note particularly is the allusion to *Yin* and *Yang*, the two principles that act at all levels of reality, and which, according to the Chinese tradition, condition all things on all planes, including the

---

2. See Chapter I, p. 20.

3. *Ibid.*

4. *Tao Te Ching* 25.

social. The harmonious equilibrium of *Yin* and *Yang* determines the social harmony as well as the physical and psychic health of the individual. The role of the king is to organise or maintain the division of the realm, established according to certain numbers: the myth of Yu the Great, the hero, sage, and sovereign at the origin, determined the 9 provinces, the 9 mountains, the 9 courses of the water, the 4 cardinal directions, parcelled out the lands, and gave the family names. "A wise prince," says Liun-Yu, "gives to things the names which correspond to them, and each thing must be treated according to the meaning of the name it has been given." Similarly, the king assigns to men very different kinds of work; and in classifying beings and things he prevents confusion between ordinary and sacred activities, a disordered contact between Heaven and Earth.

POLITICS · In traditional societies[5] politics in the modern sense does not exist. Everything concerning government legislation—the acts of public life, as well as those of private life—is included in the universal life, subject to the heavenly powers, and the government of men is only one dependence upon the religion, this last term taken in its broadest sense. In these societies, the human community is placed in harmony with the cosmic order and thereby reflects the divine order; and the king is charged with maintaining these harmonious relations between human society and the supernatural powers, the dynamic principle of life and of spirituality. That is why a bad king is a disaster, even on the plane of physical nature, for, say the *Laws of Manu*, "he disturbs the harmony with the Invisible."

It is perhaps difficult for the modern Westerner to understand this conception of politics and to acknowledge this dependence of the social structure and life with the order of nature, which is itself dependent upon the divine order, although his ancestors in the Middle Ages—just as man has at all times and in all places—considered it altogether normal, without ever calling into ques-

---

5. Let us specify that we use the expression "traditional society" in a much stricter and above all much different sense than that given to it by ethnologists generally: every society that is based on a superhuman sacred tradition which governs its entire structure and life is traditional.

tion its soundness. For this conception of politics is a simple requirement of traditional and universal anthropology and ontology, which teach us that man is a microcosm, a synthesis of the world, which means that his nature synthesises the nature of the other beings: all that is in the creation has its representation and its correspondence in man, hence the correlations that exist between the modifications of the cosmic order and those in the human order, and conversely.

SACRED HISTORY · The peoples that are termed "primitive" are very aware of all this. For them, events are produced not by contacts with spatial matter, but by the influence of an internal energy upon another internal energy. And their principal concern is not to feed themselves or to fight amongst themselves, as most ethnologists think; it is to enter into a relationship with the true world, with the Invisible,[6] and to be in harmony with it.[7] And the epithet "primitive" given to these peoples suits them in a certain manner, although by no means in the sense given to it by modern scholars, for whom "primitive" is synonymous with "savage", in accordance with the evolutionist dogma to which we have already alluded at the beginning of this book, and according to which the first man was close to being an animal, and from which he is supposed to have issued. For the sacred tradition, however, it is the exact opposite which is the truth; primitive man was the perfect man, resembling not the animal, but the angel. Let one refer to the narrative in *Genesis*, which is in conformity with all the analogous narratives of the other particular traditions. This man perfectly realised the microcosmic

---

6. See the work, already mentioned, by Jean Servier, *L'homme et l'invisible*; cf. p. 17.

7. "The more primitive ones at times have very rich rites; all their intelligence ends in being absorbed in religious concerns. Such is the case with the Australian aborigine; from the moment he is initiated, he divides his life into two sections: ordinary life, consisting in finding food and making necessary tools, and then life dedicated to holy or secret things. And he becomes more and more interested in these latter concerns, which end by occupying his entire mind; the ceremonies are very serious matters, because through them he enters into contact with real beings" (Spencer and Gillen, *The Northern Tribes of Central Australia*, 1904, pp. 33-34).

synthesis of which we spoke above; he grasped intuitively and immediately the essence of things and at the same stroke found himself effortlessly in total harmony with the world, and thereby with the divine. After the spiritual catastrophe that caused him to "fall" from the primordial state, man lost this beatitude and found himself in his present state, wherein he perceives all things *from without*, coming up against the screen of dense matter. But he did not find himself all at once in the present stage, wherein the world is apprehended as a simple aggregate of sensations; at least this perception did not constitute the true world for him. Even though seeing things *from without*, which was his new manner of knowing, he continued to act as before, whereby he entered into contact with them instantaneously and *from within*. He kept his initial "preternatural" mentality, as the theologians say, and transmitted it to his descendents in the form of the sacred and religious tradition. Throughout the thousands of years of the cycle of our humanity, man maintained this mentality which the moderns term "pre-logical", but which in reality is *ontological*. This is the mentality that is found in today's "primitive" peoples, which justifies this epithet in a sense which is altogether opposed to the one given to it by modern people. It is true that these "primitives" are often very degenerate peoples in certain respects; this is undeniable, but what we wish to say is that, despite everything, they continue to possess a primordial mentality and that they conceive the world not as dense matter, but as a living energetic world, full of forces with which it is necessary to be in harmony. What is interesting in these peoples is that they perpetuate, in the modern era, a conception of the world which tends to be progressively eclipsed—under the influence of the West, moreover—in the societies of the great nations which for a long time were traditional, such as India or China: for this conception of the world was that of all the great civilisations of the past, including the Christian civilisation.

This reminder of sacred history was necessary in order explain and make understandable the traditional conception of the role of the king as the conservator of the harmony between the society of men and the rest of the world.

"KING OF THE WORLD" · This aspect of the royal function is indicated by a title found in a number of ancient civilisations, according to which the sovereign is called "universal king", "king of the universe", or "king of the world". In Iran, for example, he is the "master of the world", or again, "Lord of the Seven Lands", the earth being divided into seven zones in Iranian cosmology. In India, he is the "universal king", and the same occurs in ancient Egypt, where the pharaoh was called the sovereign of the "whole Earth". It is necessary, however, that these expressions be understood correctly: they do not mean that the king is literally the king of the universe, that he reigns over the entire earth, nor still less over all of nature. They mean that the king, over a given territory, reigns in conformity with the universal order. In this way he participates in the archetype of the divine king who is the real king of the universe. In India we have seen that the prince represents *Prajapati*, who is the ruler and the life of the entire world; in Iran, he is, for his kingdom, like the archetypal king *Yima*, to whom, according to the *Avesta*, the goddess *Anahita* gave all powers over the "earth of the Seven Parts".

ARCHITECTURE · The correspondence thus established between the total world and a given particular kingdom causes it to be identified, as it were, with a model of the universe. We have seen this with the *Ming-tang* in China, and we shall have occasion to return to it; it is also seen in urban architecture and in the royal palaces of the Near East. Their general plan was circular, in the image of Heaven. Darabgerd, the city of the Parthians, in eastern Iran, was a wall with a trench forming a perfect circle. A second interior wall formed a concentric circle; the surface thus delimited was divided into equal sections by avenues radiating from the centre towards the gates of the walls, four of which were situated at the four cardinal directions (see plates p. 53). Firuzabad, the city of the Sassanid dynasty, was constructed in exactly the same fashion (see plates p. 54); and likewise, during the Islamic period, Baghdad, the "round city" of Mansur, founded in 762, at a date chosen by the Naubakht, the official astrologer of the Caliph. These royal cities were continuations of the oriental encampments of the same structure, as is shown by the reliefs of the palace of Kalash (see plate p. 54).

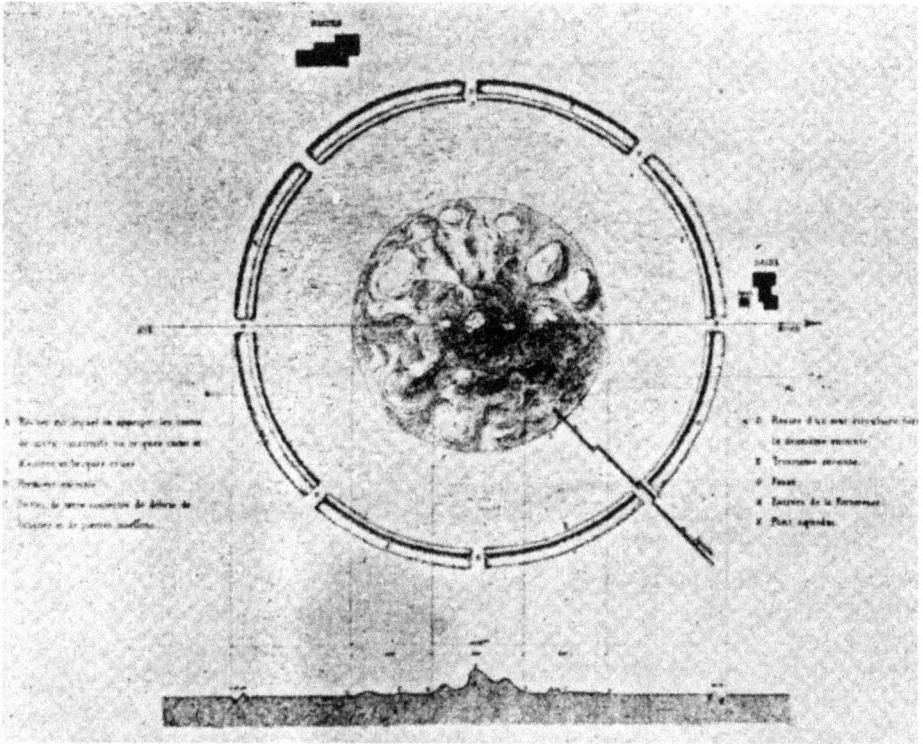

Darabgerd (according to Flandin and Coste, *Voyage en Perse*).

The city of Mansur

Assyrian camp (Kalash palace relief).

Firuzabad (aerial view, by Ghirshman).

Trelleborg, Viking fortress (aerial view).

Subsequently, on the model of Baghdad, other cities were built throughout the Middle East, for example, Hiraqla, the city of Harun al-Rashid, or Sabra, that of the third Fatimid caliph, Ismail. And under Arab influence, this type of construction passed to the West, where it is represented by the Viking camps and the castles of Trelleborg and Aggersborg.

These constructions aim at reproducing an image of the movement of heaven, the king himself being an image of the sun, in this part of the world as well as elsewhere, more or less. It is curious that the ideal city of Plato presents an analogous form: it is divided into twelve sections (the signs of the zodiac) by which the laws and the proportions of the cosmos penetrate it, Plato tells us; the inhabitants are also placed under the influence of these cosmic laws. "We must think," continues Plato, "that each part is sacred, because it is a gift of God, and follows the months and the revolution of the Whole. Thus the entire city is regulated by its relationship with the Whole, which sanctifies the parts."[8] It is vain to ask whether Plato borrowed from the Near East this vision of the ideal city; it is possible, but he could just as well have inherited it from another source, for we are faced here with a quasi-universal conception.

---

8. Plato, *The Laws* 745 ff.

The cities which we have pointed out are divided, then, into four quarters by the two great avenues oriented according to the cardinal directions; they represent the cosmic wheel, the movement of the heavens that determines the rhythm of the seasons and of life; at the intersection of the two great avenues, the central point is a reflection of the axis of the cosmic wheel, and it is there that the royal palace is raised, the king thus being identified with the *Axis Mundi*—like the emperor of China, as we have seen—moreover, one of his titles in the Near East is "Axis and pole of the world", which refers to the royal power considered as the universal motive power by participation in the celestial power. The royal city appears as an image of heaven; it is an *ouranopolis*, and for it, the king plays the part of this celestial Power for the universe; it is he who "turns the cosmic wheel", a Hindu expression which we shall encounter later, when the prince is considered as *chakravartin*.

In the royal palace, the throne room presents, along with other details, the same symbolism. It is round with a vaulted ceiling like the sky and turning on its own axis. The mediaeval legend of Prester John tells of this mysterious personage who possessed such a revolving room. In any case there was one in the residence of Chosros, the king of Iran, at Ganzaca; the vault was decorated with the image of Chosros presiding in the sky in the midst of the sun, the moon and the stars; this room was turned by means of horses placed in the area underground. We know, through Firdausi, that the throne of Chosros turned in accordance with the seasons and the signs of the zodiac, and that around the throne were to be seen, along with the signs of the zodiac, the stars and the planets, each of these elements moving and turning around the throne. Thus, the king, in the midst of his vassals and his satraps, presented an image of the celestial hierarchy: the great officials surrounded the sovereign as the other orbs around the sun. During the feast of the New Year, which was of great importance in Iran, the prince distributed or redistributed offices: it was then said that he made the destinies of men, in the image of the signs in the sky whose influence also determines human destinies.

There is yet another illustration of this scene in the decorations of the royal tombs and the reliefs of the palace of Persepolis (Achaemenid era). For example, during the course of a solemn ceremony, the nobility can be seen surrounding the king wearing a cydaris, holding a bow and placed on a small three-stage dais, which the inscription indicates is a throne. This dais is on a platform carried by bearers with raised arms; the figures turn towards the right when advancing the left foot, and the throne moves in the same direction. The Achaemenid king, like the Sassanid king, is placed in an environment of astral symbols. He always faces the sun and the moon, depicted before him in the direction of the movement followed by the throne: the sun in the form of a winged disk joined to the bust of *Ahuramazda*, and the moon in the form of the disk of the full moon inlaid with the crescent moon. The ritual movement of the scene is in relation to the astral gods; likewise, the gesture of the king in prayer and the fire altar before him. What occurs here is an act of worship by which the king is placed in harmony with the heavenly movement, and thereby manifests his divine power, as in the feast of the New Year, which is also portrayed on the relief of the palace

On the right, Iranian representations of the solar disc as a shield. On the left, Ahuramazda atop the world circle (Persepolis relief, G.L. Winthrop collection).

at Persepolis: in the "Chamber of a Hundred Columns" the king is shown on his throne as we have just described.[9]

We have enlarged somewhat on these architectural works because they are very typical and graphic symbols of the traditional conception of royalty and its function. Let us add immediately that they are not "gratuitous" symbols, to put it thus, or have a merely suggestive value; this point has to be emphasised, for men today readily see in symbols a merely suggestive value or "artistic procedures"—ideas which are completely foreign to traditional culture and to the reality of things. The symbolic cities and palaces we have evoked had a *ritual* value, and in reality constituted *petrified rites* authenticating the royal function. Indeed, in the societies we are speaking of, architecture was, and in some places still is, in its spirit and in its procedures, a completely different science than the empirical and profane art it has become for the modern world. In the traditional conception, the architectural *rite* has the effect of fixing on the ground an image of the source of a celestial influx.[10] This architecture springs

---

9. This type of Oriental rotunda was imitated in the West. Nero's famous *Domus Aurea* was one. Suetonius (*Nero*, 31) described it as turning on its axis day and night "like the world", and Nero was depicted in it with the features of Apollo-Helios. Septimius Severus, in his residence at Palatine, was depicted between two planetary gods, in the middle of the cosmos, as the lord of the seven celestial spheres, and the throne room had a ceiling imitating the starry sky.

10. We have developed this subject in our book on the *Symbolism of the Christian Temple*. Let us point out, without being able to dwell on it extensively, that the form of buildings is not a matter of indifference; it not only has a suggestive value for the mind, as we said above, but also, its action extends much further: it favours or hinders (!) subtle influences, which in turn are the vehicle for spiritual influences, for the spiritual world comes to us, and we go to it, through the visible world. Regarding this, we shall limit ourselves to just one observation. Today, scientists are beginning to rediscover the existence of the "waves of forms", which traditional sciences have always known, and which can be either beneficent or not. By way of information, we shall cite the example of a relatively recent and very significant experience, the effect produced by the waves of forms on human behaviour. An architect had the idea of constructing an office building in the form of an inverted pyramid, and it turned out to be uninhabitable, and had to be evacuated because the personnel suffered from intolerable

from sacred geometry, one of the traditional sciences which in the last analysis pertains to the spiritual Authority, and which the temporal power is in charge of maintaining and applying. These sciences play a great part in societies governed by a sacred royalty, for they make it possible to apply to different activities the general principle of conformity to the order of the world. The most important science, because it is directly related to this end, is cosmology—traditional cosmology, of course, which has little to do with what is today designated by the name. This cosmology is constructed, not only from the observation of phenomena, but above all, and in the first place, starting from the principles of ontology and, ultimately, of metaphysics, the sole means—whether rationalist and materialist scholars like it or not—of giving a science an indisputable foundation.

SOCIAL ORDER · In one form or another, cosmology has served to establish the structure of a society and the constitution of its groups. For example, it is the basis of the institution which aims at maintaining the conformity between the human and cosmic orders on the social plane. Indeed, the castes are founded on the primary data of cosmology, namely, the *elements* and the *tendencies*. The elements air, fire, earth, and water, are the constitutive principles of corporeal beings, their substantial determinations.[11] The tendencies are the constitutive qualities of bodies, and are three in number: the ascending tendency (*sattva*), the expansive tendency (*rajas*), and the descending tendency (*tamas*). The play of the elements and tendencies determines

---

discomforts. A good lesson for ignorant people who take no account of the inversion of symbols!

11 To these four elements it is proper to add a fifth element, the *ether*, which is their common source (the *quintessence* of the Western middle ages). Let us specify that the words *air, fire, water, earth* do not designate the visible forms of current language: they are symbolical designations of *substantial principles*, inaccessible to the senses. Moreover, every physical body is constituted of a mixture of all the elements, with one of them predominating. Let us also add that, to the elements the *substantial determinations* of bodies there correspond the *essential* determinations, which are designated by the sensible qualities corresponding to them: hearing, smell, etc.

individual natures, and the castes are the distribution of these individual natures into homogeneous groups. Individuals in whom the ascending tendency and the element fire dominates are the *brahmins*; those in whom air and the expansive tendency dominate are the *kshatriyas* (warriors, nobles); those in whom water and a mixture of the expansive and descending tendencies dominate are the *vaishyas* (merchants, craftsmen, farmers, etc.); finally, those in whom earth and the descending tendency dominate are the *shudras*, the low end of the social scale. These four categories of individuals are characterised, in the final analysis, by the end which they aim at attaining in life and which is the fruit of their nature: for the *brahmin* it is *dharma*, that is, "righteousness" in the Biblical sense, wisdom and holiness; for the *kshatriya* it is power and glory; for the *vaishya* it is power through possession of material goods; for the *shudra* it is satisfaction of the most material needs. It goes without saying that at the interior of each caste the individual has, of course, the possibility of rising spiritually, and there are records of *shudras* who have attained the highest degree in this domain. We have no intention of passing judgment on the system of castes nor of studying its situation in India. We employ it as a system of reference which, if one sets aside the particular modalities that determine it in the Indian society, is valid, *mutatis mutandis*, for other societies, for the very simple reason that this division of individual natures and their activities corresponds to the nature of things, and that this division has moreover existed elsewhere, based on the same principles and in an analogous form, for example, that of the three "Orders" in the Christian Middle Ages.

Another science, which directly issues from cosmology, moreover, is astrology, which, aside from its application to medicine, played a great part until relatively recently in the courts of princes. Its primary object, at least during the great ages, was not primarily divination and prediction; above all, it allowed the prince to know the favourable moments to undertake this or that action in harmony with the state of the world and nature.

To return to architecture, the works we have noted above have the advantage of throwing light on the situation of the king considered as a centre, the axial position of which we have already mentioned in relation to the emperor of China.[12] This importance of the centre cannot be emphasised too strongly in relation to traditional conceptions generally, and in particular in relation to royalty and the manner in which its function is exercised. To repeat, this function is to maintain the harmony between the human group and the order of the universe, represented respectively by the Earth and Heaven; these communicate by the axis which passes through the centre of the universal sphere, measuring the extension of the cosmos and marking the hierarchy of the states of manifested Existence. The sacred king, who by his function is identified with the "true man", is situated at this central point where the powers of heaven and earth are united. He is the tangible point of contact with the immutable Essence and the eternal Will which rules things. For this reason his person constitutes a *dynamic centre*, symbolically identified with the centre of the world, and from which the forces of the four directions of space radiate. Consequently, the king plays the part of a double receptacle, that of the "earth" and that of "heaven": in fact, he is the receptacle of the collective life of the human group, because it is in him that the people are united and as if incorporated; but he is also the receptacle of the "celestial influx", of "blessings" which descend from On High, which he receives and which through him pass to the people. Thus the king is a mediator between God and his people.

How does he exercise this function?

Firstly, in a manner which could be termed "passive", although this term is only a first approximation which it will be appropriate to rectify. In reality, through the axial position which we have just analysed, the prince plays somewhat the part of a *channel* by which the earth communicates with heaven. And this is an aspect of his function worth dwelling on a little, for the modern mentality believes that a chief of State fulfils his mission best by being active and multiplying his personal interventions in all domains and at all times in the manner of a businessman. Nothing could be further from the way of looking at things of traditional societies, for which the king is firstly a *presence*, the

---

12 See Chapter I, pp. 19ff.

presence of that *radiating centre* which we evoked above. The extreme form of this conception is found in ancient China, for which the ideal sovereign is a sage who civilises the world by the efficacy of his virtue; he *rules* without *governing*, leaving this latter activity to his functionaries: he dedicates himself to creating, or rather to "emanating" order. This virtue is of course moral virtue, as the emperor Wen (167 BC) used to say: "According to what I know of the Heavenly Way, calamities come from evil acts and happiness follows from virtue. The faults of all functionaries must have their origin in me. Now, the functionaries who are in charge of the secret prayers transfer calamities to their inferiors: it is to make manifest that I have no virtue"; and he ordered all to "reflect on the faults he, the emperor, may have committed, in the imperfections of his knowledge, his opinions, and his thoughts, and to declare them to him clearly." The body of functionaries which represented the conscience of the Empire was the conscience of the Emperor extended and propagated; the value of this body of functionaries was the value of the "unique man", for the efficacy of the imperial "majesty" bettered the administrators. On the contrary, the loss of virtue amounted to the loss of the country; that is why in the Chou-King one reads that "king Hsia extinguished his virtue and exercised violence," and for that reason was dethroned. Similarly, with the ancient Turco-Mongols, the human-celestial order was broken if the *kagan*, the emperor, committed grave faults, if he usurped power or exceeded the mandate which had been entrusted to him. But one can see by these very examples that the notion of imperial "Virtue" transcended its simple meaning as moral rule. This is perfectly normal, moreover, for morality is not, as is too often believed, a code of conventional and altogether relative rules; morality, ethics, in its fundamental prescriptions, which are universal, is nothing other than an art of living deduced from the science of "actions and concordant reactions", which is itself an application of cosmological realities, the aim of which is precisely to maintain man in harmony with the natural world and the divine world. Thus the virtue of the emperor, in the sense of moral virtue, was only an aspect, and in the final analysis a consequence, of a virtue in a much broader sense, and which the documents also term his "efficacy", that is, the superhuman strength and power (the meaning of the word *virtus* in Latin) that reside in him and radiate outside him: it is in this that his imperial "majesty" consists, termed *mnatan* by the kings of ancient Tibet.

Returning to our topic concerning the way in which the royal function is exercised, this *mnatan* acts by itself without the prince having to act: it merely allows the power of "majesty" to radiate. The same idea exists in China, of course. The ideal sovereign *acts through Non-action (wu-wei)*, according to Taoist doctrine. Chuang-Tzu writes:

> The emperor concentrates on Non-action, which is the Way of Heaven.... The ancient rulers abstained from acting on their own, allowing Heaven to govern through them.... At the summit of the universe, the Principle influences Heaven and Earth, which transmits this influence to all beings, and which, entering the world of men, becomes good government, and causes talents and capacities to appear. Conversely, all prosperity comes from good government, the efficacy of which is derived from the Principle through the intermediary of Heaven and Earth. Because the ancient rulers desired nothing the world was filled with abundance; they did not act and all things were modified according to the norm; they remained immersed in their meditation, and the realm enjoyed the most perfect order. The ancient adage summarises it thus: everything prospers for the one who is united to Unity; even the genies submit to him who has no interest of his own.

The meaning of Non-action has to be clearly understood. Naturally, it does not mean sloth; Non-action is the giving up of all outward activity along with, as the text above says, the "desire" which generates such activity. However, from a certain point of view, Non-action is the most powerful activity, the power of meditation, in which, as Chuang-Tzu says, the emperor "was immersed", which is to say the inward activity which maintained him in contact with the powers of On High. It can now be grasped how the emperor could govern without any *administrative* involvement; he ruled without any particular act. Insofar as his will is in accord with the universal order so too are the actions of others: it suffices for him to be "true man";[13] the energy which in him is concentrated in its pure state will determine, as by a subtle inductive current, a unanimous convergence of desires and actions. The imperial will thus upholds the entire Empire.

The same held true in ancient Japan. One of the rites of the palace consisted in the emperor remaining seated motionless several hours upon the throne every morning, with the crown on his head, in order to assure the peace of the empire, a rite which later was replaced by a hetimasia;[14] they were satisfied with leaving the imperial crown on the throne, but this did not change the rite at all, for both throne and crown, as we shall have occasion to repeat, were charged with the "virtue" of the prince, with his *barakah*.

The conception of power was no different in essence in Indian royalty. The prince, as "universal king", by assimilation to the King of the world, the primordial *Manu*, or in Buddhist lands the Buddha himself, was like them called *chakravartin*, "He who turns the wheel", the great Wheel, symbol of cosmic becoming. Now, he who turns the wheel is he who is situated in the empty hub, and who therefore is the "motionless mover"—another way of expressing the doctrine of Non-action.[15] At Angkor can be seen a *mandala* in the form of a wheel with eight spokes at the centre of which is enthroned a Buddha in the effigy of the king; the kings of Angkor all bore the title of *chakravartin*. At Barabudur the *stupas* played an analogous part. The *stupa* is the cosmic Law concentrated in an architectural object, an image of the *Dharma-raja*, "the King of the Law", the *chakravartin*.[16]

---

13. *Ibid.*

14. Perhaps the reader will recall that in Christian surroundings a similar hetimasia was practised in solemn ecclesiastical assemblies: a throne was raised, which remained empty, but upon which the Gospel was placed, which amounted to having Christ preside over the assembly.

15. Cf. Chapter II, p. 63.

16. All this had been luminously analysed by P. Mus in his monumental work, *Barabudur*.

In its absolute form, this doctrine of royal Non-action constitutes a limit which is never really attained; but it draws the "profile" of the function of sacred royalties and its essential mode of operation. Of course, in the exercise of power the ruler is led to accomplish certain actions, but these are very specific and limited in number—the prince is not a meddler and, above all, these actions are always subordinated to the fundamental attitude; it could be said that for him action is only the outward aspect—necessary in certain circumstances—of the essential Non-action of his function.

These actions of the ruler are fundamentally diverse ritual acts and sacrifices.

Thus, in ancient Tibet, the king, in order to radiate his *mnatan*, his beneficent "Virtue", executed a particular dance under the direction of the chief shaman; in addition, for this ceremony he dressed in the white garb of the shaman.

CHINA · In China many sacrifices were celebrated: to the Sun, the Moon, the stars, the Six Venerables (the cosmological elements), the four Directions, the five Mountains, etc. All these sacrifices were in principle accomplished by the emperor; in reality, of course, the emperor alone would not have done them all, but they were all done in his name. However, only the emperor accomplished the great Chinese sacrifice, the Sacrifice to Heaven, in the circular temple at Peking, a sacrifice whose object was to thank the heavenly King and to assure the peace and happiness of the realm and the people. Here is how an anonymous poet of the eighth century BC sang this great liturgy in the *Book of Songs*:

> The august Emperor-Father betakes himself to the temple of
>   Heaven.
> He bows at the motionless centre of the Middle Empire and says:
> The brambles and wild bushes of my domain have been burnt;
> The tilled fields yield a rich harvest;
> Our granaries are full, and I make an offering to powerful Heaven.
> The fairest heads of our flocks shall be flayed and roasted,
> And the purest wine shall fill our cups.
> Bells, drums and flutes shall celebrate the sacrifice.

The ceremony has been celebrated at its time, it has been fully
accomplished;
May our sons and the sons of your sons celebrate it always.

The imperial cult of Heaven was at first celebrated each year,
then every three years, at the first day of the first moon; in Hue
it was celebrated until 1915. It is not surprising that this rite was
reserved for the emperor, since he is the "Son of Heaven" and
thereby executes the principal act of his function as mediator
between Earth and heaven.[17]

The emperor also accomplished the sacrifice to the Ancestor
Emperors, an act which aimed at maintaining alive the "virtue"
proper to the founding ancestors and which had to pass to their
successors.

Another important rite, the most important after the sacrifice
to Heaven, because it is the act of the sacred government, is the
ritual of the *Ming-tang*. The *Ming-tang* is the place where the science of governing, which is the science of the *Tao*, is truly exercised. The *Tao*, as we have said, is the principal regulator of the
universe, of Space and of Time. The science of the *Tao* is the art
of organising the world, and it is the attribute of the prince. The
Tao is also wisdom and holiness, virtue, the practical knowledge
of the famous Hexagrams. The emperor participates inasmuch
as he is "true man" situated at the axis uniting Earth and Heav-
en. And this axis, as we shall see, is materialised in the *Ming-tang*.

This edifice referred to the division of ancient China into nine
provinces, one at the centre and the rest at the cardinal points
and the intermediate points, according to the following diagram:

4	9	2
3	5	7
8	1	6

---

17. See Chapter II, p. 47ff.

This division of the Empire was determined by the origin myth, which refers back to Yu the Great, the Hero, the Sage who, at the origin, organised the world—and thus China—in order to measure it in accordance with the form of a square: he constructed the world by means of his "virtue", fixed the 9 provinces, the 9 mountains, the 9 rivers and the 4 cardinal points, and distributed the lands. He accomplished all these acts imitating in his progress the movement of the sun, which is the "heavenly way". The diagram in our text constitutes what is termed—improperly, moreover—a "magic square"; the Empire was an image of the universe, and at the centre was the number 5, the mid-point of the first nine numbers and the number of the Earth:[18] it was the central province, the imperial residence, and the "Invariable Middle".[19]

The *Ming-tang*, or "Temple of Light", reproduced this pattern: like the cities and palaces of the Near East which we pointed out above,[20] it is an image of the Empire and of the universe concentrated in one place, and in which spatial symbolism is placed in relationship with the course of the seasons, hence its designation sometimes as the "house of the calendar". The *Ming-tang* had a square base, symbol of the earth, and a round roof, symbol of Heaven. The square base included 9 rectangular halls, the measurements of which were symbolical and corresponded to the 9 provinces, and 12 openings, 3 for each of the 4 sides oriented towards the cardinal points. The 12 openings corresponded to the 12 months, and the sides to the 4 seasons: the East to spring, the South to summer, the West to autumn, and the North to winter. The building was therefore a veritable zodiac. The central hall was properly the imperial hall par excellence, the "Invariable Middle" and point of departure of the *Axis Mundi* which linked Earth (the square base) to Heaven (the roof); the Emperor, situated between the base and the roof, was himself this axis.

---

18. In China, as in all traditional civilisations, numbers played a part of primary importance in order to determine different architectural structures, of course, but also social ones, which is less well-known.

19. Hence the designation of China as the "Middle Empire".

20. See Chapter II, p. 52ff.

The *Ming-tang* was the place where the monthly ordinances, valid for the entire realm, were promulgated, and the aim of which was to harmonise the occupations of men with the movements of nature ruled by Heaven, which ordered the seasons. To make the promulgations the Emperor circled the *Ming-tang*, in the manner of the mythic rulers, in the direction of the movement of the sun: at the East he issued the times and ordinances of spring; at the South, those of summer; at the West, those of autumn; and at the North, those of winter. There were a total of 12 stations[21] of the Emperor, and each time there was a return to the centre which indicated the half of the year and the axial function of the prince. By these different royal acts, founded on a strict adherence to the "times" and the "spaces", he maintained the paired order of the "Cardinal Points" and the "Seasons"; the "Son of Heaven" extended his regulatory "Virtue" to the empire, acting as regent of the course of time for the realm and the people in the name of Heaven. Regarding this, the meaning of the return to the centre after each "station" should be noted. In circulating the *Ming-tang* he put into motion the "cross" of the four cardinal directions, and, in consequence, the sun and the seasons in accordance with order and the "Way of Heaven" (*Tien-Tao*); but he always returned to the centre in order to clearly indicate that he is the pivot which turns the cross of the spaces and times: which amounts to saying that he is, in Hindu terminology, a *chakravartin*, "he who turns the (cosmic) Wheel".

EGYPT · As with the emperor of China, the king of Egypt, "son of the gods", received omnipotence in order to maintain the order defined by them, the *Maat*. In order to preserve this harmony, what could be termed its "motive agency", the activity of the gods in the world, has to be assured, on the one hand; and on the other hand, the elements of this order in accordance with its defined plan must be maintained. The last task is that of legislation and justice; the first and most important is worship of the divine. The pharaoh is the first, and in principle the only,

---

21. The same occurs, of course, in the authentic Christian world, although the official representatives of the Church are no longer aware of it. See our work, *The Symbolism of the Christian Temple*.

agent of this worship; he is the arch-priest, although he necessarily delegates his priestly powers to the clergy of the various temples. This is what is shown in all the representations—bas-reliefs or paintings—in the sanctuaries: the ceremonies and the sacrifices carried out in them are always accomplished by the king. But some essential acts of worship were accomplished by him in person: for example, the foundation of a temple, which is explained by the altogether primary part played by this building in Egypt, as it is, moreover, in all traditional societies, given that the temple is precisely the place where the divine order coincides with the earthly in order to give it form, and where the rites of worship are carried out to maintain its harmony.[22] In the bas-reliefs of the temples of Edu and Esna, for example, the pharaoh is represented with a shovel in hand, digging the foundation trench and placing the stakes for fixing the building's orientation—all these gestures, as is well known, being so many rites charged with symbolism.

In addition, there were two great feasts requiring the presence of the king as officiant: the feast of the god *Min* and the *Sed* feast. The god *Min*, presiding over vegetation and prosperity, was closely linked to the royal function. In this connection it is moreover important to point out that in Egypt, as in other traditional societies, the gods of fertility and the rites of fertility have a completely different scope than that which is attributed to them by modern scholars, who see in them nothing more than "agrarian magic", as they say. It has to be understood that in these cults the fertility of the vegetation is not the essential thing; the principal aim of the so-called agrarian cults is to collect the vital cosmic energy for the greatest good of the equilibrium of the individual and of the society, the vegetation being no more than a portion of the domain of this beneficent action, and serving above all as the symbolical support of the ritual whose purpose is to have this energy descend. The feast of *Min* was celebrated in the month of Pachons; it is well known to us through its depictions in the bas-reliefs of the temples of Ramses II and Ramses III at Thebes. It began with a double procession:

---

22. See Chapter I, p. 9ff.

that of the king going to the temple of *Min,* and that of the god leaving his temple, preceded by a white bull, to meet the king, a meeting which took place on the sanctuary's terrace. There took place a rite which was celebrated also during the coronation:[23] the king released four birds towards the four directions of space; this gesture was considered to be an announcement of accession to the throne during the coronation, but its profound meaning, like that of the four arrows shot towards the cardinal directions, is the extension of the royal power, the energy of the king, inherited from the gods, towards the entire extent of the kingdom. Then, the pharaoh, after having offered a sacrifice to the statues of the ancestors, would cut a sheaf of spelt and deposit it before the god *Min* as an offering of the first harvest: this was the properly "agrarian" aspect of the feast.

There were many analogous sequences in the Sed Feast, which was not annual, but was repeated at variable intervals of several years. The aim of this feast was essentially the "renewal of the king", of which we have already spoken, and its two essential rites were the ritual traversing of the countryside and the erection of the *djed.* The traversing of the countryside was an affirmation of the royal power over the realm and a fixing of the order of the society, and at the same time an offering to the divinity. Here is how the king, in the text entitled *Memphite Theology,* describes this traversal: "I have travelled ... I have crossed the earth and have touched its four sides; I have traversed it according to my wishes," says the king. "He travels, crossing the ocean of the four sides of the sky, penetrating as far as the rays of the solar disk, traversing the earth, giving the land its (divine) mistress." This, then, is yet another rite of extension of power, and ultimately of the irradiation of the royal energies over the lands; the traversing of the king over the countryside, like the stations of the emperor of China in the *Ming-tang,* is assimilated to the course of the sun spreading its strength over the world. The traversing of the countryside is like a horizontal extension

---

23. *Ibid.*

of its energy. The erection of the *djed*, already mentioned,[24] constitutes a strengthening of power and a consolidation of order.

JAPAN · The emperor, "for the Japanese, is the supreme Being
in the world of Japan, what the Divine is in the universe....
From him everything emanates, in him everything dwells....
He is supreme in all temporal matters of State, as well as in all
spiritual things"; this is how Etsujiro Uyehara, at the beginning
of the twentieth century, expressed himself. As the high priest
of his people, the emperor is responsible for their spiritual
and, consequently, their material well-being, a role which is
necessarily accompanied by great requirements. He must lead
a very strict life, "live without desire, in order to be a symbol of
the Void," says Teikichi Sato; in other words, explains K. Kumar
Ue, he must keep his mind in the state of a spotless mirror in
order to reflect in it the divine Life and make it shine on the
people. In fact, it is a rule of Shinto, but a rule common to all
sacred traditions, that an unbreakable link exists between the
"service to the gods" (*matsuri*) and the government of the country
(*matsuri-goto*). This rule is the direct consequence of the grand
principle which governs the Nipponese political philosophy,
the *sai-sei-ichi*, namely, that the "religious practices and public
affairs are but one and the same thing," and that one must "in
politics conform to the will of the gods". "True politics," wrote
the prime minister Hiranuma in 1939, "consists in executing the
will of the gods; it is in placing the gods in the temples and
worshipping them that one is placed in communion with the will
of the god." In a book published by the Minister of Education
in 1937 one also reads, "The worship of the gods by the Emperor
and the manner in which he administers the country are one
and the same thing..." Although the "religious ceremonies, the
government and education each have their particular domain, in
the last analysis they are but one and the same thing."

In this perspective it is considered that the emperor must celebrate a certain number of rites which constitute the *Koshitsu-
Shinto*, or the Imperial House Shinto, in honor of the divine and
human ancestors of the dynasty. Their aim is to maintain a per-

---

24. *Ibid.*

fect harmony between the Emperor and the *kami*, in order to assure the perfect conformity between the religious ritual and the government, and thereby guarantee the purity and happiness of the people. For this worship the emperor has three temples at his disposal: one is dedicated to all the gods, the second is the pantheon where the Spirits of the imperial ancestors dwell, the last shelters the reliquary containing the copy of the divine Mirror, the icon of *Amaterasu*.

There are a total of eighteen ceremonies celebrated by the emperor, arranged throughout the year. We shall mention only the main ones, those more particularly related to our subject.

In the first place, on the first of January, there is the *saitan sai*, the feast of the New Year, celebrated before the three temples, and preceded by the *shihosai*, or "worship of the four cardinal points": the prince turns successively towards Ise, where *Amaterasu* resides, towards Nara, the tomb of Jimmu Tenno, towards Omiya, the dwelling of the protector *kami* of the imperial family, and lastly, towards the temple of the divine Sword. On the third of January, the emperor celebrates a feast of the anniversary of the descent of Prince Ningi, and he himself recites a *norito* (invocation). On the eleventh of February, there is the anniversary of the enthronement of Jimmu-tenno. On the seventeenth, the office to obtain a good harvest. On the 17th May, there is a purification ceremony. On the 17th of October, there is the grand *Kanname-sai*, the festival of the first fruits, an offering to the gods of the first sprouts of rice. On the 23rd November, there takes place the most important feast, the *Niiami sai*, which is the Japanese version of ceremonies we have encountered in Egypt, and which pertain to almost all traditions, and whose object is the renovation of the royal power. The *Niiami sai* was celebrated for the first time by *Amaterasu* herself, and then institutionalised by Jimmu-tenno. It is the repetition of the *Daijo-sai*, the rite of investiture of the new emperor, as we have seen. It thus has the same role that the *Sed* feast has for the pharaoh. The emperor personally officiates as the High Priest of Shinto, in white priestly dress, holding the *shaku*, a kind of sceptre of flat wood, the insignia of priests; he sits on the divine Couch with *Amaterasu*, and with her partakes of the new rice, white sake and black sake, in the name of the Japanese people. This last detail constitutes the point of union between the divine reinvestiture and the irradiation of heavenly graces on the people by means of the communion meal.

Aside from these annual feasts, celebrated at fixed times, there is also, at shorter intervals, a rite called *jirei hai*, or "rite of self-purification", the aim of which is somewhat similar to that of the *Niiame-sai*; according to Fujisawa, it is a question of intensifying "the spiritual power which the emperor possesses of clarifying and making transparent every physical and mental disturbance".

INDIA · The Hindu king was not the grand officiant of the worship of the divine, which was reserved to the caste of *brahmins*; he did however play a priestly part in the ceremonies related to royalty, among which was the *Festival of Indra*, and also one of the most important ceremonies of Hindu worship, the *Ashvamedha*.

The *Festival of Indra*, or more exactly, the *Feast of Indra's Standard*, was celebrated by the king in his capital. The "standard" was a tree cut in the forest, then planted in the central square, and decorated with garlands and various fruits. For seven days there was an uninterrupted series of offerings to the tree and popular celebrations. In this ceremony of the erection of a tree, which in certain respects reminds one of the erection of the Egyptian *djed*, the reader will have easily recognised the Hindu version of the universally known rites of vegetation and fertility of which we spoke above, and with all the reservations we made regarding its profound meaning.

Much more imposing was the *ashvamedha*, the "sacrifice of the horse". Although it was practiced only very seldom in historical times, owing to the enormous costs it entailed, and despite the fact that the last celebration goes back to the ninth century, it is worth mentioning here, because it maintains its primary importance in Hinduism as the very archetype of the sacrifice. It was essentially a royal rite and a royal feast, but also a popular feast, a ceremony in which, precisely, king and people met to accomplish the act intended to assure the prosperity of the kingdom. The *ashvamedha* was celebrated in February-March and lasted three days. The previous year, a horse was chosen to be sacrificed: it was let free towards the Northwest in order to roam at will for one year. It was escorted by young noblemen with the prince heir apparent who protected and watched over it. During this time, at the capital, daily offerings were made. At the end of a year, once the horse had returned to the point of departure at the end of its "supervised freedom", the sacrifice was prepared. A brick altar was erected towards the East, at which twenty-one posts were set up for as many sacrificial victims to be sacrificed to *Agni*. That was the first day. The second day, the horse was solemnly sacrificed, cut into pieces and thrown to the fire as an offering to *Brahma*, *Vishnu* and *Shiva*, and its blood spilled as a libation. On the third day, the solemn oblation of *soma*—the well-known drink of immortality—was celebrated.

The *ashvamedha*, as we have said, was the sacrifice par excellence. In fact, according to the *Brhadaranyaka Upanishad*, the victim was assimilated to the entire universe, each of its organs being assimilated to part of the world: the eye to the sun, the back to heaven, the belly to the atmosphere, the rib bones to the regions of space, the veins to the seas, the mane to the trees, etc. The path of the horse accomplished precisely this assimilation of the animal to the world. But, as is the rule of all sacrifices,[25] it was also assimilated to the one offering the sacrifice—in this case, the king, and with him, his people. And once again, it can be seen that such a rite, which aims at assuring the prosperity of the king and the kingdom, also comprises a loftier end, which is the regeneration, not only of the country and the earth, but of the human being, as the *Brhadaranyaka Upanishad* also affirms: "The one offering the sacrifice must know well that he himself is the figure of the horse. All beings endowed with intelligence act with an end to gather the fruits of their works; the fruit which results from the *ashvamedha* is to facilitate man's harvesting the fruit of his works. It is the way by which he arrives directly at the end to which his endeavours lead."

The horse sacrifice was common to several Indo-European peoples. It was practiced in ancient Iran by the king. Through

---

25. See our *Divine Liturgy*, Chapter 1, and for India particularly, A.K. Coomaraswamy, *The Doctrine of Sacrifice*.

Philostratus, we know that Apollonius of Tyana, during his journey in this country attended this rite celebrated by king Vardanes.[26] The Iranian king possessed a markedly priestly quality: he was a sacrificer, but also the fire priest—more exactly, the *fratadara*, the "custodian of the fire"—and this in truth was his principal sacred duty,[27] which is understandable when one knows the importance the cult of fire had for the Iranians, and which has been perpetuated to our day by their descendants, the Parsis. It is also an Indo-European heritage that we encounter as well in ancient Greece, where we have seen that the public Hearth in some wise conferred the investiture upon the king.

IRAN · But the great religious feast of Iran was the *Noruz*, the Feast of the New Year, in which the ruler played the main part. The rite was also a rite of prosperity, like those we have studied above, and once again we see that this type of religious rite pertains specifically to king, since for him it is a means of exercise of one of the main activities of his function, which is to assure the prosperity of the kingdom. In it the king played the part of the mythic hero *Thretaona-Fereydun*, the slayer of the dragon *Aji-Dhaka*, responsible for aridity: his victory freed the waters, guarantors of fertility, and at the same time the female prisoners of the monster, the two sisters of the primordial king Yima, with whom he consummated the customary *hieros gamos* in these rites.

RITES OF RENEWAL · These rites were based on the well-known scheme of the battle of the hero with the monster; a scheme which serves to organise a great number of cosmogonic myths, in which the creation is depicted as the victory of light over darkness, of order over the primeval chaos. This is the scheme comprised in the first verses of Genesis in the Bible. And precisely, the feasts of the new year are repetitions of the creation, ritual reiterations of the creative act; the new cycle of manifestation, which is the commencing year, symbolises at its level the complete cycle of the manifestation of the world. The initial instant of creation is that of the irruption of the divine

---

26. Philostratus, *Vit. Apoll.* 1.31.

27. On many monuments he can be seen depicted in worship before the fire altar.

Energy, which is then at its maximum intensity, and we know that afterward, in the measure that the cycle unfolds, the cosmic energy diminishes; the same occurs in any cycle, large or small. It is important, therefore, to renew this energy, by seeking it at its source; this is the function of these rites of renewal which we are now studying, and which aim at making the divine Energy descend again, abundantly, if one may say so, on a tired world. Each beginning year, with the new growth of vegetation, is a new stage of life for man and the entire community, a new stage in which the divine power is invoked that it might pour out the vital force which it dispensed on the first day of the world.

These rituals, which above all are royal rituals, for the reason already mentioned, have existed everywhere and at all epochs. We have seen them in Iran, and they had special importance in the Mesopotamian empire, in Babylon and in Assur.

The celebration there lasted six days. The first five were days of mourning and penitence, then was celebrated the (provisional) exile of Marduk, the divine hero who had assisted the gods at the time of creation, battling against the monster Tiamat (Chaos). On the evening of the fourth day, the *Enuma Elish*, the epic of creation, was solemnly recited. The fifth of *nisan* was the Day of Expiation: the king entered the sanctuary with the high priest, who removed the king's insignias: the crown, the ring, the sceptre, and the sword, and left them on a seat before the god; then he struck the face of the king who, kneeling, made a "negative confession" in the Egyptian manner, saying: "I have not sinned (regarding such and such a matter), I have not been negligent as regards your divinity, I have not let Babylon perish..." The high priest, who played the part of Marduk, had the prince arise, promised him the favour of the god and returned his insignias. What took place there was a reinvestiture of the sovereign. The next day, the sixth of *nisan*, commemorated the resurrection of Marduk, who returned from the hells. The king played the part of the hero Nabu, the son of Marduk, and received again from the ruling gods the power of fighting against the forces of chaos. A procession, presenting the victorious army of the gods destroying the forces of Tiamat at the origin, celebrated the victory of Marduk by going to the *Bit Akitu*, the "House of Prayer", where perhaps the victory was depicted. Finally, there took place the royal *hieros gamos*. This last phase of the feast is not mentioned in what follows in the narratives which relate it to us, but it surely took place, as can be deduced from a passage of the Hymn to Ishtar, the Evening Star, wherein the husband of the goddess, who bears the epithet of Tammuz (a divine personage playing the same part as Marduk), is in reality the king *Idin-Dagan*; it is said that he is her husband, "in order to safeguard the vital breath of the whole land", and at the same time the ritual of the New Year is alluded to. No doubt, what is in question is the royal *hieros gamos* of the said festival.

It would be tiresome to enumerate all the analogous ceremonies that can be found in the different religious areas. To close this list of examples let us simply mention the case of ancient Scandinavia, which, of course, is attached to the Aryan branch. The king was the officiant at the typical Scandinavian sacrifice, the *blot*, intended to regulate the right order of the annual cycle and to assure the peace of the realm. For this ceremony the king made use of two special insignias: the *ring*, the famous Scandinavian ring, an object impregnated with numinous force, and the branch, "the branch of life" (let us recall the "golden bough"), which he used to brush the blood of the sacrificial victim on all who participated in the sacrifice.

ASPECTS OF THE ROYAL FUNCTION

We would like to enlarge a little more on this aspect of the royal function—which refers more especially to material prosperity and the fertility of the soil—for two reasons. In the first place, this subject occupies a large amount of space in all the works which deal with the history of religion and with traditional royalty, and deservedly so; however—and this is the second reason—the manner in which official scholars view this problem, and the explanation given to it, do not in any way correspond to the reality of the thing, and it seemed necessary to replace it in its true perspective, and to recall in this respect the doctrine conforming to the sacred tradition.

An affirmation of an African chief, Etatin, in southern Nigeria, perfectly summarises the situation and clearly poses the problem: "By means of the rites I procure game for the hunter, I make the yams grow, I give the fisherman fish and I make the rain fall." These words are reported by Frazer in his work cited above,[28] which contains an impressive number of analogous documents concerning "primitive" peoples. Let us recall the case, also in Africa, of the king of the Shilluk, of whom we have already spoken; that of the Masai (a people of Kenya and Tanzania) where the king is "he who makes rain"; that of Bangkara (Sumatra), whose prince also "makes rain", as well as, at the opposite end of the Pacific, the chief of the Natchez, who governs the growth of the corn and is likewise the lord of the rain.

These "rainmakers"—a term which we owe to the official scholars, and which in its authors reflects a certain irony that accompanies the conviction of the scientific and rationalist white man's superiority—are not found solely in "primitive" peoples; this will have been noted by what we have said previously, and in particular regarding the rites of Iran and Mesopotamia. The Indian king also is the lord of the rain. Likewise, the Egyptian pharaoh regulates the right order of the floods: the *Teachings of Amenemhat* tell us that in his time no one went hungry because the king made the wheat grow, and the Nile obediently flooded all the accessible lands so that they could be cultivated. And similarly, in *The Tale of Sinuhe*, we read (the king is being addressed): "The sun rises at thy will; the water flows in the river..."

In reality, whether it be a question of bringing about rain, making the wheat or the corn grow, assuring the harvest of the fruit, etc., what is involved is not, as the official scholars imagine, magical operations, except perhaps in cases encountered in very degenerate peoples. To be sure, there are rites for rain-making or to make vegetation grow, but what is at issue are religious rites, which are included in a very hierarchic ensemble of sacred attitudes in the chief or the sovereign. That is why, wherever an authentic tradition exists, these "powers" are conditioned by the "virtue" of the prince, virtue in the broadest sense, but

---

28. *The Magical Origins of Royalty*, 1920, p. 118.

including moral virtue. Let us read again, for example, the portrait of the "perfect king" (*basileus amymon*) in Homer: "He fears
the gods and lives according to Righteousness. Then, thanks to
him, the black furrows bring wheat and barley; the tree is heavy
with fruit; the flock grows without cease, the sea, appeased, offers its fish, and the peoples prosper thanks to him."[29] We find
the same in India. The *Laws of Manu*, describing the effects of a
good reign, say: "In this land, where the king avoids seizing the
goods of the mortal fishermen, people are born at the proper
moment and enjoy long life. And the grains of the farmers reach
maturity, each according to as it was sown, and the children do
not die, nor are they born deformed." On the contrary, misfor-
tunes, famine, disorders of every kind occur if the king does
not conform himself to *dharma*; the bad king brings disasters,
even on the plane of nature, because, continue the *Laws of Manu*,
"he disturbs the harmony with the Invisible." In Tibet, when
the *mnatan*, the "majesty" of the king—that is, the essence of his
power—is corrupted, the fields dry up, we read in the chronicles,
and things go badly. If the kings of Ireland observe the customs
of the ancestors, that is, if they conform to the "heavenly mandate", the seasons are gentle, the harvests good, the trees are
laden with fruit. On the contrary, the faults of the prince bring
on catastrophes. There is a brilliant demonstration of this in the
"Breton" novels, especially in the cycle of the Grail; in Wolfram
von Eschenbach's *Parsifal*, king Anfortas is tormented by a mysterious malady, the result of his pride, and this decadence entails
the decadence of the kingdom; all his time is spent awaiting the
hero who will heal him and to whom he will deliver the celestial mandate which he is no longer worthy of carrying out. All
the novels of the Grail cycle are dominated by the theme of the
wasteland, of the fisher king, and, at the same time, of the search
for a spiritual restoration which will also bring back material
prosperity.

It is important to insist upon this correlation between spiritual reality and physical reality, for it is a point of view which
totally escapes modern man, who does not understand how a

---

29. *Odyssey* 19.109 ff.

spiritual behaviour can act at such a material level, because he no longer has the sense of the continuity linking all the levels of existence. Thus, to take the example of rites intended to make it rain, it must be understood that, above all, they have a symbolical significance, because the art of making it rain is in the first place the power of making celestial "blessings" descend, which almost everywhere are symbolised by rain. In ancient Tibet, it was said that king Gnakri in the beginning descended to earth like a fertilising rain, and prince Spude Gun Rgyal offered himself to be the fertilising rain from heaven. And one cannot avoid relating this tradition with the famous passage from Isaiah referring to the coming of the "Righteous one", of the Messiah King: "Rain down, you heavens, from above, and let the skies pour down righteousness" (Isaiah 45:8). The power of making the rain fall, is in the first place the power of bringing down all the different celestial blessings, the spiritual rainfall; this does not mean that the kings in question did not *also* have the power to make the material rain fall, for this power is very real, whatever incredulous rationalists may think, and there are even proofs of this in our day. But what has to be said and repeated is that this last power is merely a consequence of the former one, and it is in the last analysis its least important aspect. What is essential is the royal "virtue" which acts efficaciously upon nature and upon man through celestial power. These remarks evidently hold true as well for the other royal powers; the power of healing, especially, from the chiefs of the islands of Tonga in the Pacific, to the chiefs of the Ualos and the Fan in Africa, or the dignitaries of the Amerindian tribes; even to the Norwegian kings, whose "healing" hands were a gift of God, according to an ancient strophe in the Eddas; and of course, to the kings of France, to which we shall return later.[30]

It must be said that the sacred king assures prosperity and health by his efficacy as the organ of integration, which participates in the divine and the human: power thus concentrated in

---

30. The gift of healing is another face of the gift of fertility and of health; in the Middle Ages, German mothers presented their newborn to the King of Denmark, Waldemar I, to be touched and thus favour their growth.

him is spread over nature and over his subjects. This phenomenon will easily be understood once one discards the modern way of thinking, which results from the individualism that has cut man off from his surroundings. For modern man there is the isolated individual and the world facing him, and there is no longer a real and living link from the one to the other; all the more so inasmuch as modern man believes that the world is an aggregate of sensible, material phenomena, subject only to quantitative knowledge. Now, in reality, the world is a *vast living being* and man is immersed in the cosmos to which he is attached by a thousand links conditioning his being and earthly existence. Between man, the summary of the world, a microcosm, as we have recalled, and the world, the macrocosm, there is woven a web of analogical correspondences which the mediaeval West still knew perfectly; for example, to cite no more than one set of corporeal correspondences, the principal parts of the human body, its main organs, are related through analogical correspondences with the zodiacal signs, which constitute one of the bases of traditional medicine. These astral influences which, by virtue of the macro-microcosmic analogy, operate both within the domain of the individual man and in that of nature, can be vivified, "exalted", by the inward, spiritual attitude of man. In the king, *thanks to his consecration*, these harmonic correspondences are exalted in fact, and confer upon him powers which other men possess in principle, but not in fact. Having become "true man" by his axial function—to return to the Chinese terminology, which is applicable in all cases—he enters into contact with the heavenly influences, and brings them to this world in order to join them to the earthly ones, firstly within himself, and then in the cosmic surroundings, by irradiation.

When these powers are employed, they are manifestations, among others, of the harmony reigning between human society on the one hand, and the cosmic and divine orders on the other. This harmony is properly *justice* in the most precise and complete meaning of the world: the state of *justness*, the *just* state, that is, perfectly coherent in itself and in relation to universal Law.

Justice is the first virtue of the king and his first duty, for the exercise of justice is, firstly, the maintenance of that state of harmony. Justice in the restricted and ordinary sense, which is exercised in "judicial" surroundings, results directly, as is easily seen, from justice in the most universal sense: to judge and punish the evil doer and the criminal, and to re-establish the rights of the victim, is to suppress disorder and restore order. But at the same time, it can be seen that a true justice in the domain of the judiciary cannot exist in a satisfactory manner unless it is founded on a transcendent order, itself the guarantor of a just social order, which is to say regular and in conformity with the universal Law.

WAR · The function of the prince as righter of wrongs leads us quite naturally to speak of the extraordinary and terrible face of justice—war—the legitimacy of which is determined by the necessity—altogether analogous to that which exists at the level of individuals within the same social group—of suppressing disorder and restoring order in the relationship between two social groups or two countries. Our intention is in no way to treat the problem of war in all its aspects, as this would require digressions that would take us far from our subject, but to envisage the manner in which war is conducted in a traditional society. What we wish to say is that war is then a *sacred act*, a sacred action, for the same reason as those we have studied up to now, undertaken by the king in the name of his "heavenly mandate", and which is undertaken, in principle, in accordance with a *ritual*, as a veritable *sacrifice*, a notion to which it is closely related—at times, totally so.[31]

To be brief, we shall take only two examples: those of classical Antiquity and Egypt; but it would be easy to make the transposition so as to apply them to other ethnic and cultural groups.

In Athens, and above all in Rome, the ritualisation extends to all the essential acts of war, from its preliminaries to its conclusion. In Rome, even the insignias were sacred, at least originally, as symbols of guardian divinities; on the field, they had a chapel, and their porters, the *signiferi*, were clothed as priests.

---

31. Heroic death, considered as a sacrifice to the divinity, is at the basis of the lofty ethics and spirituality of chivalry; that of the Christian Middle Ages and, in Japan, that of the Samurai.

In Greece, the *herald* (*keryx*) in charge of uttering the declaration of war also had a sacred character. But in Rome, the ritual aspect was also extended to the preliminary of the declaration of war and, as a series of sacred acts, were entrusted to the *College of the Fetials*, founded by king Numa. If Rome felt injured by a neighbouring people, the Fetial considered the gravity of the injury and offered a demand for reparation: crossing the border of the enemy people, he expressed the claims of his country and, in solemn formulations, his demands. If at the end of a delay of thirty-three days satisfaction had not been obtained, the Fetial would decide whether the war were just, and it is he who would declare it.

To do so, the body of Fetials, heads covered with wool, would go to the enemy's border, and putting the gods of Rome's legitimacy as witnesses, would declare war by means of a sacramental formula accompanied by a symbolical gesture: throwing a bloodied lance against the enemy territory.[32]

Prior to departing for the campaign, while in Rome, the king or the consul, in priestly dress, would open the temple of Janus (which remained closed in times of peace). There followed prayers and a sacrifice, as in Greece.[33] Before initiating battle, an essential rite consisted in taking the auspices (in Greek, *oiônoi*)[34] in order to decide whether or not the combat would proceed, according to whether or not the omens were favourable. This custom has been greatly mocked, for it has been viewed as a ridiculous superstition or as a sign of blind fatalism. It would be good to pause for a moment at this question, for it is perhaps here that the justification of the sacred character of warlike activity can best be grasped. The art of augury, like other analogous disciplines of the Indo-European peoples, was not a practice born of blind fatalism, but quite the contrary; it was intended to discover the points of juncture with invisible influences, so as to graft onto them the forces of men in order to "exalt" and multiply

---

32. Livy 1.32.

33. Livy 1.49; Xenophon, *Hellenica* 3.4.3; 4.7.2; De rep. Laced. 13 (14).

34. As in the battle of Plataea (Herodotus 9.61.62).

them and have them act on a higher plane so as to overcome all material and spiritual obstacles. For the Greek, for the Roman, as for all traditional men, it is a transcendent force, more than a human value, which makes for attaining victory. To this conviction is attached a practice like that of the *devotio*: at a particularly critical moment, if the outcome seems unfavourable, the chief throws himself against the enemy to his death, a death which takes on the significance of a *sacrifice*, of an *offering* (the meaning of the word *devotio*) in order to bear upon destiny and to attract the transcendent strength mentioned upon the soldiers. Moreover, during the battle it is the gods, more or less symbolised by the insignia, who are the essential combatants.[35] And again, it is the divinity who is present at the victory celebration, for acts of thanksgiving take place during it, and a sacrifice is offered. In Rome, to this was added a most significant rite, of which we have already spoken:[36] the *Triumph of the king*, originally, and later of the *general* (but this latter fact is of little importance, for the rite is of royal institution). In reality, for the triumph, the vanquisher donned the insignia of the god of the capital in order to place before this god the victory laurel, a gesture clearly indicating that the god is the real conqueror; moreover, the "disguise" of the chief showed that in a certain sense he was "overtaken" and transfigured by a force coming from On High, a *numen*.

Finally, there was a rite during the last act of the campaign: the establishing of a peace treaty. At such an occasion we see in the *Iliad* that the king celebrated a sacrifice and, with his hand on the victim's head, after offering a prayer, he pronounced an oath: "O immortal gods, make it that just as this victim has been struck by iron, so may be broken the head of the first to break his oath."[37] In Rome, a hearth was placed between the two armies and an altar was raised to the divinities they had in common; a priest brought in the victim; the two chiefs made the li-

---

35. Christianity changed nothing in this. Constantine placed the chrism on his standard, and all the banners of Christendom were symbols of the divine power in action during the combat.

36. See Chapter I, p. 38.

37. *Iliad* 3.245-301. Cf. Thucydides 5.45; Xenophon, *Anabasis* 2.2.9.

bations, uttered their promises, and sacrificed the victim, which was burnt on the altar.[38]

The Egyptian customs open other perspectives on the ritual of war. The archetype of war is here the combat of the god Horus against the enemies of his father, and more generally, against the forces of the enemies of light. In the temple of this god, at Dendara, this victory is celebrated the first day of the month of *pakhon*, the day of the new moon. The statue of the god was brought out in procession towards the river and crossed it in his barque while the priest recited the text recounting "how the enemies were killed". The ground was scattered with sheaves of wheat representing the enemies, which were trod upon while a hymn was sung: "Thou hast annihilated thine enemies, O Harsomtis. Thou hast slain thine adversaries. They have fallen at thy feet, thou hast crushed them as though they were grains." Now, it is interesting to know that certain indications of dates of expeditions of war are in relation with the calendar of feasts; the *Decree of Raphia* informs us that Ptolemy IV Philopator left Pelusia to march against his enemies, the army of Antioch III, on the first of Pakhon of the year 217, and that he slayed his enemies "as of yore Horus, son of Isis, vanquished his adversaries." Similarly, the strategy of Ptolemy Epiphenes was determined in large measure by this liturgical point of view; in the year 196, he marched against the rebels of Lycopolis, and vanquished "as Ra and Horus, the sons of Isis and Osiris vanquished of yore the rebels in the same place".[39] These two examples pertain to the last epoch of the history of Egypt, but everything tends to make one think that this manner of acting of the princes was that of previous epochs, since all the written or figured documents concerning the battles of the pharaohs refer analogously to the relationships between the actions of war of men and those of the gods.

These examples are interesting for they enable us to know the fundamental conception of war in traditional civilisations, a conception which precisely converts it into a ritual and sa-

---

38. Virgil, *Aeneid* 12, 118-20, 170-74, 200-15. Cf. Livy 9.5; Polybius 3.25.

39. Inscription on the Rosetta Stone.

cred act. According to this idea, war undertaken by men is an imitation of the spiritual combat that divinity maintained, and in reality has not ceased to maintain, against its enemies, the demonic forces; a combat which generally takes the form of a battle against the darkness; and thus the warrior myths are derived directly from the cosmogonic myths, in which the action of the light against the darkness expresses the creative act, the establishment of order over chaos. Examples of this, to mention only a few, are the battles of Vishnu, of Indra, of Shiva, in India; in Iran, that of Mithra against the emissaries of darkness up to the moment of the appearance of Saoshyant, the lord of a future kingdom; in Mesopotamia, that of Markuk against Tiamat, which we have analysed. Thus we return to what we said at the beginning of this exposition on war, recalling that it has no other legitimate aim than to re-establish the social order—image of the heavenly order—once it has been disturbed. To conclude, let us add that this spiritual, metaphysical, counterpart of war, as it is conceived in traditional civilisations, is what enables it to be a starting point for spiritual realisation for the individual, eminent examples of this being the order of the samurai in Japan and the chivalric orders in mediaeval Christendom.[40]

---

40. Regarding Japan, there is the interesting book of Shinsho Hanayama, *La Voie d'Eternité* (tr. Pierre Pascal, Paris, 1976), in which it will be seen that the chivalric ideal was perpetuated in Japan until our times.

CHAPTER III

THE "TWO SWORDS"

Throughout the course of the previous chapter, it will have been noted that the kings of the different civilisations that we have studied continually fulfilled a religious role in the exercise of their functions, especially in the offering of sacrifices. We have seen it in the case of the emperor of China and of the Egyptian pharaoh, in the kings of Mesopotamia and of Iran, etc. This amounts to saying that in the "sacred royalty" we are studying, the king possesses a priestly quality or, in other words, he is a *priest-king*. This is so not only in the case of the "divine" royalties, as in Egypt and China, but also in those which are royalties "by divine grace". For example, it is said expressly that the Mesopotamian king is a "priest" (*sangu*); he heads the clergy, names the high priest, and is responsible for the cult, although the duty of accomplishing it in fact is left to the clergy, and he officiates only during the important festivals, at the founding of a new temple, or at the great festival of the New Year, of which we have already spoken extensively. In Iran, the twofold character, priestly and royal, of the sovereign is underscored by his dress: he wears two robes, one *red*, which for Indo-Aryan peoples is the colour of the "warriors", and one *white*, which is that of the Magi. From a Syriac text, *The Cavern of Treasures*, we know that the king wore the white robe over the red robe when he celebrated a sacrifice or made some other offering to the gods. The royal headdress was also red and white.[1]

---

1. It will be noted that these two colours are also those of the Pope's vestment: white robe and red cape. No doubt this is not by chance, and we shall speak of this again, when later we have occasion to study the relationships between the priesthood and the royalty in Christianity.

The twofold character, priestly and royal, is frequently attached to the chiefs of so-called "primitive" societies. The King of the Jukun (Northern Nigeria) is a priest-king. Similarly, that of the Gallas in Ethiopia and that of the Shilluk people, already mentioned: in this latter people, as we have said, the king is considered to be the reincarnation of the divine hero Nyakang, and he is the mediator between men and the great god Juok, for which reason he has priestly status.

The union of royalty and priesthood is very close in classical Antiquity, in Greece and in Rome.

GREECE · In Homeric society, it is the king who is the high priest and who offers the sacrifices: he cuts the hair on the head of the victim, spills the lustral water and the sacred barley, recites the prayer, immolates and presides over the preparation of the ritual meal.[2] The palace of the Homeric king is a prytaneum; his hearth is the public hearth where offerings are made prior to the deliberations of the council. In Aeschylus, the Dyanides tell king Argos: "Thou art the master of the altar, the sacred hearth of this land."[3] In Sparta, the two kings who are, as we have already said, "sons of the gods", in this capacity offer the public sacrifices, the one to Zeus Lakedaimon, the other to Zeus Ouranios.[4] It is again the king who offers the sacrifices to Hestia, goddess of the public Hearth, to Kos, to Mythilene, Chios and to Theos.[5] All these examples show that the king is priest, *prytane*, in relation to his function at the public Hearth, to the *Hestia* of the city, from which, as we have already said,[6] his dignity and power are derived.[7] In a very interesting page, Aristotle writes textually that the priestly function is the first function of the king: "According to religious rule, the care of the public sacrifices of the

---

2. *Iliad* 2.402 ff., 3.171 ff.

3. Aeschylus, *The Suppliants*, 370-73.

4. Xenophon, *De rep.Laced.*, 13, 15. Cf. Pindar, Pyth. 5.131.

5. Aristotle, *Politics* 3.14.13; Demonsthenes, *Against Nearchus* 74; Plutarch, *Roman Questions* 63; Livy 2.2.1.

6. See *supra* pp 36-37.

7. Aristotle, *op.cit.* 7.5.11.

city does not pertain to special priests, but rather to those men to whom the dignity comes from the public hearth and whom we call kings."[8] To the augurs and the priests properly so-called (*hiereis*) are left the appendages of the cult, but the official religion does pertain to them.

This primacy of the priestly function in the king was so anchored in the customs of the Greek city that, at the time during which royalty disappeared as a political magistrature in order to make way for the aristocratic regime and then the democratic one, the Athenians always kept, religiously, it must be said, a magistrate who bore the royal title and was called the *archon-king*. To designate this magistrature the word *royalty* (*basilia*) was employed until a rather later period, for we still find it in Pausanias.[9] At first, this magistrature, like primitive royalty, was hereditary; later it became elective. But the archon-king always kept certain prerogatives inherited from ancient royalty, for precisely, these prerogatives were uniquely of a religious order: presiding at feasts and judging in cases wherein religion was implicated. In particular, and it is very significant, the *archon-king* played a part of primary importance at the feast of the Anthesteria, the Dionysian feast of fertility. It is he who, taking on the personality of the god, consummated the *hieros gamos*, the final act of the feast, with his wife, the "queen" (*basilinna*), incarnating *Terra Mater*;[10] a ceremony which, as we have seen, concluded analogous royal rituals in other civilisations.

ROME · In Rome, the evolution of the institution followed a similar course to that which can be observed in Greece. During the primitive era the king is the high priest. As high priest, Romulus carried the augural staff,[11] as did Pico, an ancient king of Latium, along with the *trabea*, a white garment adorned with bands of purple which the augurs as well as the king wore, and

---

8. *Ibid.*

9. Pausanias 14.5.10 & 13.

10. Aristotle, *The Constitution of Athens* 3.5. See H. Jeanmaire, *Dionysos*.

11. Cicero, *De Divinat.* 1.17; 1.48.

which later passed to the knights (*equites*) and the consuls.[12] The Latin king possessed a building for worship, the *Regia* (the "Royal"), near the public Hearth of the *Vesta* (the same word and the same divine entity as the *Hestia* in Greece), where he fulfilled the sacred function of the public cult. It is known that the king was designated by a double election: a first election to confer upon him the title of *rex*, "king", corresponding to the religious power, and a second to confer upon him the *imperium*, the po-litical-military power.[13] When the royalty was abolished, the *im-perium* passed to the consuls and the title of *rex* was transferred to a magistrate—the exact replica of the Athenian archon—who became the *rex sacrorum*, and who continued to fulfil the sacred functions at the *Regia*, the sacrifices in the public Hearth and the ones which preceded the electoral meetings. His wife also bore the name of "queen" (*regina*).[14]

If we have dwelt somewhat at length on the Greek and Ro-man usages, it is because their historical evolution and the situ-ation which resulted show, by two extreme examples, how the priestly character was intimately linked to the person of the king in the most ancient forms of sacred royalty.[15]

At this point a question will not fail to arise in the mind of the contemporary reader: How to explain this phenomenon of the priest-king, so foreign to the political institutions of the modern West? How to explain the coexistence, in one and the same per-sonage, of attributions pertaining to the religious domain and to the political domain, two domains that are increasingly distinct, if not separated, in the modern world?

SOCIAL ORDER · The reply to this question requires, first of all, reference to the regular organisation of society, that is, to the

---

12. Virgil, *Aeneid* 5.187.

13. Cicero, *De Republica* 2,13 ss.

14. Livy, 2.2.1; 6.41.9.

15. Another vestige of the priest-king is the case of the "King of Nemi", a priest in charge of the cult of Diana Aricina in the sacred wood of Nemi, near Mount Albins. Frazer wrote a long dissertation on this, in his usual manner, of course.

system of castes, to which we have already alluded,[16] but which it is worth considering now from a new point of view.

The simplest way to begin is to start from the myth of the origin of the castes, as it is found in the Hindu tradition. When Brahma created man, it is said, he made him quadruple: there were originally four men. First came Brahmin, who came from the mouth of Brahma, and Brahma gave him the *Vedas*, the sacred Scriptures, to teach and in order to accomplish the rites; then, from the right arm of the god emerged Kshatriya, whose function is to defend Brahmin, his brother, so that he can dedicate himself calmly to divine things. In the third place, from the right thigh of Brahma, came Vaishya, whose mission is to work, and thus to feed his two elder brothers. Finally, from the right foot, came Shudra, to serve the first three. In other versions of the myth these four men are sons of Purusha, who in the Hindu tradition corresponds to Universal Man or the creative Logos, which, obviously, does not change the teaching that is intended.[17]

The first caste, that of the *brahmins*, is dedicated to knowledge and to teaching; the second is that of the men of action, and above all of government; the third is dedication to the more material action of exploiting the world, of economic, artisanal, and agricultural activity; finally, for the fourth caste are reserved the menial tasks, purely material and mechanical work.

To forestall any objection, let us say immediately that if we make use of the Hindu system for our exposition, this is not because we wish to present it as the sole model to follow, although, without first examining them, neither is there any reason to accept uncritically the bitter criticisms that frequently have been, and continue to be, levelled at it by prejudiced persons who have not understood its true nature. But whatever the criticisms which can be directed to the castes in India at the present time— and there be such—this does not take away the fact that they

---

16. See Chapter II, pp. 59-60.

17. The myth is given in different forms in the *Purusha-sukta* of the *Rig Veda* (10.90), the *Vishnu Purana* (1.6), and the *Laws of Manu* (*Manavadharmashastra* 1.31).

are perfectly legitimate in principle, because they conform to the natural order to which we alluded in the previous chapter,[18] and to which we shall doubtless return several times. Moreover, the Hindu system of castes is the most complete and the clearest: thus it can serve as a system of reference to explain, *mutatis mutandis*, the analogous systems that exist in other traditions, and also to study the natural institution of castes in itself and in its principle.

In reality this principle is very simple: it is the difference in individual natures which exists among men, and which, like it or not, naturally establishes a hierarchy among them. If this natural hierarchy is not integrated in a society so as to determine its structure, it is doomed to fall into disorder; egalitarianism, in effect, is contrary to natural facts. The Indian word to designate caste, *varna*, means precisely "individual nature", and what determines the functions is not merely inheritance, as is believed, but the differentiated characteristics of different men. In summary, the distinction of castes is reducible to a natural classification of men with a view to a distribution of functions in society. Each man possesses an aptitude for this or that thing; and in a correctly ordered society, founded upon traditional bases, these aptitudes will be determined by precise rules. The end sought for is to have the functions correspond to the division by classes of the individual natures—each in its proper place—and to have the social order conform to the hierarchical relationships created by the nature of the individuals, and thereby to be in accordance with the order of the world, as we have said and continue to repeat. In summary, the castes designate functions that exist in *every* society, just as in all places there exist qualifications which constitute the aptitude for this or that function. Let us note in passing that we are here faced with a social structure totally different from that of modern countries where only *social classes* exist, which are something completely different from the castes, or rather, they are their falsification, as will be made clear further on. In a word, if a society is correctly ordered and normal, there

---

18. See Chapter II, p. 60.

will always be found in it a structure which can be reduced fundamentally to the system of castes.

As we have expounded it, this system, then, corresponds to the structure of a normal society; but we must immediately add: in the present state of humanity, what does this mean? The concordant teaching of all traditions teaches us that humanity has not always been in the state in which it is presently found. Everyone is at least aware of the four ages of gold, silver, bronze and iron transmitted to us by Greco-Latin antiquity, and which has its exact counterpart in the Hindu tradition of the four *yugas*. It is also known that these accounts attest to a progressively descending evolution of humanity from a perfect state (the *golden age* in the Indo-European tradition, and the *earthly paradise* in the Judeo-Christian tradition), passing through states increasingly remote from the primitive perfection until arriving at the *iron age*, the *dark age*, or the *Kali Yuga*, according to the Hindu terminology. This is not the time to consider this evolution; we shall examine it in the last chapter, in relation to the history of the degeneration of political power and of modern society. For the time being, we shall say only what is necessary to explain the phenomenon of the priest-king, which becomes clear only by comparing the present state of man and his former one.

ORIGIN OF PRIESTLY ROYALTY

The Hindu tradition tells us that at the beginning of the cycle of our humanity there were no castes, or what amounts to the same, there was only one: the caste of *hamsa*. We find the same affirmation in other traditions. If in this initial state the castes did not exist, that is because the corresponding functions did not exist either, in a differentiated manner. This state of undifferentiation disappeared the moment the original unity was broken. Thus, returning to the present topic, the two functions, priestly and royal, co-existed, as it were, the one contained within the other in the common divine principle from which they are derived and of which they are the two aspects, united in a synthesis within that state of *hamsa*, the reign of a lofty spirituality. Subsequently they separated, but the separation was not total; indeed, it was not really total until the recent era, with the appearance of lay societies; until then, both functions, to speak precisely, were *distinct* more than *separated*, and this same *distinction* was realised by degrees, so that a line of clear demarcation cannot be drawn between the attributions of the priest and those of royalty. Primitive society was assuredly theocratic, and the representative of the priesthood exercised political power; an examination of ancient civilisations here supports the traditional sacred teaching. To cite no more than one example familiar to all, the history of the Hebrew people is a striking proof of this. The Hebrew people lived first under the rule of the strictest theocracy, and the Bible affirms repeatedly that God is its only sovereign.[19] A leader like Moses and his successor, Joshua, are direct representatives of God with the status of "prophets" in the broadest sense, including the two powers, priestly and royalty; after Joshua, the *Judges*, who governed Israel until the appearance of royalty, were also elected directly by God. Egypt offers another example of theocracy, and this example is interesting, for it is a question of a theocracy persisting through a structure of royalty, and allows us to understand the fact of the priest-king. In a certain sense it is a vestige of the primitive state, or if preferred, an intermediate stage between the integrally theocratic primitive state and the following state, for example that of the royalties of the Western Middle Ages, when the distinction between the two functions is much more accentuated. Let us note, however, that in this status of priest-king, the distinction is far from vague. In effect, what can be seen is that the king, in this case, exercises only one of the two activities of the priesthood, namely the accomplishment of the rites and the sacrifices, or rather of *some* rites and sacrifices; in turn, the other activity of the priesthood, the principal one, which is the teaching of sacred science, is reserved for the priesthood. Such is the case in Egypt and in Mesopotamia, to speak only of these two countries, but the same holds true absolutely everywhere.

---

19. For example, 1 Kings 8:7; Judges 8:23.

This fact is important, and after our observations on the priest-kings, it introduces us directly to the consideration of the two functions in themselves, which will definitively clarify the nature of royalty as well as that of regular traditional societies.

Indeed, what conditions the nature and the state of a society is precisely the relationship between the priestly and royal powers. The question was greatly debated during the mediaeval West, in which the theologians discussed the doctrine of the "Two Swords". The expression designates the two powers, the spiritual sword and the temporal sword, and is taken from a passage in the Gospel in which exegesis, above all that of St. Bernard[20] saw the basis for the attribution of the two powers to the prince of the Apostles. In question is the scene shortly preceding the arrest of Jesus in the garden of Gesthemane: "And he who hath no sword, let him sell his garment and buy one... Then they said, 'Lord look, here are two swords.' And He said to them, 'It is enough'" (Luke 22: 36-38). Fathoming this teaching, mediaeval theology specified the nature of the two "swords" as distinguishing the notions of *auctoritas* and *potestas*: *auctoritas* designating the *spiritual sword* and *potestas* the temporal. This distinction is worth bearing in mind, for it really characterises the proper nature of each of the two as well as their difference: one is the *spiritual authority*, and the other is the *temporal power*, and from here on we shall employ these two expressions more than those of spiritual power and temporal power, which have the disadvantage of introducing a certain confusion in the two ideas, as we shall see immediately.

The *spiritual authority* is that of the *brahmins*, to use the Hindu terminology in its most general sense, and as we have explained it, that is, referring to the members of the caste characterised by the ascending tendency, or *sattva*;[21] its domain is that of intellectual power, wisdom, truth. These three notions are of course to be understood in their loftiest sense: *sacred* intellectuality, integral wisdom, and divine truth. The temporal power, for its part, pertains to the *kshatriyas*, the members of the caste in which the

---

20. In his *De consideratione* addressed to Pope Eugene III.

21. See Chapter II, p. 59.

"expansive" tendency, *rajas*, that is, *strength*, dominates, as more-over is indicated by its name, since *kshatra* signifies "strength". Its domain is that of administration, justice and war, as we have said. The role of the spiritual authority, in turn, is that of conserving and transmitting the traditional supra-human doctrine, the foundation of the society. It is the domain of the sacred, of the priesthood, which has a double function: first, knowledge and teaching of the sacred science; then the rites, which depend on sacred science. But it must be clear that we employ the word priesthood in a very broad sense, wider than it tends to have in the West. The priesthood not only includes the officiates of the cult, but also and especially all those who have the function of knowing the orthodox doctrine, and of preserving it and deepening their knowledge; it is exactly those who, in the Middle Ages, were termed the *clergy*, as opposed to the *laity*, or again, the "Church teaching" as opposed to the "Church taught".

Thus, the domain of the spiritual authority is in the first place that of knowledge, which it must transmit by distributing it to all according to a hierarchical order, as Dionysius the Areopagite says. Every authentic knowledge, whatever it may be, has its source in the teaching of the priesthood. What is reserved to it primarily is the science of principles—metaphysics—and secondarily theology. But in addition, it must promote and control the development of the applications of these principles and of the sciences derived from it, and which pertain to the other castes, above all the aristocratic caste to which the king belongs.

The relations between the two swords are clearly determined in the various traditions. The *brahmins* give the *kshatriyas* the intellectual guarantee of their power; conversely, the *kshatriyas*, through their strength, create conditions favorable for the accomplishment in peace of the work of knowledge and teaching. Thus it is, in Hindu mythology, that Skanda, the son of Shiva, and the lord of war, protects the meditation of the other son of Shiva, Ganesha, lord of knowledge.

In the philosophical language of the Middle Ages, St. Thomas Aquinas developed the same doctrine: according to him—and on this point he merely follows the most constant theological teachings—all human functions are subordinated to contemplation as to a higher end, "so that when considering them aright, all seem to be in service of those who contemplate the truth," and that the true reason for the government of civil life is to assure peace for this contemplation.[22]

No doubt these assertions are surprising to our contemporaries. And yet they conform to the strictest orthodoxy once we consider what the true destiny of man is. Let us also add that this principle of the superiority of contemplation over action does not exclude the interest that the social life in itself and the material conditions of human existence may have; this, precisely, is the function of certain derived sciences, which we have mentioned just above, including the most usual ones, such as morality, law, or the "arts", in the mediaeval sense, namely, the traditional techniques proper to the different trades. But this does not contradict the affirmation of St. Thomas, in the sense that all these sciences and all these "arts", not only derive, in different hierarchic degrees, from the pure sacred science, but that they also have as their essential object to help man to participate in it in the measure of each person's possibilities, and thereby fulfil their destiny and reach "salvation". That is why Christ said, "Seek ye the kingdom of God; and all these things shall be added unto you" (Luke 12:31). Let us point out, in addition, that the spiritual authority may not always be visible, even while not ceasing to act on the whole of the social life, of which it is like the axis or the pole.

The relations between the spiritual authority and the temporal power are determined by those of their respective domains. These are, on the one hand, those of knowledge or of contemplation, and on the other, those of action. In order to be exercised, the temporal power needs *certain* kinds of knowledge, but not *the* (supreme) knowledge; and these kinds of knowledge, as we have said above, derive from the supreme knowledge as its applications. At this level, knowledge is not considered in itself, but rather insofar as it gives action its *law*.

It is true that today, for most minds imbued with egalitarianism, it is offensive that the pure and supreme knowledge be

22. St. Thomas Aquinas, treatise *On Kingship*.

reserved for some and not offered to all; being enemies of all hierarchy in this domain as in others, they readily qualify as "elitism", as they call it, this intellectual privilege; and for them this term is the worst of condemnations, accompanied by rebellion and sometimes by hatred. And yet nothing could be more normal than the intellectual status of the traditional social order. If the priesthood is the guardian of the supreme knowledge, it is not because of some jealousy, but quite simply because it alone—in principle, yet the rare exceptions end by being resolved in a normal society—possesses a nature made for this type of knowledge. Conversely, the man of action with difficulty arrives at the supreme knowledge, and moreover, generally does not desire it. Thus, in a normal society each person does that for which he is qualified. And experience unfortunately shows us that outside this principle social life is only confusion.

Always and everywhere, except in the modern West, the superiority of knowledge and contemplation over action, and consequently of the spiritual authority over temporal power, has been affirmed. It is not necessary to insist on the case of the Hindu tradition, which properly serves as a reference in this domain. The same is the case in ancient Tibet, where the *mnatan*, the royal "majesty", was submitted to the *mtu*, the "spiritual authority", master of the "religious Law" (*cos*), prior to the revolution that turned the country into a lamaist theocracy; in China, where the relationships are those of Taoism, possessor of the metaphysical knowledge, and Confucianism; and among the ancient Celts, where the priesthood, pertaining to the Druids, held such importance that, according to Dio Chrysostom, it dominated the kings to the point that they could decide nothing without the Druids, and that it would be more accurate to say that it was the Druids who ruled, whereas the kings, seated on thrones of gold and living in magnificent mansions, were their ministers and the servants of their thought.[23] If Dio is not exaggerating, we are faced with a situation in which the role of the priesthood is especially augmented, which is not the case usually. There are also cases in which the two functions, the spiritual and the tem-

---

23. Dio Chrysostom, 48.8.

poral, are correlative and complementary, more than they are in hierarchy, corresponding to the binomial body-soul. This point of view is not false, moreover, for it is certain that both functions are complementary in fact, as the two principles commonly considered[24] constitutive of man, along with the two domains of his existence, the "natural" and the "supernatural". This intimate union is expressed in India by means of the image of matrimony,[25] and even through the figure composed of Indragni, that is, Agni, the archetype of the spiritual leader, and Indra, the archetypal king. A *kshatriya* expresses it thus: "I destroy my enemies and lead my subjects with the help of the spiritual power."[26] But this point of view does not eliminate the first one, which is the essential one: the complementary exists only in appearance, and "horizontally", which is that of equality. The real situation of the two functions is, on the contrary, established according to the vertical hierarchy of the superior and the inferior, which does not in any way contradict the complementarity

This hierarchy is the essential point of view, in fact, because it is that of the nature of things. The superiority of knowledge over action exists owing to the fact that the former is the mover of the latter, but it is, according to Aristotle's words, a "motionless mover". For action pertains to the world of change and it cannot have its principle within itself; the reality which it can possess comes to it from a principle situated beyond it, in knowledge. The spiritual authority possesses this immutability that comes to it from its supra-human nature, from the divine knowledge; whereas the temporal power is subject to the vicissitudes of contingency, of the transitory, unless it is linked to a principle which assures its stability.

ROYAL CONSECRATION · Hence the temporal power needs to be consecrated by the spiritual authority, a consecration that constitutes its legitimacy, that is, its conformity to the order of things. This is the point of the *royal initiation*, which prop-

---

24. We make this restriction, for in reality man is constituted of three principles: body-soul-spirit.

25. *Mahabharata* 1.69.25.

26. *Shatapatha Brahmana* 6.315.

erly constitutes what has been termed—while often falsifying its meaning—the *divine right*, which is nothing other than the exercise of the temporal power in virtue of a delegation by the spiritual authority. This point is of capital importance, and it will have to be borne carefully in mind when we come to speak of the interminable disputes which arose concerning it during the Western Middle Ages.

The royal initiation is conferred by the spiritual authority, and it could not be otherwise, for the very simple reason that the superior (priestly) function contains "eminently" the inferior one, as the principle contains its consequence or its application, as superior forms contain "eminently" the inferior ones, according to Aristotle. A curious confirmation of this, in the realm of linguistics, is to be found in the word "druid", which is linked etymologically to the form *druvid*, composed of two roots: *dru*, "strength", and *vid*, "wisdom",[27] a form which expresses the doctrine of the cohabitation of the two functions in the spiritual authority in a brief and striking way.

However, in the present state of humanity, the spiritual authority does not as a general rule exercise the temporal power; it transmits it to the king. Thus his dependence is established, the sign of which is the coronation: the king is legitimated only if he has received the priestly investiture and consecration, which imply a spiritual influence necessary for the regular exercise of the royal function, so that normally the king is merely the depository of the power, and can lose it; and this is what occurred numerous times during the Middle Ages, during the course of which the Pope, for grave reasons, and in virtue of the "power of the keys" "released" the subjects from the obligation of fealty to a prince. This power of the keys is precisely related to the cohabitation of the two functions. There are two keys, one of gold and the other silver, which are respectively the sign of

---

27. The Indo-European root *dru* is originally the name of a tree; it refers to the power of growth; later it designated the *oak* (in Greek, *drys*), a striking symbol of the vigour of vegetation. The root *vid*—and its alternate form *weid/wid*—means "to know" in Greek, *(w)idein*; in German, *wissen*; and in English, *wisdom*; and in Latin, the idea of "seeing": *videre*.

priestly authority and temporal power, contained "eminently" in the priesthood. This symbolism of the keys will be developed in the following chapter. What we have wished to recall here is the fundamental principle of the legitimacy of the political power— the condition for the regularity of human society and its organic character—which is its attachment and submission to the order of things and to the divine Law. In effect, society as such is not an organic being, nor even an organisation; only that is organic which possesses a principle superior to the multiplicity of its elements. Now, in itself, society is merely a "collectivity", that is, a sum of individuals. But the spiritual authority introduces a principle of unity into it, a superior principle, because it is supra-individual, and in which it plays the part that the soul and the spirit play in the body of the individual. But this principle cannot establish and animate the society otherwise than in accordance with the norms that we have recalled, outside of which, in fact, and as is the case today, there are simply collectivities, that is to say, herds, or almost so.

CHAPTER IV

THE KING OF THE JEWS AND
THE KING OF THE WORLD

Now the Lord had told Samuel in his ear a day before Saul came, saying, Tomorrow about this time I will send thee a man out of the land of Benjamin, and thou shalt anoint him to be captain over my people Israel. And when Samuel saw Saul, the Lord said unto him, Behold the man whom I spake to thee of. This same shall reign over my people ... they went out both of them, he and Samuel, abroad. And as they were going down to the end of the city, Samuel said to Saul, Bid the servant pass on before us, (and he passed on), but stand thou still a while, that I may shew thee the word of God. Then Samuel took a vial of oil, and poured it upon his head, and kissed him, and said, Is it not because the Lord hath anointed thee to be captain over his inheritance?.... After that thou shalt come to the hill of God, where is the garrison of the Philistines: and it shall come to pass, when thou art come thither to the city, that thou shalt meet a company of prophets coming down from the high place with a psaltery, and a tabret, and a pipe, and a harp, before them; and they shall prophesy: And the Spirit of the Lord will come upon thee, and thou shalt prophesy with them, and shalt be turned into another man.... And it was so, that when he had turned his back to go from Samuel, God gave him another heart: and all those signs came to pass that day.... And Samuel said to all the people, See ye him whom the Lord hath chosen, that there is none like him among all the people? And all the people shouted, and said, God save the king (1 Samuel 9 and 10).

Thus was royalty born in Israel.

If until now we have omitted mentioning the Hebrews among the diverse monarchies studied, it is because of the special role that monarchy played as the inspiration of Christian royalty, which will occupy us in what follows in this book; this has led us to reserve it a place apart.

But at the same time, there is no lack of links and analogies between the Hebrew royalty and those of the Near East which we have already presented; hence, this royalty truly constitutes a junction between the most ancient neighbouring monarchies—and all others beyond, which do not fundamentally differ from them—and the monarchies which were constituted in Christian lands.

Hebrew royalty is not as well known to us as that of the neighbouring peoples or that of India, because the religious texts of Israel are much less interested in the institution of monarchy than are most of those found elsewhere. Royalty never had the same importance for the Hebrews as it did for other peoples, since the general experience in Israel had been a system of theocracy. It is possible, none the less, starting from historical texts of the Bible, such as Samuel, Kings and Chronicles, to arrive at a quite precise idea of the institution of royalty and of accession to the throne; moreover, the royal hymns which occur among the Psalms are full of elements that indicate important aspects of royalty on which historical texts are silent.

In the sacred narrative concerning Saul, the feature which first strikes the attention is the direct intervention of God in choosing the king: Saul is God's chosen, and so too will be his successors, especially his immediate successor, David.[1] The dynastic principle was established starting from David, but the accession to the throne always took place by the grace of God; God made a covenant with the House of David, nevertheless a choice is made each time. Thus, it is Solomon who accedes to the throne, and not Adonijah, even though he is the elder brother,

---

1. The accession of David to the throne took place more or less in the same manner as it did for Saul, and through the intermediary of Samuel as well (1 Sam. 16:13). For Solomon, see 1 Kings 1:38-39.

"for it was his from the Lord" (1 Kings 2:15). Each enthronement implies a renewal of the covenant with David. Indeed, the same held true for the neighbouring peoples and at all times. In Mesopotamia, for example, Gudea is called "the shepherd distinguished in Ningursu's heart. Of Nabonidus it is affirmed that "Sin and Nergal designated him to rule when he was as yet at his mother's breast." Regarding Cyrus: "Marduk designated his name for royalty over the universe."[2] Regarding Bar-Rekub, the king of Zenjirli: "My master Rekub-El hath seated me on the throne of my father." There is no point in repeating here analogous affirmations cited regarding the pharaohs, the princes of Iran, etc. Suffice it to note, once again, to what extent it was important for traditional civilisations to recall, by such formulations, the non-human origin of power.

The king of the Jews is therefore the chosen of God. The starting point of royalty is God's covenant with David, a covenant which is the realisation of the pact on Sinai; and this pact is renewed by the anointing of each new king. It is God Himself who recalls this in Psalm 89:

> I have made a covenant with my chosen, I have sworn unto David my servant,
> Thy seed will I establish for ever, and build up thy throne to all generations ...
> I have laid help upon one that is mighty; I have exalted one chosen out of the people.
> I have found David my servant; with my holy oil have I anointed him.

Therefore it is God who chose the king, and also He who proclaims him, as one can see by a verse from one of the most well-known Psalms—Psalm 110—a royal hymn, of which we shall speak again:

> The Lord said unto my lord, Sit thou at my right hand, until I make thine enemies thy footstool.

---

2. Cf. Isaiah 44: 28: "That saith of Cyrus, He is my shepherd..."

This "oracular" Psalm was assuredly recited at the coronation, as were other Psalms we shall look at.

Indeed, we know that during the course of the coronation ceremony, which took place at the temple,[3] the high priest bestowed the royal insignia upon the prince, namely the *nezer* and the *edut* (2 Kings 11:12). The *nezer* is the royal crown; as for the *edut*, it signifies "testimony" and, according to the best commentators, it designates a testimony concerning the Davidic covenant. In fact, the word *edut* is employed as a synonym of *berit*, "covenant", and also *hoq* "decree"; now, Psalm 89, verse 39, sets forth in parallel fashion the royal diadem and the *berit*, and similarly, Psalm 2, a royal Psalm, speaks of the sacred in relation to the "decree" (*hoq*) of the Lord. The *edut* would have been a kind of protocol of adoption by God, of the type in Psalm 2, and a reminder of the Davidic covenant of the type in Psalm 89.

Next came the essential act, the anointing with holy oil, which, as we have seen in the case of Saul and David, sufficed unto itself to consecrate a king. Thus the king was called the *Anointed*, in Hebrew *mashiah*, a word which has passed into our language in the form of *messiah*. In the ancient world, especially in Egypt, but in all the East as well,[4] oils and ointments were considered divine substances, emanations of God, because they are solar substances, the sun itself being one of the great symbols of divinity. We have seen this in the narration of Saul's coronation: when he had been anointed, the spirit of God came over him. The same occurred with David (1 Sam. 16:13).

The anointing with oil served also to consecrate the priests: it was this which conferred perpetual priesthood, according to Exodus (40:12-15). Thus, as with the priest, the king, the "Anointed of the Lord", participated in the holiness of God.

---

3. We have two accounts of the coronation of the kings: Solomon's coronation (1 Kings 1:32-48) and that of Joash (2 Kings 11:12-20). Solomon was crowned at Gihon, but that was an exception. The other following coronations took place at the Temple.

4. The rite of anointing was practiced in Canaan (Judges 9:8-15). Elijah received from God the order to anoint Hazael as the king of Aram (1 Kings 19:15). Moreover, the rite of anointing was known by the Hittites, and one of the royal epithets of the king was *The Anointed*.

The ceremony ended in the temple with the blowing of horns and the acclaim of the people crying "Long live the King!"—an acclaim which signified their acceptance of the choice made by God.

The last part of the coronation feast, the enthronement, was celebrated in the palace. The king was seated solemnly on the throne, which constituted the assumption of power—for the throne is synonymous with royal power—and there he received the homage of the great. But here, too, the emphasis is on the divine origin of the power, for the throne of the king is expressly designated as the "throne of Yahweh" (1 Chron. 29:23) and "the throne of the royalty of Yahweh over Israel" (*Ibid.* 28:5).

Regarding the king of Israel, this rite of coronation manifests the typical features of sacred royalty as we have highlighted in other traditions. In the first place, as we have mentioned previously, the king, as a result of his anointing, acquires a divine character, the Spirit itself having invested him. For this reason the king becomes "son of God", adopted by him as such at the time of his advent to the throne and by the grace of the anointing. It is Yahweh Himself who, through the mouth of the prophet Nathan, announces to David that he will be succeeded by Solomon, and says: "I will set up thy seed after thee, which shall proceed out of thy bowels, and I will establish his kingdom ... I will be his father, and he shall be my son" (2 Sam. 7:14; cf. 1 Chron. 17:13, 22:10 and 28:6). What is remarkable is that this adoption as son is mentioned at the moment of the investiture of the king, as is shown by Psalm 2, recited upon this occasion, in which this is sung:

> Yet have I set my king upon my holy hill of Zion. I will declare the decree:
> the Lord hath said unto me, Thou art my Son; this day have I begotten thee.

And in Psalm 88, God also says:

> He shall cry unto me, Thou art my father, my God, and the rock of my salvation.

As "son of God", the king receives the promise of eternity for his throne and of universal sovereignty: "... I shall give thee the heathen for thine inheritance, and the uttermost parts of the earth for thy possession" (Psalm 2).

"Thy seed will I establish for ever, and build up thy throne to all generations" (Psalm 88), which is easily understood, since, as said before, the king of Israel is placed on the "throne of Yahweh" Himself.[5]

We have seen previously how it is necessary to understand this universal sovereignty attributed to the king by all traditions. What it signifies is a virtual universality, in the sense that the prince governs his people in accordance with the Law by which God governs the entire universe.

The adoption of the king of Israel as "Son of God" makes him, in a certain sense, participate in the divine nature. Without going as far as the Egyptians or other peoples, the Hebrews have at times considered their king as divine. Thus in Psalm 45, which is a royal epithalamium, the king is addressed saying:

> Thy throne, O God, is for ever and ever: the sceptre of thy kingdom is a right sceptre.

And in the book of Samuel (2 Sam. 14:17-20), David is called "Angel of God". Now, the expression "Angel of God", "Angel of Yahweh", is scarcely distinguished from the word "God" Himself (Cf. Gen. 22:11-12).

These relationships between God and the prince explain the latter's priestly character. No doubt the Israelite king is not a king-priest in the full sense, as were the pharaoh or the emperor of China.[6] Nevertheless, it is undeniable that he participated in the priesthood. He is seen wearing the *ephod*, which is a ritual

---

5. Analogously, the king of Egypt sat on the "throne of Ra".

6. With the exception, however, at the end of the history of Israel, of the Hasmonean princes who combined the royal crown and the high priesthood. Simon, the first prince of the Maccabean dynasty, son of the priest Hasmon, and some others, were kings and priests. But it seems to us that here it is a question rather of *priest-kings* than of *king-priests*.

vestment of the priest: this is the case of David, who danced before the Ark "girded with linen ephod". (2 Sam. 6:13-14). The king offers sacrifices: prior to the dance before the Ark, David sacrificed a bull and a fattened calf (*Ibid.*). Solomon made offerings with his own hands on the heights (1 Kings 3); he built the temple—an essentially priestly function—dedicated it, and on that occasion sacrificed, blessed the people and consecrated the interior courtyard (1 Kings 8:54, 62 and 64).

In any case, the priesthood of the king is affirmed expressly in Psalm 110, which is the oracle of God pronounced, as we have seen, during the coronation: "The Lord hath sworn, and will not repent," is proclaimed before the prince, "thou art a priest for ever after the order of Melchizedek." Priesthood and royalty are thus intimately linked in the Covenant of God with the House of David; a covenant which is merged more or less with God's Covenant with the people, upon which depends the entire life of the Israelites. The affirmation of the king's participation in the priesthood of Melchizedek is of such importance that we shall return to it, but after having first considered the problem of Hebrew royalty in connection with messianism, which will clarify it definitively.

Meanwhile, let us note that the king also bears a title that pertains to Yahweh, that of "Shepherd of Israel", of the "Good Shepherd" (Psalm 79; 2 Sam. 5:2 and 7:8; Num. 27:17), a title which was already known in Mesopotamia, where Hammurabi was called the "beneficent shepherd". The king, as the "good shepherd", is he who brings justice and prosperity. Both things, moreover, are intimately linked.

Justice and prosperity are the characteristics of "peace," *shalom*. Now, *shalom* has a wide scope, like *Maat* in Egypt; *shalom* designates the normal state of things, the social, no doubt, but also the cosmic situation, and in particular, fertility, abundant crops and the rates of the flow of water. The royal virtue is exercised in this domain as well, as in all sacred royalties. It is thus expressed in Psalm 72, which is a prayer for the king who accedes to the throne:

> Give the king thy judgments, O God, and thy righteousness
> unto the king's son.

He shall judge thy people with righteousness, and thy poor with judgment.

The mountains shall bring peace to the people, and the little hills, by righteousness ...

He shall come down like rain upon the mown grass: as showers that water the earth ...

There shall be an handful of corn in the earth upon the top of the mountains; the fruit thereof shall shake like Lebanon: and they of the city shall flourish like grass of the earth.

But this equilibrium, the condition for justice and prosperity, is the fruit of watchful action, for it is perpetually threatened, on the plane of nature as well as on the social plane, by the pressure of the forces of disorder. It is then that the function proper to the king must be exercised, his function as *kshatriya*, as a combative hero and saviour hero of his people, of which Psalm 45 offers a magnificent portrait:

My heart is inditing a good matter: I speak of the things which I have made touching the king: my tongue is the pen of a ready writer.

Thou art fairer than the children of men: grace is poured into thy lips: therefore God hath blessed thee for ever.

Gird thy sword upon thy thigh, O most mighty, with thy glory and thy majesty.

And in thy majesty ride prosperously because of truth and meekness and righteousness; and thy right hand shall teach thee terrible things.

Thine arrows are sharp in the heart of the king's enemies; whereby the people fall under thee.

In this role, the king is closely united to God on the one hand, and to his people on the other. This is a point which it is important to emphasise in order to fully understand the nature and meaning of the Israelite royalty, which is a quite remarkable case of sacred royalty. It is defined by the trinomial God-King-People, whose terms are linked immiscibly by the pact of the Covenant and its corollary, the Davidic covenant. By the first one, God is bound to his people, by the second he is bound to the king, whom He has chosen as the executer of His will; at the same time, God binds the people to the king, and in this way an intimate union of the king and the people is made, with the result that the prince is, as it were, the embodiment of the people: it is in the king that the community is manifested and integrated, because the king, the middle term of the trinomial, is the mediator between God and the people, the channel by which descends the divine power which vivifies it. The king is a source of strength for the people, he is its "breath of life", the "light of Israel", the bearer of divine powers without which Israel cannot live (Hosea 3:4).

It is this divine power of which the king is the bearer that enables him to maintain the equilibrium, the *shalom*, and to re-establish it if necessary by means of combat against hostile forces, whether coming from men or from nature. The king leads God's combat. Upon his faithfulness depends the salvation of his people; he trusts totally in God, that He might show the universe that the king is His anointed.

> Arise, O Lord, in thine anger, lift up thyself because of the rage of mine enemies (Psalm 7).

> O ye sons of men, how long will ye turn my glory into shame? how long will ye love vanity, and seek after leasing?
> But know that the LORD hath set apart him that is godly for himself: the Lord will hear when I call unto him (Psalm 4).

> I will be glad and rejoice in thee: I will sing praise to thy name, O thou most High.
> When mine enemies are turned back, they shall fall and perish at thy presence.
> For thou hast maintained my right and my cause; thou satest in the throne judging right (Psalm 9) (Cf. Psalm 17).

> Plead my cause, O Lord, with them that strive with me: fight against them that fight against me (Psalm 35).

RITES OF RENEWAL · The covenant by which the king is the possessor of the divine strength is renewed at the beginning of each reign with the anointing of the coronation, and during the course of the reign it is renewed each year. It is a matter of necessity, for the equilibrium which must be obtained has to take into account the cosmic rhythm to which biological rhythms and human behaviours are subject. More especially, the rhythm of the annual cycle, the cycle of the seasons, with its ascending and descending phases, takes on prime importance for the life of men, and conditions the rhythms of human behaviour as well as the life of nature. Throughout this cycle the vital energy develops to its furthest extent and then decreases until it is exhausted, which leads to a loosening of tension on all planes and runs the risk of leaving the field wide open to hostile forces, the forces of death.

To fight against this, then, the king needs to recharge, so to speak, his energetic potential at its source, that is, in divinity. To this end are celebrated the particular feasts that we have already encountered and analysed in different traditional feasts situated at the beginning of the New Year, of the new annual cycle.[7]

This feast also existed among the Hebrews, with the same object and the same setting, or at least an analogous setting, in which the king played the role of primary importance, demonstrating his twofold character, royal and priestly.

The *Feast of Tabernacles* or *Feast of the Tents* (*hag ha sukkot*), celebrated at the end of the harvest in the month of *tisri*, and beginning the civil year, is the continuation of a New Year feast celebrated in both Hebrew kingdoms.[8] The agrarian nature of this feast is undeniable, although other elements are superimposed upon it; its primitive nature is clearly brought out in a passage of a post-exile text, that of Zech. 14:16-17, in which the prophet says: "And it shall be that whichever of the families of

---

7. See Chapter II, p. 75ff.

8. Concerning the Feast of Tabernacles, see Exod. 33:16, 34:22; Deut. 16:13,16; Lev. 23:34ff. The feast was celebrated under tents of foliage in memory of the dwellings of the Israelites in the desert, according to Leviticus. Lasting eight days, it is mentioned in the Gospel of St. John with the Greek name of *skenopigia* (John 7:2), and in Plutarch (*Quaest. conv.* 5).

the earth do not come up to Jerusalem to worship the King, the Lord of hosts, on them there will be no rain." The gift of rain, therefore, depends on the feast, which in turn is closely linked to the conception of Yahweh as the king whose enthronement is celebrated. However, let us hasten to recall what we have already said concerning fertility rites: namely, that their end and efficacy must not be seen as limited to the physical domain and the material life, which is inseparable from the rest of the life of a people, the social, political, and spiritual life.

Meticulous studies of the book of Psalms have allowed us to prove that a certain number of these are songs or recitations that pertain to the ancient feast of the New Year, the setting of which it has been possible to reconstruct as follows. It comprised the commemoration of the victories of Yahweh, Leader of the powers of light, over the powers of darkness; next an enthronement of Yahweh as king, the repetition of the cosmogonic act and the putting to death of Rahab, the monster symbolising the primordial chaos, and as a result, the revivification of nature for the year to come, and at the same time that of the king and of all the people.

These different themes are expressed in the ritual drama that took place at the temple and of which the Psalms offer us the principal sequences.

Yahweh appears in them as the master of the waters. The rain results from the fact that God opens the heavens (as in Gen. 6 ff., 7:11, 8:2): The Lord, "gathereth the waters of the sea together as an heap: he layeth up the depth in storehouses" (Psalm 33); "Thou visitest the earth, and waterest it: thou greatly enrichest it with the river of God, which is full of water: thou preparest them corn, when thou hast so provided for it" (Psalm 65). The power of God is affirmed on the cosmic Sea, the source of all the rivers (Cf. Amos 5:8). These texts explain the meaning of the "Sea of Bronze", so important in the temple of Jerusalem: as a replica of the cosmic ocean, it therefore had to play an important part in the rite.

The Psalms offer us numerous passages insisting upon this aspect of God as master of the waters enthroned as the King who frees the waters, making the torrent roar. Particularly interesting is Psalm 29:

> The voice of the Lord is upon the waters: the God of glory thundereth: the Lord is upon many waters ...
> The Lord sitteth upon the flood; yea, the Lord sitteth King for ever.

This recalls the Babylonian *Creation Poem*, with Marduk battling against Tiamat, the chaos, and the forces of darkness; a poem recited by the high priest on the fourth day of the Babylonian Festival.[9] Psalm 29 must have been recited at an Israelite Feast celebrated in honor of Yahweh the king. In both cases the justification of the earthly king is assured by it.

Psalms 46 and 67 refer to the enthronement procession of Yahweh as king in the Temple:

> God is gone up with a shout, the Lord with the sound of a trumpet ...
> For God is the King of all the earth: sing ye praises with understanding ...
> God reigneth over the heathen: God sitteth upon the throne of his holiness (Psalm 47).

As with Psalm 47, Psalm 68 describes this procession, which no doubt took place before the Ark of the Covenant:

> Let God arise, let God arise, let his enemies be scattered: let them also that hate him flee before him ...
> They have seen thy goings, O God; even the goings of my God, my King, in the sanctuary ...
> Sing unto God, ye kingdoms of the earth; O sing praises unto the Lord ...
> Ascribe ye strength unto God: his excellency is over Israel, and his strength is in the clouds.

---

9. See Chapter II, p. 76ff.

Consequently, God also gives strength to the king. This Psalm has the aim of celebrating the ritual triumph of Yahweh, the Great King who brings salvation to his people, gives victory over death, grants rebirth to all things, the renewal of life. The Psalm that follows, Psalm 48, is in the same spirit. It is the re- cital of the total victory of Yahweh over the allied "kings of the earth". These "kings of the earth" or "kings of the nations" have a double meaning, at once historical and cosmic: the expression designates the enemies of God and of his people, Canaan, etc., but also, in a much vaster sense, all the forces of darkness and death, of which the political enemies of the nation are merely the instruments and of which they represent but one aspect:

> God is known in her palaces for a refuge.
> For, lo, the kings were assembled, they passed by together.
> They saw it, and so they marvelled; they were troubled, and hasted away.
> As we have heard, *so have we seen in the city of the Lord of hosts* ...

This last line, which we have deliberately highlighted, shows that we are faced with a ritual combat; also, we have another proof of this in the following verse:

> We have thought of thy loving kindness, O God, in the midst of thy temple.

This feast in celebration of the victories of Yahweh and the salvation of His people pertains to the monarchic period, as is shown by this passage from Jeremiah, which says:

> Is not the Lord in Zion? is not her king in her? ...
> The harvest is past, the summer is ended, and we are not saved (Jer. 8:19 ff.).

This means that salvation comes when Yahweh manifests as king during the time of harvest. That being so, it is certain that the feast of the New Year has a precise relationship with the human king of Israel, who is the force of life of the nation. This is really

115

the significance of Psalm 89, which sings of the triumph against the primeval monster, Rahab (the chaos of the Waters), and his allies, as well as of the work of God, the Creator:

> Thou rulest the raging of the sea: when the waves thereof arise, thou stillest them.
> Thou hast broken Rahab in pieces, as one that is slain; thou hast scattered thine enemies with thy strong arm.

After which it is said that the salvation of the people is assured,

> For our shield belongs to the Lord, and our king to the Holy One of Israel.

There follows a reminder of Yahweh's covenant with the House of David. In it, it is the king himself who speaks and who concludes the liturgy. He reproaches God for having allowed the humiliation of His anointed and he implores Him:

> Remember, Lord, the reproach of thy servants; how I do bear in my bosom the reproach of all the mighty people;
> Wherewith thine enemies have reproached, O Lord; wherewith they have reproached the footsteps of thine anointed.

These lines show that during the course of the feast the king appears as the humbled and "suffering servant". It is a question here of a ritual abasement, which is a lesson: deliverance, victory over death, depend solely upon God; in the battle against the forces of evil, it is only when things look darkest that God intervenes and saves. For, ultimately, He does save. As Psalm 18 said, when the king thanks God for having wrested him from the hand of his enemies, for He drew him out of "many waters" ready to engulf him. The entire Psalm is also a story of the battle against the dark forces. The king is saved because of his righteousness (*tsadek*); he is justified as righteous (*tsadik*):

> The Lord rewarded me according to my righteousness; according to the cleanness of my hands hath he recompensed me.

116

For I have kept the ways of the Lord, and have not wickedly departed from my God.

For all his judgments were before me, and I did not put away his statutes from me.

I was also upright before him, and I kept myself from mine iniquity.

Here we reach an important phase of the ceremony, which unfolds in two parts: the abasement and the exaltation of the king. A certain number of Psalms (25, 38, 40, 41) show us the king overwhelmed by evils and speaking of the "sins of his youth"; in reality, regarding this he speaks in the name of his people whom he represents, whom he *incarnates*, and the "I" that he employs is "collective". In the ritual abasement, the king bears the sins of his people, he is humiliated by them, but thanks to his fidelity, which he affirms in this "confession of innocence" recalled above, he receives forgiveness. And it will not be forgotten that, during the course of the parallel festival in Babylon, the king, initially humiliated and struck by the high priest, made confession of his innocence and received anew the insignia of power which had been removed from him; after which the high priest said, in the name of Marduk, that his prayer had been granted, and that he would triumph over his enemies.[10]

---

10. See Chapter II, p. 76. Since the Mesopotamian king, like the king of Israel, represented the people, he has to answer for the conduct of his subjects before the gods, hence for the sins of the community, and he subjects himself to the penitential rites to which we have alluded, following which he obtains reconciliation. The same idea is found in India: according to the *Laws of Manu*, the sins of the people pass to the king if he falls; in China, the emperor, as "true man", takes upon himself the expiation of the faults of his people: he must expiate for all, and to this end make the necessary sacrifices. This understanding, founded on the idea that people and prince form a psychic and spiritual union, has not disappeared, and we have a striking and moving example of it in the recent history of Japan. After the defeat of his country, the emperor Hirohito came of his own accord to MacArthur and told him: "I have come to you, General MacArthur, to submit to the judgment of the powers that you represent, given that I solely am responsible for all the political and military decisions

The same theme is developed in Psalm 118, which is associated with the Feast of Tabernacles (Neh. 8:9-18). It is a song of victory and of the action of graces meant for a procession:

> All nations compassed me about: but in the name of the Lord will I destroy them.
> They compassed me about; yea, they compassed me about: but in the name of the Lord I will destroy them ...
> The Lord is my strength and song, and is become my salvation ...
> The Lord hath chastened me sore: but he hath not given me over unto death.

It can be seen that, here again, it is the king who speaks and who celebrates the liturgy, after which he cries:

> Open to me the gates of righteousness: I will go into them, and I will praise the Lord:
> This gate of the Lord, into which the righteous shall enter.

The king has suffered a humiliation and has come close to death. But the Lord has delivered him because he is "righteous"; and with him all the people, of which he is the "focus", are delivered from death and justified. The life of the king is renewed and that of the people with him. The procession passes through the "gates of righteousness", in order to follow the rite with another ceremony at the altar. At that point the last act of the feast is accomplished, the renewal of the Davidic covenant and the re-investiture of the king, his re-adoption as "son of God", as attested by Psalms 2 and 110, which surely were sung here as they were during the coronation. God strikes fear into the enemies and there is the cry:

> Yet have I set my king upon my holy hill of Zion (Psalm 2).

---

that were taken, as well as for all the operations which were undertaken by my people during the course of the war." Only a sacred king could behave in such a manner. (In Shinsho Hinayama, *La Voie de l'Eternité*, translation of P. Pascal, Paris, 1972, p. 132.)

At this moment the king himself takes part in the liturgy and repeats the oracle received from God proclaiming the adoption as son and the supremacy over enemies:

> I will declare the decree: the Lord hath said unto me, Thou art my Son; this day have I begotten thee.
>
> Ask of me, and I shall give thee the heathen for thine inheritance ... (Psalm 2).

The confirmation of this was given by the recitation of another oracle, that of Psalm 110 (no doubt recited by one of the "prophets of the cult"):

> The Lord said unto my Lord, Sit thou at my right hand, until I make thine enemies thy footstool ...
>
> In the beauties of holiness from the womb of the morning: thou hast the dew of thy youth.
>
> The Lord hath sworn, and will not repent, Thou art a priest for ever after the order of Melchizedek.

Here the twofold character, royal and priestly, of the sovereign is affirmed.

This last point is important; if we have dwelt somewhat at length on this feast of the New Year, it was in order to show how it reveals the particularly sacred character of the king, who participates in the cult in a typically priestly role, a role attributed to him by God Himself in affirming that he is a priest according to the order of Melchizedek. The Anointed of the Lord, the *meshiah*, the suffering and humble servant, is in this annual rite once again adopted as son, assured of victory over the forces of death, and, to express his function as mediator between the people and Yahweh, a priest of the order of Melchizedek.

* * *

JESUS AS KING · This understanding of the king as saviour of his people was sublimised, after the exile, in messianism, the expectation of a Messiah, of an exceptional *meshiah*, who would

119

re-establish royalty in Israel in order to definitively bring it salvation and power; and was fully accomplished in Jesus Christ. This is a subject at which we must pause, and which it is appropriate to examine closely, for it lies at the very heart of the political doctrine of Christianity, which is itself fundamentally in perfect accord, despite specific differences, with that of the universal sacred Tradition.

Jesus' role as spiritual Master has so been emphasised that it has been somewhat forgotten that he was also—and perhaps, from a particular point of view, first of all—King, as is proved by a certain number of royal Psalms that we have cited, especially Psalms 2 and 110, which are termed messianic, and have in fact been related to Christ, He having applied them to Himself in the Gospels. Moreover, the Gospels insist throughout on the royal character of Jesus in the story of His life.

The fact that governs everything is that Jesus was not born into the priestly caste, the tribe of Levi, but into the royal caste, the tribe of Judah in the House of David, and that he bears the title of "Son of David" (Matt. 1:1; Luke 1: 32-33), a title that the Jewish people acknowledged in Him. Thus the blind man in Jericho, whom Jesus would heal, implored Him crying: "Jesus, son of David, have mercy on me" (Mark 10:47 ff). Other analogous cases are in Mark 7:24-31 and Matt. 9:27-31, 15:21-28 and 21:9. Upon the entry to Jerusalem on Palm Sunday, it is to the cry of "Hosanna to the Son of David" that the people acclaim Christ (John 12:16). As well implicitly acknowledging this title at the scene of the healing of the blind man in Jericho, Jesus also did so before the Pharisees (Matt. 22:41-46), when on this occasion He cited Psalm 110:

> The Lord said unto my Lord, Sit thou at my right hand, until I make thine enemies thy footstool.

The title is taken up again by St. Paul (Rom. 1:3) and in Revelations, where Christ in glory is called "He who has the key of David" (Revelations 3:7 and 4:5) after Isaiah (22:22): "The key of the house of David I will lay on his shoulder; so he shall open, and no one shall shut; and he shall shut, and no one shall open" (that is to say, he will have all power).

As "Son of David", Christ is also "Son of God", as it is said expressly in the story of His conception (Luke 1:26-38), at the time of His baptism, and as He Himself proclaims before Caiphas: "'Tell us if You are the Christ, the Son of God!' Jesus said to him, 'It is as you said'"(Matt. 26:63-64). This title of "Son of God" was borne by the Israelite king, as we have seen; but it was attached to his function, not to the individual. In the case of Christ, of course, it is different, since he is Son of God as the Divine Word; but nonetheless, what is important to note is that he bears this title as a man, and above all as a king, as is shown by Psalms 2 and 110, an aspect concerning which there is no need to return (see Mark 12:36).

The Gospels insist on this title of king for Jesus, above all in the Gospel of St. John, where His royalty is affirmed as many as sixteen times.

Jesus is proclaimed king-messiah by God Himself at the time of the Annunciation, when the angel says to Mary: "And behold, you will conceive in your womb and bring forth a Son, and shall call His name JESUS. He will be great, and will be called the Son of the Highest; and the Lord God will give Him the throne of His father David. And He will reign over the house of Jacob forever, and of His kingdom there will be no end" (Luke 1:31-33). The proclamation is completed by that of the angels to the shepherds of Bethlehem: "I bring you good tidings of great joy which will be to all people. For there is born to you this day in the city of David a Saviour, who is Christ (Messiah—Meshiah) the Lord" (Luke 2:11-12).

The title of *saviour* of the people pertains, as we have seen, to the Israelite king; as for the name *messiah*, it was his specific designation; the king was the anointed of the Lord since it was the sacred anointing that signified his adoption as son and conferred upon him the divine power. At His birth, Jesus was moreover acknowledged as king by the Magi, to whom we shall return later.

As king, Jesus is also the "good shepherd" of the people (John 10:1-21), and he announces the establishing of the Kingdom of

God, which will be that of righteousness and restored order, at the same time that he affirms his cosmic power (Matt. 28:18), and an era of prosperity, the sign of the period of salvation (Matt.14:13-21). The figure of the Messiah, the glorious king of the whole universe, had already appeared in the prophetic text of Daniel:

> I was watching in the night visions, and behold, one like the Son of Man, coming with the clouds of heaven! He came to the Ancient of Days, and they brought Him near before Him. Then to Him was given dominion and glory and a kingdom, that all peoples, nations, and languages should serve Him. His dominion is an everlasting dominion, which shall not pass away, and His kingdom the one which shall not be destroyed (Daniel 7:13-14).

To which Revelations responds wherein Christ is called "Prince of the kings of the earth"; on His robe can be read, "King of kings and Lord of lords" (Rev. 19:16).

It is above all in the events of the last days of the earthly life of Jesus that His royalty appears with splendor. The Gospel of St. John, as we have said, mentions Christ's royal title sixteen times. Now, of these sixteen, twelve are accumulated in chapters 18-19 which relate the events in question. First of all, of course, there is the triumph of Palm Sunday and the entry into Jerusalem—recalling the royal procession of coronation and the Feast of the New Year to which we have alluded above—a triumph in the course of which the multitude acclaims Jesus as "king of Israel" (John 12:12-19). But paradoxically, it is the story of the Passion, the crucifixion and the death, which definitively brings to light the royal character of the messiah. Before Caiphas, Jesus is accepted as king; to the question of the High Priest, "Tell us if you are the Christ, the Son of God!" (that is to say, the *Messiah*), Jesus replies, "It is as you say. Nevertheless, I say to you, hereafter you will see the Son of Man sitting at the right hand of the Power, and coming on the clouds of heaven" (Matt. 26:63-64; John 18:33-40). The three elements of Jesus' affirmation are royal titles: Messiah, Son of God, and Seated at the Right Hand of God (cf. Psalm 110). This is made still clearer during the trial before Pilate (John 18), for this trial refers entirely to the claim of Jesus to the title of king. The Jews accused him of perverting the nation and of "deciding that he is Christ (Messiah) King" (Luke 23-2). Hence the question of Pilate: "Are you the King of the Jews?" to which Jesus declared: "It is as you say." (Matt. 27:11); and again, "You say rightly that I am a king" (John 18:37). Then we are taken to the painful scene during the course of which the soldiers, to mock Jesus, undertake a parody of royal investiture: Christ is dressed with a purple mantle, receives a crown of thorns and a reed by way of a sceptre; after which the soldiers bow mockingly, saying: "Long live the king of the Jews!"—a parody of the traditional scene of the homage of the great, which would follow the enthronement of the new king. However, let one beware; this scene has not only the meaning of the pitiful and unbearable mockery that its authors wished to give it. It must be "read" at two levels: the visible, which is distressing, and the invisible, which means something altogether different. Involuntarily, the insulters have also, in their own way, declared that Jesus is indeed king. And that, moreover, is how the first Christian ages understood this scene in which today we see only the outrage done to the sublime martyr. The scene of the *Mocking* has been a subject especially treated in Byzantine iconography, where it is represented, not in the realistic manner corresponding to the visible historical reality, but with the features of the coronation ceremony of an emperor: Jesus is seen dressed in the imperial purple, and before him are not Roman soldiers but personages making the *proskynese*, that is to say the great reverential prostration, accompanied by musicians.[11]

And this is the way that other acts of the tragedy must be interpreted. When Jesus is again taken to Pilate, he has Jesus sit[12] in the court built on the place called *Gabbatha* and exclaims:

---

11. See A. Grabar, *l'Empereur dans l'art byzantin*, p. 66.

12. The translation that we give of this passage is not the usual translation according to which it is Pilate who is seated in the court. The interpretation that we adopt is based on the transitive value of the word *ekathisen* (*kathizo*); it was adopted by Justin, the *Gospel of Peter* (s. II), and the Ethiopian versions of the fourth Gospel. It is accepted by several modern exegetes, in

"Behold your King!" (John 19:13-15); a caricature, to be sure, of Christ seated at the right Hand of God to participate in the judgment of the world (cf. Psalm 110 and John 12:31), but which at the same time manifests this glory of Christ as king and judge.

But it is the crucifixion that is the most complete expression of Christ's royalty. The supreme humiliation—of which the humiliation of the Israelite king was but a pale image—coincides here with the supreme victory. Christ Himself called His ordeal a *raising*, and the Gospel of St. John closely relates Christ's royalty to the raising on the cross: "Now is the judgment of this world: now shall the prince of this world be cast out. And I, if I be lifted up from the earth, will draw all men unto me. This he said, signifying what death he should die" (John 12:31 ff.). Similarly, at the meeting with Nicodemus, Jesus said: "And as Moses lifted up the serpent in the wilderness, even so must the Son of man be lifted up: That whosoever believeth in him should not perish, but have eternal life" (John 3:14-15). The elevation on the cross is already the elevation to the right Hand of God: "This Jesus God hath raised up ... being by the right hand of God exalted" (Acts 2:32-3).

The crucifixion hence has a double aspect: priestly and royal. Priestly, because Christ acts here as the high priest, accomplishing the sacrifice of which he himself is the victim. But this sacrifice also takes on a royal character, firstly because Jesus has willed it thus: the inscription fixed on the cross, and giving the reason for the condemnation, reads: "Jesus of Nazareth, king of the Jews"; it was Pilate who wrote it, and St. John emphasises this by adding that Pilate changed nothing despite the protests of the Jewish priests (John 19:19-22), thus attesting, despite himself, before the world and from then on thereafter, that *Jesus died a king*.

---

particular, I. de la Potterie, "Jesus roi et juge d'apres Jean 19,13" in *Biblica* 19:13 (960), pp.217-47. Let us add that this interpretation fits the context better than the usual one, for in effect Pilate says: "Here is your king", which is quite natural if Jesus is seated in the court. Besides, why would Pilate seat himself at this court to say those words?

The *Titulus Crucis*, cross inscription as drafted by Pilate: "Jesus of Nazareth, King of the Jews," in Hebrew, Greek and Latin, kept in Rome, at the Basilica of the Holy Cross in Jerusalem.

What characterises the king—the *kshatriya*—is a heroic and combative nature. Christ is heroic in sacrificing Himself, and this sacrifice is at the same time the decisive combat by which he becomes—as is the role of the king—the saviour of his people. The combat of the cross is the supreme combat against the forces of darkness, that combat of Yahweh and His Anointed evoked in the Feast of the Israelite New Year. It is to this that Jesus alludes in his words recalled above: "...now shall the prince of this world be cast out." Christ here engages on a universal scale that "combat against the monster" which is the essential act of the heroic destiny; a combat which, according to Cyril of Jerusalem, had already begun at the moment of His baptism, an event evoked by the liturgy of the Blessing of Water:

> Having come to the shores of the Jordan, Thy Son saw the dreadful Dragon lurking in the water with gaping maw, impatient to devour mankind, but Thy only Son, by His great power, tread on the water and gave hard chastisement to the vigorous beast, according to the prophecy of the prophet: Thou brakest the heads of the dragons in the waters (*Psalm* 74).[13]

This combat ends with his descent into the hells, from where He delivers the captives. That is why the liturgical hymns, of both East and West, sung on Good Friday contain expressions of victory:

> Sing, O my tongue, the triumph

---

13. Cyril of Jerusalem, *Catecheses mystagogicae*; blessing of the waters according to the Armenian and Byzantine rite.

Of that glorious battle!
And of the cross, bright trophy,
Sing the splendid victory
By which the world's Redeemer
Himself sacrificing victor was.[14]

The banners of the King advance;
'Tis the mystery of the Cross,
Upon it Life did death endure,
And yet by death did Life procure.[15]

The cross is celebrated as a "throne" in this response pertaining to the gothic liturgy of Spain:

From the heights of the throne of Thy cross
Cast a look upon us, wretched and captive
In the bonds of our passions;
O Redeemer, deliver us
Of the ordeals we've deserved.[16]

In ancient Byzantine and Roman iconography, the Crucified is not represented as cast down and bleeding, but erect, living and wearing the royal crown (see plate p.127). The image which translates the invisible reality hidden behind the visible event is impressive by its grandeur. It expresses powerfully the victory of Christ symbolised by the four directions of the cross, witnessing that this victory against darkness extends to the entire universe according to the four cardinal directions,[17] and that Christ, conquering king, extends His reign over all Creation, and is in reality the King of the World.

The scene of the cross already potentially contains the glory of the Resurrection and the epiphany of the conquering Christ

---

14. Hymn *Pange lingua gloriosi* (Good Friday).

15. Hymn *Vexilla Regis* (Passiontide).

16. Text and translation in Dom Guéranger, *L'Anée liturgique*.

17. See St. Irenaeus, *Epideixis* 1.34. See our work, *La divine Liturgie*, p. 105 ff.

Glory crucifix, with Christ wearing the royal crown (12th cent.,
Amiens cathedral).

of the Apocalypse, in which the sacred writer describes in detail the battle against the forces of darkness, the dragon and his armies, the final victory of Good over evil, of Life over Death, assured by Christ the sacrificed Lamb. And the defeat of the Dragon is celebrated by the wedding of the Lamb, which recalls the royal hierogamies of the conquerors, and which were a prelude to the universal reign of righteousness and peace prophesied in the messianic Psalm (Psalm 85).

"KING OF THE WORLD"

Speaking of Christ, St. Paul writes: "For by Him all things were created that are in heaven and that are on earth, visible and invisible.... And He is before all things, and in Him all things subsist" (Col. 1:12 ff.). And Jesus Himself proclaimed: "All authority has been given to Me in heaven and on earth" (Matt. 28-18). These two texts give us the foundation of the universal royalty of Christ who, according to traditional terminology, is the *King of the World*. Christ's royal power is rooted in His very person: He is king because He is the Word of God (John 1:1-14), master of the creation which was made in Him and by Him; and it is through Him that creation returns to its divine source; it is why He is the supreme mediator. However, two aspects can be discerned in Him: firstly, He is the Divine Word, the eternal Word, the pure spiritual Light issuing from the Divinity (*phos ek photos*, says the *Credo*), the supreme Intelligence in Whom reside the "Ideas", in the Platonic sense, of all beings; next, He is, at a lower degree, like a reflection of the pure spiritual Light, the cosmic Intelligence, and it is under this aspect that the Word is termed *King of the World*. As such, He formulates the Law that regulates the course of the world and of humanity—the *dharma*, to employ again the Hindu terminology. That is why He is represented in the attitude of the *chakravartin*, "He who turns the cosmic wheel."[18] Thus, in the rose window of the Apostles in the cathedral at Reims, God the Creator is seated at the centre, the immovable hub, surrounded by angels, whereas the circumference of the rose consists of twelve circular spaces containing the twelve apostles; and as is well-known, the twelve apostles are in symbolical correspondence with the twelve signs of the zodiac.[19] The zodiac is seen again on the circumference of the great rose window of the facade of Notre Dame in Paris, at the centre of which is seated the Virgin in Majesty with the crown and royal sceptre and holding the child Jesus. In both cases we are faced with a representation of the great cosmic wheel in its relationship with the invisible, and these are in reality quasi-sacramental images of the King of the World.

As King of the World, Christ possesses fully the two functions of pontiff and king: king, inasmuch as He formulates the law and "turns the cosmic wheel", and pontiff inasmuch as He is the mediator, as we have said above; as a sign of this He holds the two keys, the golden key of the pontiff and the silver key of

---

18. See Chapter II, p. 64.

19. See our book, *Symbolisme du temple chrétien*, p. 95 ss.

the king, the two keys which were also entrusted to Peter, as we shall soon see, and which are the "keys to the kingdom".[20]

Christ depicted as Janus and representing the
month of January in an ancient calendar. He
holds in his hands the key and the sceptre,
attributes of the two powers, royal and priestly.

The King of the world is normally manifested within an earthly spiritual centre, an organisation charged with conserving the sacred deposit, and whose leader may bear the title and the attributes of the King of the World, inasmuch as he represents Him. This personage is himself a pontiff and a king by participation; his function is that of maintaining equilibrium and harmony, that is to say, the reflection within the created of the divine immutability. His attributes are those of the divine Word which we have spoken of: Righteousness and Peace, two terms that the Bible cites each time it speaks of the messianic reign.

---

20. A certain relationship between this aspect of Christ and the Janus of the Latins must have been established, as is shown by an ancient iconography published by Charbonneau-Lassay, "Un ancien emblème du mois de janvier," *Regnabit* (March, 1925); we see a Christ with a key in one hand and a sceptre in the other and the mention of "January"; it is a question, then, of a Christ-Janus (see plate 17). The Latin Janus, who carries two keys, is in fact the god of the mysteries and of the initiations, the one who "opened" the spirits just as he "opened" the year, of which he was the "door" (*Janua* in Latin). In the emblem mentioned above, note that just the one key functions as the symbol of the priesthood, and that the sceptre, symbolising royalty, substitutes for the second key. Cf. the antiphone of Christmastide, in which the Messiah is called "key" and "sceptre".

MELCHIZEDEK · During the epoch when the Hebrew people were formed, the king of the world on earth was Melchizedek, representing primordial orthodoxy, and who invested Abraham with his mission. Genesis recounts that:

> Melchizedek king of Salem brought out bread and wine; he was the priest of God Most High. And he blessed him and said: "Blessed be Abram of God Most High, Possessor of heaven and earth; And blessed be God Most High, Who has delivered your enemies into your hand." And he gave him a tithe of all (*Gen.* 14:19-20).

The name and the titles of the personage are significant: Melchizedek signifies: "King of righteousness" (*melek, sedek*), and his title "King of Salem" means "King of peace" (*shalom*); these are the two attributes of the King of the World. St. Paul, in his Epistle to the Hebrews, has given us an exegesis of this biblical passage, quite enigmatic, as is the person of Melchizedek:

> For this Melchisedec, king of Salem, priest of the most high God, who met Abraham returning from the slaughter of the kings, and blessed him; to whom also Abraham gave a tenth part of all; first being by interpretation King of righteousness, and after that also King of Salem, which is, King of peace; without father, without mother, without descent, having neither beginning of days, nor end of life; but made like unto the Son of God; abideth a priest continually (Hebrews 7:1-3).

These last lines of St. Paul are interesting; Melchizedek has neither father nor mother, without descent; in other words, his origin is superhuman. This, of course, does not apply to his human representative, encountered by Abraham, but to the King of the World *in divinis*. And he is without beginning or end, he is not subject to birth or death, and his priesthood is perpetual; these traits apply also to the King of the World *in divinis*. Nevertheless, both characteristics pertain also, not to a given representative at a particular moment in history, but to the institution each of whose successive representatives directs its activity.

One last important point in the passage of St. Paul is the one which tells us that Melchizedek "is made like unto the Son of God", which clearly defines the nature of the King of the World on earth and his relationship with the King of the World *in divinis*. Above, we have seen that Psalm 110 expressed an oracle of Yahweh to the Israelite King: "You are a priest forever according to the order of Melchizedek." It is also known, moreover, that this Psalm is messianic and that it stands for the eternal investiture of the Messiah. At the same time we can grasp the importance of these texts for knowing the root and foundation of sacred royalty firstly in Israel, then in the Christian world, as well as the intimate union which exists between royalty and priesthood.[21]

THE MAGI · The presence of Melchizedek in Scripture is a first witnessing to Christ as King of the World. A second one, far better known and still more significant, is the episode of the adoration of the Magi at the time of the Nativity of Jesus. The importance of this scene cannot be exaggerated, which certain ecclesiastic exegetes, on account of rationalism and "Bultmann-ism", consign to the store of Biblical folklore which, thanks to their works, increases daily, to the great detriment, alas, of orthodoxy. The Christian tradition, however, has always seen the importance of the Magi in the Gospel message, since the liturgy also has always celebrated this event in one of its most solemn feasts, that of the Epiphany, that is to say, of the "Manifestation" of Jesus to the entire world. Why? Because according to the teaching of the Church, the Magi represent the non-Jewish world, the world of the "nations", according to Biblical terminology.[22] Great efforts have been made in trying to know from what country the Magi came; it is very difficult, even impossible, to answer this with precision. Nevertheless, the text of the Gospel is categorical: they came from the East; also, a detail of this

---

21. Our work was completed when the book of J. Tourniac, *Melkitsedek et la tradition primordiale* (Paris, 1983), appeared, thus we regret not being able to have made use of it.

22. Whereas the appearance of the Angels to the shepherds was a manifestation of Jesus to the Jewish people.

text, that the Magi offered *three* presents to Jesus corroborates the tradition that tells us that the Magi were also three. The number three as well as the eastern direction of their place of origin, leads us to say with some certitude that the Magi pertained to the Irano-Indian area.[23] Now, a teaching of the Indo-European tradition allows us to clarify the meaning of the scene of the Magi. At the basis of the political conceptions of this tradition, we find the doctrine of the Three supreme Functions related to the tripartite structure of the world (*tribhuvana*): heaven, the intermediary world, and earth, of which the correspondences in man are spirit, soul, and the physical body. The Three supreme Functions are designated respectively by the terms *Brahmatma*, *Mahatma*, and *Mahanga*, which are principles, but which are represented on earth by men. *Brahmatma*, corresponding to the world of the spirit, is called the "Master of the Three Worlds", as well as "King of the World", which amounts to the same thing; it possesses the fullness of the powers both priestly and royal. These two powers are then distinguished, in order to be manifested in *Mahatma*, the priesthood, in relation to the world of the soul, and *Mahanga*, royalty, in relation to the corporeal world. From *Mahatma* and *Mahanga* issued the two superior castes, the *brahmins* and the *kshatriyas*.

Now, the role of the Magi at the Nativity relates perfectly to this conception, as can be seen from the nature of the gifts they offer Jesus, so that it could be said that the Magi of the Nativity were representatives of these three functions: the *Mahanga* offers *gold*, which is proper to the king, the *Mahatma* offers him *incense*, which is proper to the priest, and the *Brahmatma* offers *myrrh*, the balm of incorruptibility, which is proper to the prophet, to the spiritual master. Hence the meaning of the scene can be understood: they are the authentic representatives of the primordi-

---

23. The *mage* more particularly designates members of the priestly caste of Iran. But it seems to us that it is difficult to deduce automatically that the personages of the Nativity scene were Persians, for it is evident that in the Near East, as in the Greco-Roman world, the term *mage* was employed to name persons pertaining to diverse nationalities of that region; the Chaldeans, for example.

al Tradition, who come to acknowledge and worship the *avatara*, to use the Hindu terminology, that is to say, the divine incarnation, the coming to earth of him who really and absolutely is the "King of the World", as Divine Word.[24]

These Magi are therefore the same thing as Melchizedek, who had represented the eternal orthodoxy at the time of Abraham. And thus it can be seen how the texts of Genesis and St. Paul and the gestures of the Magi agree with one another in order to demonstrate the universal Royalty of Christ, the Messiah, King, Priest, and Prophet.

ROME · The question of the transmission of power of Christ-King and Priest is a delicate one, and would require developments that we cannot take up here. We shall simply recall the important points which condition the conception of royalty in Christian lands. One thing is certain, and that is the preeminent role entrusted to the Apostle Peter and his successors. Without entering into the theological considerations relative to the status of the Roman pontiff, we will simply note some of his attributes that are highly significant. First of all, and perhaps the most important, the pope bears in his coat of arms the *two keys*, the gold key and the silver key. Now, we already know that these symbolise respectively spiritual authority and temporal power;[25] they are the "keys to the Kingdom", as Christ said in giving them to Peter; keys in the plural, because they relate to the two domains, heavenly and earthly. In addition, the Pope bears the tiara of three crowns, a symbol of royalty, firstly, because of the crowns, the proper attribute of the priesthood of the "bishop of Rome" being the mitre. And the three crowns clearly relate to the Three Worlds, of which we have spoken previously. There is no doubt that this is a question of the attributes of the representative of the King of the World, master of the Three Worlds. Other attributes confirm our observations and carry the same meanings: the *white* vestment and the *red* cloak, *white* being the colour of

---

24. We have mentioned that the East had knowledge of prophecies announcing the coming of the Saviour (Chapter I, p. 32).

25. See this Chapter, pp. 128-129.

the priesthood and *red* that of royalty, as we have seen.[26] Finally, the Pope bears the title of *Pontifex Maximus*, "Sovereign Pontiff", a title inherited from Roman Antiquity—we shall return to this in the following chapters—which signifies that he represents the supreme spiritual authority.[27]

TEMPORAL POWER OF CHRIST

The universal supremacy of Christ King is the foundation of the entire political doctrine of Christianity. This is something that there is no reason to contest. Nevertheless, at the very interior of Christianity, and from the first centuries, voices were raised claiming that the royalty of Christ, being purely spiritual, had nothing to do with the government of men, and did not concern the actions of the temporal domain; in short, that there was no need to look for the origin, principle and foundation as well as the justification for temporal power in Christ's royalty, such as it is declared in the Gospels. That is why, although our exposition has amply demonstrated the contrary, it is worth focusing on this matter even more closely, and in so doing refute the false reasons put forth by the adverse party.

Their principal argument is drawn from the very words of Christ in the course of his interrogation by Pilate. To the procurator's question: "Art thou a king then? Jesus answered, Thou sayest that I am a king." And He adds, "My kingdom is not of this world" (John 18:33-37). It is by supporting themselves on these last words that they try to deny the temporal royalty of Christ; by these words, it is said, Christ wished to affirm that his power had in view only the regency of souls and spirits, that he did not think of reigning over another domain and that he left men free to organise their society and the actions of temporal affairs without Him.

---

26. See Chapter III, p. 87.

27. Here a matter arises which we cannot delve into at this time: that of Prester John, of his existence and his role. This very delicate question starts to become clear with the books of J. Tourniac, *Lumière d'Orient*, Paris 1979, and *De la Chevalerie au secret du Temple*, Paris 1975.

In reality that is a totally false interpretation of the Gospel text, and it is impossible to justify it not only from the theological point of view, as will be seen, but even from the philological and grammatical point of view. Certainly the translation into our language is ambiguous and lends itself to confusion, owing to the fact that the preposition *de* (of) in Latin languages serves to designate possession as well as origin; but in the original Greek it is not subject of discussion: the phrase *e basileia mou ouk estin ek toutou tou kosmou* means, and can only mean, one thing: "My kingdom does not proceed from this world," for the preposition *ek* can only indicate origin. Moreover, this is confirmed further in the text by the words, *ouk estin enteuthen*, "it (My Kingdom) is not from here" (*hinc* in the Latin translation). The meaning would certainly be clearer in our language if it were translated as "My *royalty* is not of this world," which is perfectly possible, since the world *basileia* has both meanings, "kingdom" and "royalty", in the Greek of the New Testament as well as in classical Greek. If Jesus says that his royalty does not come from this world, it is as much as to say that it comes from Above, that it is not a royalty according to the world, but an infinite and eternal royalty. In a word, Jesus is dealing here with a question of *origin*, not of *terrain* and *competence*.

Moreover, the following words of Christ in the dialogue with Pilate demonstrate it; He tells the Roman: "Thou couldst have no power at all against me, except it were given thee from above," that is, from God, hence from Jesus, since He has declared Himself Son of God and God Himself. He means to tell Pilate: your power is political and juridical, and the very fact that I come to you to declare that this power comes from Me proves that the royalty that I claim, although it is not *from* this world is nonetheless exercised *over* this world, individuals and nations, because I am the Son of God, principle and master of the universal order.

This exegesis, in these or in other terms, is that of the entire orthodox Christian tradition. All the Fathers rejected as heretical the theory of those who claimed that Christ's royalty did not extend to the domain of the temporal. Thus, St. John Chrysostom, commenting on the Gospel of St. John, cried:

Is the kingdom of Jesus Christ not of this world? It certainly is.... These words: "It is not of" do not mean that Jesus Christ does not command in this world, but that He also has His kingdom in Heaven; and this kingdom is not human, but far greater and more brilliant. He said: "I am not of the world" (John 17:14); He says that His kingdom is not from here in this sense; which does not exclude the world from His kingdom, but rather shows, as I have said, that His kingdom is not human, nor passing, nor perishable.[28]

To hold that the words "My kingdom is not of this world" mean that Christ has no power over the temporal, is to introduce a contradiction into Scripture itself, since Jesus proclaimed: "All power is given unto me in heaven and in earth," and in the Our Father: "Thy kingdom come, Thy will be done on earth as it is in Heaven." Now, the reign of the Father comes through the Son, and how could the will of the Father be done on earth if the person of the Son, "First-born of all creation", be excluded from life on earht?

Continuing to speak to Pilate, Jesus says: "I am a king. To this end was I born, and for this cause came I into the world, that I should bear witness unto the truth" (John 18:37), that is to say, to re-establish normal order to the temporal as well as to the spiritual, to inspire laws, sanctify customs, clarify teaching, guide counsel and regulate the action of governments. The power of Christ over society is implicit in His incarnation; by it the temporal world was converted into the moving sacrament of the entire world, and the "Kingdom of God" embraces the whole man, that is, man in whom the temporal and the spiritual are intimately linked and cannot be separated; it embraces all of society, and it is inconceivable that human institutions, their projects, their meaning, should develop according to their own laws while the spiritual organisation, which possesses the message of Christ, that is, the Church, should in parallel fashion

---

28. St. John Chrysostom, *Hom. 83 in Johann.* A number of citations from other Fathers, with the same meaning, can be found in the *catena aurea* of St. Thomas Aquinas on this passage in the Gospel.

realise on a superior plane another and independent development without touching the former one. For ultimately, spiritual life and salvation are the final end of the entire universe; hence nothing should escape, and everything should be subordinated to this supreme reason, in particular the life of society, which is an essential aspect of human life.

TRANSMISSION OF SPIRITUAL AUTHORITY

After having said, "All power is given unto me in heaven and in earth," Jesus adds, addressing His Apostles: "Go ye therefore, and teach all nations..." (Matt. 28:16-20). With this, He invested His Apostles with the spiritual authority and the power to teach, that is, to make known the Doctrine and the Law which must regulate human activity, hence to inaugurate the Kingdom of God on earth, in all domains, including the temporal. From the Apostles this mission naturally passed to the Church which, in conformity with what we have just said, has always, in one manner or another, claimed this universal authority over man.

In the social and political domain this teaching of the Church was not formulated in a complete fashion from the beginning; and it is easy to see the reason: Christianity was plunged into a society belonging to another tradition, against which it often had to defend itself, and all its forces were mobilised to bring about the spiritual conquest of this society. Nevertheless, from the first centuries the principle of the royalty of Christ over civil life was affirmed, as can be attested, for example, with the previously quoted words from St. John Chrysostom. In the fifth century, in the West, Saint Augustine lays the foundations for what will be Christian society in his celebrated work, *The City of God*, stating the rule that the "earthly city" must be at the service of the "heavenly city"; in other words, that it must help man on the way toward the latter and try to model itself on it, so that the heavenly Kingdom might already, as it were, be inaugurated on earth. With the Christian princes, emperors and kings, civil life becomes progressively imbued with this principle.

It is above all after the re-establishment of the Empire in the West that a true political doctrine was constituted, and this, in great measure, from a Biblical perspective; what is rediscovered then, is the sacral value of Hebrew royalty, in which the prince is designated in order to make the law and the exercise of worship respected, whilst at the same time there is an awareness of all the consequences that must be drawn from the royal ancestry of Christ. We cannot follow all the stages of the development of this doctrine, since this would take us away from our subject, so we shall confine ourselves with recalling the most noteworthy, in order to show the continuity of the doctrine.[29]

Its clearest expression was the work of Pope Gregory VII (1073-1085), who had to define the position of the spiritual authority in the face of certain claims of Emperor Henry IV. Gregory VII taught that the king holds his power from God, but that the divine action is not accomplished directly; the people, or the law of heredity, designate the person who must reign, and the Church, taking note of the contract thus established between the people and the prince, judges whether the latter has submitted to the divine law; then it concedes to the one elected the right to govern, and the government is conceded to the prince through the coronation, which includes an oath regarding the content of the contract. It will immediately be noted that this doctrine, in Christian form, conforms with that of the universal sacred Tradition, as we have explained it.[30]

The great theologian Hugh of St. Victor (d. 1141) speaks in the same sense in his treatise *De Sacramentis*: "The spiritual power is entitled to institute the royal power; the priestly dignity consecrates the royal power; it hallows it by blessing it and gives it body by instituting it.... The royal power is set up by the priesthood on the order of God." This lapidary formula perfectly summarises all the sacred doctrine concerning the political regimen. In 1202, Pope Innocent III specified this doctrine by recalling that the Roman pontiff, as was Melchizedek in times past, is at once priest and king, and he made the title of "Vicar of Christ" prevail over that of "Vicar of Peter", previously employed; the emperor, he says, receives his power from God, but it is the

---

29. The reader may refer to the book of J. de Pange, *Le Roi très-chrétien*.

30. See Chapter III, p. 91ff.

Church which interprets the divine will, transmitting it through the coronation. In the thirteenth century, Gregory IX (1227-1241), recovering the symbolism of the Two Swords, writes: "The two swords were given to the Church, but it only uses one; the other it entrusts to the secular prince, who employs it for her; the one should be employed by the priest, the other by the knight, who obeys the sign of the priest."[31] This text, once again, recalls, in another form, the traditional doctrine which teaches that the priesthood is the necessary mediator to transmit the temporal power. This teaching is taken up by Innocent IV (1243-1254), which recalls that the "Power of the Keys", the power to "bind and loosen", allows the pontiff to intervene in the temporal domain. We find it also in the *De regimine principum* of St. Thomas Aquinas;[32] the Pope, he writes, has both powers; the papal *dominium* surpasses all the others because it is at once priestly and royal; it is the source of all power; the imperial jurisdiction comes from God, but through the mediation of the Church. Finally, Cardinal Henry of Suse, like Innocent IV, bases the two-fold pontifical *dominium* on the doctrine of the Two Swords in his work on the *Decretales* (1245-1253).

The two symbolisms of the Keys and of the Swords are interchangeable, for both refer to the two powers. It is that of the Swords that is called upon by Boniface VIII (1294-1302), who has at times been put forth as a terrible partisan of a tyrannical theocracy, but who in reality, despite some excesses in his language or actions, expressed only pure orthodoxy. Speaking of the Roman pontiff, he writes: "Its power includes two swords, the spiritual and the temporal.... Both swords, the temporal and the spiritual, pertain to the ecclesiastic power, but the former is drawn *for* the Church, the latter *by* the Church, the second by the priest, the first by the kings and the knights, with the consent and the permission of the priest. Therefore it is necessary... that the temporal authority be subject to the spiritual.... The

---

31. Cited in A. Fliche, *La Chrétienté romaine*, p. 226.

32. Unfinished work by the author, finished by his disciple Ptolemy of Lucca.

spiritual power institutes the earthly power, and judges it if it be not good."[33]

The permanence of this teaching can be followed in the theologian who is most representative of orthodoxy in the sixteenth century, Cardinal Bellarmin. While noting that the Church does not directly possess temporal jurisdiction, he recalls that it is able to directly exercise its authority over the rulers, when the salvation of souls demands it: in such cases it can abrogate laws harmful to eternal ends, transfer kingdoms, and even decide temporal penalties.

The official teaching of the Church has never varied fundamentally, not even in our contemporary modern era, despite appearances. It has been claimed, for example, that the famous "rally" ordered by Leo XIII marked the end of the Church's claim to regulate the workings of temporal government, since, it was said, it ordered Catholics to accept the republican regime which had just been installed and was officially laic, hence declaring itself totally independent of spiritual authority. Now, that is in no wise the case; the words of the pontiff were completely twisted, so that the Roman document was made to say exactly the contrary of what it did say, because, in reality, what Leo XIII asked for was not, of course, to rally round a laic regime, but quite the contrary, to rally all Christian forces to oppose laicism. This camouflage of truth, unfortunately, seems to die hard, and to this day goes on fueling the thought of the greater part of those who deal with these matters, including Catholic authors. To cite just one example, we have consulted an apparently serious work, which, moreover, is in several respects the work of a university specialist, on the problem of the relationships between the spiritual and the temporal, and which, without further ado, declares, without proof, as if it went without saying, that the rally had put a definitive end to the "theocratic" desires of the Church. If the author had referred to the text of the Pope itself, instead of docilely following the general opinion of previous publicists and historians, he obviously would not have been able to write such a proposition. And yet, one of the elementary rules of scientific

---

33. Register of Boniface VIII, col. 888-90.

work is to refer to the original text before making commentaries on it.

Thus, today, the dominant opinion, even in religious surroundings, is that which interprets Christ's saying, "My kingdom is not of this world," in the manner of those heretics stigmatised by St. John Chrysostom in the homily cited above, who deny the spiritual authority the right to control the temporal power and to form its structures. We have before us the special issue dedicated to Christ the King of a theological journal pertaining to this current of thought, and which, with clever evasions and smooth-talking, accomplishes the feat of ejecting the orthodox doctrine which, according to its title, this journal is supposed to promote. And it is not only theologians who speak or write in this way; often, representatives of the ecclesiastic hierarchy, through weakness, defeatism or opportunism, show themselves, in their official declarations, indulgent towards lay political regimes, and seem to renounce recalling the true doctrine; at least when they know it, for some seem quite simply unaware of it. All these persons are, more or less consciously, impregnated with ideas spread for two centuries by that modern politico-religious heresy which is liberalism, a heresy that has corrupted, and continues to corrupt, the Catholic "intelligentsia". Thus clerics with the disease of changefulness reject the social and political doctrine of the Church, accusing it of being the by-product of a former "theocracy", in its turn a product of "Constantinism". Yes, Constantine! According to them, he is the starting point of all the—in their own words—errors of Catholicism. And what is the great sin of Constantine? Having allowed the birth of a sacral society, a society that they reject with the excuse that it supposedly betrayed true Christianity, that of the first centuries, by involving it in social and political life; religion, according to them, has to return to the "primitive purity" of the time in which it was a purely spiritual institution and act only as a ferment in the midst of the social and political world, which for its part is to be organised in total independence, in conformity with purely natural norms. Complete sophistry, for if the ferment in question acted as it should, it would transform the world and would result in giving birth to a sacral society, precisely as it did in the fourth century; whereas in the opposite case, civil society, developing in independent fashion, necessarily would come into conflict with religion and finally eliminate it. So true is this, as we have said, that the temporal cannot be separated in man from the spiritual: either they are both harmonised in a fertile unity, the source of equilibrium and peace, or else, if they turn their backs to each other, sooner or later there will come a time when man will be a kind of disjointed puppet who lives in surroundings entirely given over to general subversion, which in fact is the case in our present world.

But let us return to the official teaching of the Church—because we must emphasise it here at the end of the chapter—concerning which, as we have just said, it has never varied fundamentally. To be convinced of this it is enough to read some documents published by the last popes. It is certainly true that in these texts the practical consequences of the doctrinal principles (coronation, the role of the priesthood in the investiture of governments, the right to pass judgment on them in certain cases, etc.) are passed over as if they did not exist, which is quite understandable, since all the States in Christian lands have become laic, although in varying degrees, and the priesthood is no longer in a position to wield its authority in these concrete forms. But the doctrinal principle remains, and at the proper time the consequences they imply would necessarily manifest should circumstances permit.

These doctrinal principles, which the spiritual authority cannot compromise without destroying itself, have been strongly recalled by Leo XIII, who has been characterised as a "liberal":

> Nature did not form society in order that man should seek in it his last end, but in order that in it and through it he should find suitable aids whereby to attain to his own perfection.... Therefore, they who are engaged in framing constitutions and in enacting laws should bear in mind the moral and religious nature of man, and take care to help him, but in an orderly and right way, to gain perfection, neither enjoining nor forbidding anything save what is reasonably consistent with civil as well as with religious requirements. On this very account, the Church cannot

stand by, indifferent as to the import and significance of laws enacted by the State ...[34]

The affirmation is perhaps even clearer with Pope Pius XI, who says:

> ...true peace, the peace of Christ, is impossible unless we are willing and ready to accept the fundamental principles of Christianity, unless we are willing to observe the teachings and obey the law of Christ, both in public and private life. If this were done, then the Church would be able, in the exercise of its divinely given ministry and by means of the teaching authority which results therefrom, to protect all the rights of God over men and nations.
>
> It is possible to sum up all We have said in one word, "the Kingdom of Christ".

And also:

> Authority itself lost its hold upon mankind, for it had lost that sound and unquestionable justification for its right to command on the one hand and to be obeyed on the other. Society, quite logically and inevitably, was shaken to its very depths and even threatened with destruction; since it no longer had a stable foundation, everything having been reduced to a series of conflicts, to the domination of the majority, or to the supremacy of special interests.[35]

And in order that this teaching might better penetrate minds, this pontiff instituted a special liturgical feast of Christ the King; and in the documentation that explained the reasons for his decision, Pius XI said, in speaking of Christ: "... for his kingly dignity demands that the State should take account of the com-

---

34. Encyclical, *Sapientiae christianae* 2 (January, 1890).

35. Encyclical, *Ubi Arcano Dei Concilio* 47-48 & 28 (December, 1922). Encyclical, *Quas Primas* 32 (December, 1925). *Discourse to the New Cardinals*, 20.2.1946.

mandments of God and of Christian principles, both in making laws and in administering justice, and in providing for the young a sound moral education."[36] And all the liturgical texts chosen for the office of the Feast of Christ the King deserve to be read again, for they splendidly reflect the eternal doctrine of the supremacy of the spiritual authority over the temporal power; moreover, the fact that this doctrine is proclaimed in the liturgy gives it particular force, in virtue of the well-known adage: *lex orandi, lex credendi* ("The rule of prayer is the rule of faith").

Finally, let us cite these words of Pope Pius XII: God has entrusted to the Church, he says, the mission of "raising up the whole man, and thereby of collaborating ceaselessly in establishing the firm foundation of society. This mission is essential to it ..."[37]

The chronology of the ecclesiastic declarations led us up to the first half of our century; but it is not there, unfortunately, that we can find brilliant examples of civil societies organised in accordance with divine law. We must now go back and follow the course of history to see how a Christian society was built, starting from the fourth century under the aegis of the Christian rulers in whom sacred royalty, although taking on some new features, kept on shining with the light inherited from an immemorial tradition.

---

36. Encyclical, *Quas Primas* 32 (December, 1925).

37. *Discourse to the New Cardinals*, 20.2.1946.

CHAPTER V

THE HOLY EMPIRE

Paradoxically, it is the institution that had so persecuted it that in the end furnished triumphant Christianity with the foundation and the instrument for a restoration of true political power, in accordance with the divine message, and capable of structuring the newborn society: the reader will see that we are referring to the Roman Empire.

The imperial institution, so often praised by "politicians", has been, on the contrary, reviled, and its role slandered by too many theologians to whom we alluded in the preceding chapter, and for whom "Constantinism" would appear to be the worst defect of Christianity.

It would take too long, nor would this be the place, to investigate all the motives for their censure. But there is one, in our opinion, that had to be decisive for taking such a stand: it is that most of these people have, at any rate, no idea what the Roman Empire was, and continued to be, as regards its true nature, for they have confined themselves to a purely "political" view of the institution, without being aware, or refusing to be aware, of its truly "spiritual" dimension, a dimension which, of course, is independent of those who wore the purple, some of whom were mediocre and others, unfortunately, monstrous. That is why it is important to clarify the problem at the outset; and above all to define with precision the idea of empire.

IDEA OF EMPIRE · Too often, all that has been seen is a desire for military glory and expansion springing from the heart of an ambitious personality, or even from the collective soul of a proud people. And no doubt history offers us many examples of conquerors whose careers could confirm this view. There is no doubt also, it has to be admitted, that in the most favorable cases, military glory and the desire for territorial expansion are never absent from the imperial enterprise. Nonetheless, these are not the traits that define the specific nature of the empire. The idea of empire, if considered from without, is obviously that of a unique power extending its dominion over peoples of different races and traditions. But there are different ways of dominating, and not all empires are inspired by the "law of the jungle". In places where there flourished a traditional civilisation, with normal political institutions, that is, created according to divine law, the idea of empire presented itself in the form of a mission, and above all as a spiritual one. A traditional civilisation lives from the memory of a "lost paradise", and presents itself as a direct branch, the most direct branch of the "golden age", inasmuch as it is the vehicle of an immemorial tradition or a revelation that restores the state of things.

Such was already the case, in a certain respect, of Alexander's enterprise. Despite his ambition, which was great, the Macedonian conqueror was moved by the conviction that he had received a civilising mission; he dreamed of integrating the East into Greek culture, whose superiority he held in no doubt, and even of fusing all races into a universal empire that Hellenic humanism would convey towards happiness.[1]

This idea of a civilising mission of the *Oikoumene*, opposed to the "barbarians", came from the Greek philosophers, the Stoics above all, who preached a universalism founded on the human community participating in universal reason. And from the second century AD they assimilated the Roman Empire to the *Oikoumene* and considered that Rome had inherited the mission of Alexander. Thus, the Stoic philosopher Pactios, the friend of Scipio Aemilianus, taught that the Roman conquests sought to realise the union of the civilised nations and to give peace, order and justice to them all. Similar convictions were also held by the Roman elite.[2]

---

1. Regarding this subject see the collective work, *Le bonheur par l'empire ou le rêve d'Alexandre* (acts of a colloquium at the Sorbonne), Paris, 1982.

2. Cf. Livy 1.16; Virgil, *Aeneid* 6.852 ff; R. Namatianus, *Itinerariium* 5.63;

But—and this is the important point to which we were aiming—that civilising mission was fundamentally tied to a religious idea. The profound reality of the Roman Empire cannot be understood without mentioning the religious depth inseparable from it, and which nourished its very conception; and in all this it did no more than follow the ancient Roman tradition. Valerius Maximus writes:

> Our city has always considered that all things ought to be placed behind the religion, even in those surroundings in which the splendour of his sovereign majesty has wished to manifest itself. That is why its masters have never hesitated to serve the religion, deeming it that in this way they protected the government from human things if they conducted themselves correctly and constantly as servants of the divine power.[3]

For its founders and best representatives, the aspiration of the Empire was to extend order universally, instigating a state of equilibrium and stability in accordance with a divine model that was reflected in nature, so that the Emperor commanded by a "heavenly mandate". Julius Caesar was perfectly aware of preparing the restoration of a "golden age", as well as of his providential mission as a "divine" (*divus*) man. "This is the man," writes Virgil, "this is he, whose promised coming you have so often heard, Augustus Caesar, son of a god, who will make a Golden Age again in the fields where Saturn once reigned, and extend the empire beyond the Garamantes and the Indians."[4] The "barbarian" peoples represented disequilibrium in relation to the *pax romana* and a permanent threat of allowing chaos to be established, against which the empire had to raise the bulwark of the Law. Virgil became the prophet of a veritable mysticism of the empire. But, remarkably, the Christians believed in this mission of the Empire, even during the epoch of the non-

---

Claudius, *De consulatu Stilichonis* 3.150-154.

3. Valerius Maximus, *De regno*.

4. Virgil, *Aeneid* 6.791-95.

Christian emperors, and even the persecutors. In this regard, there are astonishing passages in Tertullian:

> The Christians honour the emperor as a man who comes immediately after God and who owes to God all that he is. We, who see in the emperors the choice and the judgment of God who has given them authority over all peoples, we respect in them that which God has placed.... What more could I say about our religion and our piety for the emperor, whom we must respect as one whom God has chosen: so that I could say that Caesar is more to us than to you [Tertullian is addressing the pagans], because it is our God who has established him.[5]

At the origin of the Empire there was something "celestial" that pre-dated Christianity and which Christianity implicitly recognised. Beginning with the 2nd century the Empire ceased to be hostile to the Christians, who in turn considered it part of the providential plan and integrated it into the general perspective of the new religion. This integration was possible firstly because of the authentically religious values of the imperial institution, and secondly, because the ends they had fixed for themselves coincided: in effect, the universalist aim of Christianity, an aim required by its very mission, coincided in many respects with the universality of the Empire in its philosophical and cultural dimension, while its political dimension secured for the Christians the indispensable social and administrative order; thus the "mystique of Empire" was also recovered by the Christians. The Empire was legitimated as it were by Christ, who was one of its subjects, and it become one of the instruments of salvation for humanity; one, moreover, that was considered indispensable, to the extent that its disappearance would have left the field open to the Antichrist, as most of the Fathers thought, and as the Canon Alexandre de Roes wrote again in the eighteenth century. In particular, Christianity made the messianism of Virgil and Augustus, oriented towards the restoration of the golden age, its own, by relating it to the mission of Christ. Well-known in this

---

5. Tertullian, *Ad Scapulam* (PL 1.699); *Apolog.* 32 & 33.

connection is the way the famous Eclogue of Virgil, announcing the birth of a child who was to bring the golden age back to the world, was interpreted by seeing in it the proclamation of the birth of Christ.[6] No doubt the child of Virgil's poem cannot be identified with Jesus, all the more so in that the child is not presented as the author of universal renovation;[7] however, it is certain that the announcement of the return of the golden age, quite widespread in Pythagorean circles at the time of Augustus, corresponds completely to the climate of messianic expectation to which we alluded already in relation to Iran.[8] Dante, in Canto 22 of *Purgatory*, reflects this state of mind very well when he has Statius tell Virgil these words:

> When thou saidst: "The cycle is renewed;
> Justice returns with the men of the first ages,
> And from above descends a new humanity,"[9]
> Poet and Christian both to thee I owed.
> That thou might better see what I merely trace,
> To paint it I shall stretch my hand.
> Already the universe entire was pervaded,
> With the true belief sown
> By the messengers of the eternal realm,
> And thy verses recorded further above
> Accorded so well with the new predictions,
> That I was wont to resort to them ...[10]

There is a very serious tradition referring to this imperial mystique, according to which the Emperor Augustus saw in the sky the apparition of a virgin, borne by a rainbow, and from whom

---

6. In particular, Eusebius, *Discourse of Constantin to the Assembly of the Saints*, 19-20. Cf. Dante, *Purg.* 22.70 ff.

7. Regarding this question, see J. Carcopino, *Virgile et le mystère de la IVe eglogue*, Paris, 1943.

8. Cf. Chapter I, p. 21.

9. Free translation from Virgil, *Ecl.* IV, 5-7.

10. Dante, *Purg.* 22.70.

a child is seen to emerge. The oracle whom Augustus questioned spoke of a child already born and to whom all would have to submit. Augustus had an altar erected at the top of the hill from which he had seen the appearance, and dedicated it to the "First-born of God".[11]

Bossuet was right, in his *Discourse on Universal Reason*, to point out this convergence of different empires towards the Roman empire in view of Christianity. Everything takes place as if Caesar and Augustus had prepared everything for Christ. The ancient world and its public religion were collapsing little by little; but there were two things that emerged intact: Roman law—the social code that Christianity lacked, and which it adopted with certain reservations—and the Imperial institution. The structure of this institution and its religious values found in Christ the king and priest a new unifying centre, with a priesthood and a cult that had antecedents in the ancient civilisation in which Christianity appeared and in which sacred royalty was anchored. It is necessary, in this regard, to see clearly the scope of the work of Caesar as the founder of the Empire as an institution. Caesar united in his person the power of *imperator* and that of *pontifex maximus*, the temporal power and the spiritual authority; to which it must be added that the power of *imperator* already had a profoundly religious nature, as we have shown.[12] This means that under Ceasar the spiritual authority recovered the temporal power to establish the *pax romana*. The work of Caesar providentially foresaw the future, and the Fathers have always considered the Empire as the "shield" that allowed Christianity to expand until the time of Antichrist. The *pax romana* was the condition, as well as the effect, of the *Shekina*, personified in Christ. But the important thing is to see that the instrument of the peace, the imperial power, was a power sacred in nature; it cannot be repeated too often, and it is necessary to be able to understand the subsequent destiny of the Augustan Empire in the Christian Empire, whose hidden motive force was the "mystique" inherited from the Caesars.

---

11. A.C. Emmerich, *Vie de la Sainte-Vierge*, p. 218.

12. Cf. Chapter I, p. 37.

CHRISTIAN EMPIRE · In the fourth century, Christianity developed a set of representations in relation to the ancient conception of sovereignty. These penetrated even piety and worship. The sacred symbology of ancient sovereignty appears in figurative monuments and various other objects. There is a profusion of elements originating from the Roman, Hellenistic and Eastern Empire. God and the divine world, the entire domain of the sacred, are represented with features pertaining to sacred royalty, its institutions, its rites, and its attributes. It is the central idea of Christian art starting from the fourth century and for three or four centuries thereafter. This is a sign, moreover, that the idea of sacred royalty and the idea of the cultic-ritual position of the king persisted, by adapting, of course, to the concept of Christ as universal sovereign and King of the world.

When Constantine decides to leave Rome to establish his seat in Byzantium, he takes all that constitutes the Empire, and his successors inherit the sacred significance of the Augustan institution carefully conserved and magnified by Constantine himself. The Christian emperor in Byzantium is God's representative on earth; he unifies within himself the totality of temporal power and religious leadership of the realm. His function consists in defending Christian culture and maintaining the purity of the faith as the condition of the unity of the Empire, against the sects which tend to dissolve it. The form of this Byzantine sovereignty shines with the splendor of the imperial mystique recovered and Christianised, manifested in the symbols of art, in coins, images, court etiquette, and the rules of the liturgy.

Prior to Constantine, of course, this imperial mystique had undergone the influence of eastern monarchies which practiced a veritable cult of the sovereign; it is also linked to the point of view of the Neo-Platonists, for whom the prince was an emanation of the divine power, but also, and perhaps above all, it is linked to the Christian faith. The imperial mystique of the Byzantine era shines with the light of faith in the redemption by the *Kyrios Christos* and his return as Judge at the end of time. Thus this world is mixed with the Beyond, the temporal with the spiritual; and the superhuman character of the ancient emperor passes to the "deputy", to "God's envoy".

The ancient heritage is already manifested in the manner in which the prince accedes to the Empire. On this point there was no revolutionary change, not even any evolution, at least not at the outset. The juridical basis of the transmission of power continued to be the same as that for the pagan Emperor. The imperial dignity does not arrive by inheritance: everything occurs at the circus or the palace, the lifting up on the shield, the acclamation and a kind of coronation by means of *torcs*, an essentially military insignia. In this conferral of dignity, three groups of actors play a role: the army, the Senate, and the people. It would be a great mistake, however, to think that all this amounts to a "laic" investiture. There is nothing laic, we repeat once more, in the imperial institution in Rome. During the pagan age, it was the gods who "made" the emperor. We have an echo of this in the *Panegyric of Constantine* (310 AD), in which there is a staging of the Assembly of the gods to welcome Constantius Chlorus at his death and approve the decision of the deceased to place his son Constantine on the throne.[13] During the Christian era, it will be the "Divine Hand" that invests the emperor (see plates pp. 153 & 154); and if this mythological fabling as such was no longer assented to in this era, nonetheless, the certitude of the religious reality that it expressed remained, namely, the divine election of the *imperator*.

The true religious foundation of the imperial power resided in the fact that, above all, it came from the triumphal honour; we have said that the *triumph* in Rome had a highly religious significance, since the victor was assimilated to the god Jupiter—Jupiter Capitolinus, to be exact—whose temple in Rome was the destination of the triumphal procession.[14] Now, among the symbols of this assimilation to the Olympian god, the most remarkable and important one was precisely the purple chlamys, for purple was precisely the dress of the Capitoline statue. This is why the purple chlamys became the main article of imperial clothing, the specific sign of imperial dignity. The importance of the symbolism of purple is brought out again in the fact that it is found in

---

13. *Panegyrici latini* VII, 7.4, Galletier.

14. Cf. Chapter I, p. 37-38.

Emperor Otto II and Empress Theophanu receiving the power of Christ
(ivory, Cluny Museum).

Emperor Henry II (miniature from the Sacramentary of Henry II, Munich, Bayerische Staatsbibliothek).

the high shoes or imperial boots, another characteristic article of the emperor's attire. Other elements were naturally added to these: the *tzitzakion*, the *sagion*, the white *dibetesion* adorned with gold, and above all, the *stemma* or diadem, the symbolism of which will be studied later. Nevertheless, the purple garment, inherited from the rite of triumph, is maintained by all the emperors of Byzantium as the irrefutable sign of the continuity of the institution as well as of its sacred character.

This sacred character, we repeat, is pre-Christian, but was acknowledged by the Christian spiritual authority, as we have said. This we shall also see in the coronation ceremony. The coronation, of Hellenistic origin, was not included in the Christian liturgy, nevertheless, little by little, it took on Christian features and put itself under the protection of the Church, until finally it entered the liturgy. This occurred for the first time on the twenty-fifth of August in the year 450, the date on which the Patriarch Anatolius crowned the new Emperor Marcian, raised on the shield, in the Circus, by Empress Pulcheria, the Senate and the people. This coronation was converted into the symbol of the union of the emperor with God. Beginning with Phocas (602), the coronation was celebrated in the temple, first at the church of St. John the Baptist, and then at St. Sophia.

But the total Christianisation of the imperial ritual was brought about after the tenth century. Indeed, from then on it was enriched by the anointing of the prince with the Holy Chrism. The rite of anointing was adopted, in the East as well as in the West, by reference to the tradition of Israel, by the influence of that deepening in the Bible and the Old Testament already pointed out in another connection.[15] By this anointing, which recalled both that of baptism and that of the bishop, the emperor become the "Anointed of the Lord", like the kings of Israel. The anointing, the new sign—typically Christian—of the "divine election", turned the *basileus* of Byzantium into the sole "lieutenant" of God, the sole ruler of the world. As the pagan emperor was assimilated to the Olympic god, the *basileus*,

---

15. Cf. Chapter IV, p. 136.

through the anointing, was configured with Christ, the preeminent "Anointed of the Lord".

The sacral character of this Byzantine royalty, perfectly analogous—*mutatis mutandis* of course, taking into account its Christian specificity—to the diverse traditional royalties that we have evoked, shines forth not only in the theological conception itself, but also in the entire ritual and symbolic apparatus surrounding it.

In the first place, the conception that the imperial power comes directly from God by virtue of divine election is a constant. Thus it is said that the prince is "predestined by God" and directed by Him (*theokybernetos theothen hodegetheis*), that he has received his sceptre from God,[16] he is "crowned by God" (*theostephes*), and he commands "by the grace of God" (*dia tou theou charitos*). He is the *basileus* over whom the *megas basileus*, "the Great King"—that is to say God as "King of the World"—extends His hand, a gesture that indicates the election and the transmission of power, as well as of the spiritual influence that accompanies it—a gesture profusely reproduced in Byzantine iconography in sculptures and mosaics as well as in paintings and coins.[17] All these notes of theological import are to be found in Eusebius,[18] who also adds that the emperor is the "lieutenant" of "the Great King" (*megalou basileus hyparchos*) and, in words worthy of note, he is the "interpreter of the divine speech", or—since it can also be translated thus—the "interpreter of the Divine Word" (*hypophetes tou theou logou*).[19] Eusebius insists at length on the strict relationships uniting the emperor to the Divinity: he is the image of

---

16. *Cod. Just.* 1.29.5.

17. See plate p. 154.

18. In his work *Laus Constantini*. It is vain to say that the theses of Eusebius are subject to caution because this bishop was suspect of Arianism, for similar theses can be cited held by other perfectly orthodox theologians in both East and West.

19. It is interesting to note that the Greek term *hypophetes* pertains to the specifically religious vocabulary, being applied only to the minister of the worship charged with interpreting the oracles. See Homer, *Iliad* 16,35; Apoll. Rh. 1,1811; Theocritus 16,20.

God, as his empire is the image of the heavenly Kingdom; he is the "image of the Logos", "he who is formed to the archetype of the Great King".[20] An anonymous author of the twelfth century also proclaims: "Earthly royalty is the dazzling image of God's, and the emperor is himself the image of God."[21] An inscription of the 2nd century designates the emperors as "the sovereigns among the gods" (*hoi en theois autocratores*).[22] Constantine even received the title of "Saviour" (*soter*), for being the one who lead to the era of salvation, investing his kingdom with a messianic significance. And Eusebius is not the only one who thinks and speaks in this manner, for we find the same ideas in the majority of the theologians of both East and West.

The sacral character of the *basileus* appears clearly, moreover, in his titulary terms, such as are encountered in the diverse documents emanating from the Palace. He is *augoustos* (*augustus*), a word whose acceptance is uniquely religious, with the meaning of "consecration", "holy", "worthy of veneration owing to its sacred nature". The emperor is also "most pious" (*eusebestatos*, *piissimus*), the Greek and Latin words having a much stronger meaning than the word "pious" in our language. Still more characteristic are the titles of *hieros* "sacred" and *hagios* "holy", applied to the emperor. Thus, in the coronation ceremony the patriarch, after having placed the crown on the head of the prince, addresses him repeating three times *hagie* in the vocative, to affirm his holiness with an exclamation that strangely recalls that of the *trisagion* in the mass: "Holy, holy, holy, is the Lord God of hosts ...." These terms of *hieros* and *hagios*, moreover, not only are applied to the person of the emperor, but also to all that belongs to him and emanates from him: his palace, his words, his orders, his laws, his rescripts, and so forth.

---

20. Eusebius, *Vita Constantini* and *Laus Constantini*. Cf. also this passage from his Ecclesiastical History: He is worthy of the power of the emperor "who bears the image of Royalty from On-High ... in accordance with its archetypal model". (*Hist. eccl.* 1.449).

21. Anonymous poem (12th century) ed. Codinus Curopalata in the 15th.

22. See *Harv. Theol. Rev.* 28 (1935), p. 36.

But that is not all. There are all kinds of facts and titles which prove that Byzantine royalty not only was a *sacred* royalty, but also a *divine* royalty. Thus, at the death of Constantine, coins were struck which bore the inscription *divus Constantinus* and in which was engraved a scene showing a quadriga raising the prince to heaven where he was grasped by a heavenly hand.[23] That is the proof that Constantine had been favored with apotheosis like the pagan emperors. There is no need to be astonished at this, for all the Christian emperors who followed him, until a very late date, were honoured with apotheosis, and this apotheosis received the approval of religious personages beyond reproach. Thus St. Gregory Nazianzen, describing the funeral of the emperor Constantius, exclaims: "It proceeds towards the glorious temple of the Apostles which harbours the sacred race of the Caesars, whose honours and merits equal, or scarcely fall short of those of the Apostles and those of Christ."[24] And St. Ambrose, who never hesitated to level grave reproaches to the emperors, describes, in the funeral orations of Valentinius and Theodosius the Great, the ascension of both princes to heaven, where they are resplendent with superhuman glory.[25] It would be a mistake to see in these words mere rhetorical devices, exaggerations inherited from Homer or Virgil, or poetic hyperbole intended to flatter the memory of princes. The genre and the tone of these works prove to us that the texts cited express the sentiments of the authors as well as those of the auditors. These declarations were taken very seriously by everyone. Eutropius, for his part, in his history[26] that covers up to the death of Jovian, ends the narrative of each imperial reign with the formula: *inter divos relatus est* or *inter divos meruit referri*, "he (the deceased emperor) was taken amongst the divine beings ... deserved being

---

23. J. Maurice, *Numismat. Const.* I (1908), p. 262, pl. 18.

24. St. Gregory Nazianzen, *Invectiva* II.

25. St. Ambrose, *Orat. pro Valentiano,* 64 & 77; *Orat. pro Theodosio* 40, 52 & 81.

26. *Breviarium historiae romanae.*

taken amongst the divine beings".[27] For Christian consciences it was not too difficult, in the last analysis, to accept these apotheoses, for the ancient apotheosis was recovered and reintegrated into an authentically Christian perspective, that of the rite of beatification or of canonisation, as can be seen by the fact that the Caesars buried in the Church of the Holy Apostles bear the posthumous title of *makarioi*, "blessed",[28] a word already employed in Greek antiquity to designate both the gods and the glorified dead,[29] and which passed to the Christian vocabulary with a meaning close to that of *hagios,* to qualify the *saints.*

An anonymous epigram collected in the *Anthology* evokes the Emperor Theodosius II, the husband of Eudoxia, in a very interesting way, saying:

> The man is dead, but the god lives;
> Here below he was made man, but he was always that which he was there above.[30]

The first verse reproduces the ancient formula of apotheosis. The second was rejected by a certain critic,[31] who considered it an addition. It is in fact possible that what is in question is a gloss of a reader that later passed to the text; but it matters little for our purpose, on the contrary. In this case, in fact, this gloss, which throws further into relief the idea of the previous verse and deepens it, proves that the general feeling tended towards seeing in the emperor a species of man-god incarnate. We shall have to return later to this conception and explain it from the Christian perspective; for the moment it is enough to note that

---

27. Let us note that the formula was omitted for Julian.

28. *De Caeremoniis,* Const. Porphyrogenete 2.4.7.

29. For the gods: Homer, *Iliad* 1, 339; *Odyssey* 5, 186, etc. For the glorified dead: Plato, *Laws* 947 D and the expression *Makaron nesoi* "Isles of the Blessed", designating the abode of heroes.

30. *Anthology,* 1.105, Waltz.

31. Stadtmüller.

the emperor was considered a divine being, not only after his death and his apotheosis, but even in life.

Throughout the history of the empire, the imperial titulary proves this. In an admonishment to Justinian, the monk Agapetus proclaims that the emperor "by his dignity is like Him who rules all things".[32] An official acclamation addressed to the prince, the *polychronion*, expresses itself thus: "May God grant many years to your *divine royalty* (*entheos basileia*)!"[33] But it is not only his dignity that is termed "divine", but his very person. The emperor is "equal to the gods" (*isotheos*), he is "divine" (*theios, divinus, divus*), he is "most divine" (*theiotatos, divinissimus*). In Byzantium, Constantine had a statue built in the Circus representing him with the features of the solar god with the following inscription: *hode theiotatos autocrator*, "this is the most divine";[34] and an official acclamation is also known: "Hail, divine, most divine emperor.... Glory to the emperor our Lord, and Christ of the Lord."[35] One even goes so far as to say that he has "descended from a divine lineage" (*divina stirpe progenitus*). His subjects also call him *theiotes*, "divinity", *ainiotes*, "eternity", and certain princes speak of themselves in palace documents, saying "Our divinity" (*he hemetera theiotes, divinitas nostra*). Hence, there is no difficulty in understanding that certain panegyrists call the emperor "a god present bodily" (*praesens et corporalis deus*),[36] "a sovereign god" (*deus praestantissimus*).[37]

We are faced here with expressions that translate this conception, mentioned earlier in the case of Theodosius' epigram, of a supra-human nature that pertains to the emperor by right. During the pagan era this mysterious power was termed *Tyche* and, in Latin, the *Genius* of the emperor, a kind of entity that overlays the human individual and confers a divine status upon him.

---

32. Agapetus, *Admon. ad Justin.* 21.

33. *De Caeremoniis*, Const. Porphyr. 1.2.

34. Zosimus, *New History*, 2; Zonaras, *Chron.* 13.3.

35. *De Caeremoniis,* Theophan. 1.86.

36. Vegetius, *Epit. rei militaris* 2,5; *Paneg.* 6,22,1.

37. Pacatus, *Paneg.* 4,5.

This continued in the Christian era and oaths were administered by the imperial *Tyche*, which was termed "divine and heavenly" (*theia kai ouranios*). How could it be astonishing, therefore, that the crime of *lèse majesté* was punished with the same severity as sacrileges, that is to say, by excommunication, since the imperial person touched so closely the domain of the sacred?

The divinity of the emperor was also marked by the representation of the *nimbe*, or halo, around his head, a representation that is encountered consistently in all the works of Byzantine art, especially in mosaics and miniatures,[38] and which thereby assimilated the prince to the saints, including Christ Himself. We shall see later what the deepest meaning of the nimbus is in relation to the royal function.

CULT OF THE EMPEROR · All divinity requires a form of worship. As is known, there was a cult of the emperor in the pagan era, but it continued with some modifications during the reign of the Christian emperors. This cult appears in the court ceremony. The palace is a temple, "the true sanctuary of the monarchic religion"; as a divinity, the emperor dwells there surrounded by a cloud of mystical secrecy; the places where he is remain hidden by *vela*, in the way they are drawn before the holy doors of the iconostasis. The feet of the emperor must never touch the ground;[39] he is always separated from it by a footstool, the *suppedion*, made of porphyry, a stone attributed to divinity. At the approach of the basileus, sacred silence is observed, broken only by ritual acclamations: "Life and riches of the Romans", "Master of the earth", "Joy of the world", "Holy, holy, holy"; before him, one remains with hands crossed on one's breast, the attitude of the faithful who, during the Divine Liturgy, presents himself for communion. If one must touch the emperor, for example, to serve him, it can be done only with hands gloved, like the lesser ministers who, during the liturgy, only touch the sacred objects with gloves or with a veil. Respect is shown him through the "adoration", the *proskynesis*, that is, the great prostration, accom-

---

38. Thus, for example, the emperor Honorius, on the *Probus Diptych*, Aosta (406 AD).

39. The same interdiction existed in the imperial palace in Tokyo.

panied by the act of touching his feet, knees and hands—a rite already practiced in the case of the pagan emperor, considered as *deus praesens*, and which originated in the Near East, as we have seen.

The many civil and religious festivals celebrated in Constantinople required various public displacements of the emperor, which were organised as veritable religious processions: in front of the emperor there came lighted fire, torches and candlewood, as attributes of divinity. In the liturgical feasts, imperial hymns were performed, and doxologies copied from those of divine worship were sung in honour of the *basileus*. Moreover, in the palace, offerings of incense were made and candlewood was placed before images of the emperor, as before icons. These images of the emperor were objects of general veneration; everywhere there were moveable *laurate*, symbols of his power that were considered true sanctuaries and granted the right of asylum. They were paraded in procession in the midst of icons of the saints; they were honoured with the *proskynesis*, with candles and incense, as in the palace, and with acclamations. The extent of this veritable cult can be understood by recalling that Pope Gregory the Great placed an imperial effigy in the chapel of the pontifical basilica of Latran, before which he made the *proskynesis*.[40]

COSMIC DIMENSION · If the sovereign can be considered a divine being, it is obvious that this is not as an individual, but rather by reference to the archetype of royalty, the "King of the World". However, inasmuch as he is the image, or one of the earthly images, of this archetype, the king also bears the title of "king of the world", "king of the universe", or "universal king". We have seen before in what sense the expression has to be un-

---

40. For Constantine, the imperial cult went so far as to establish a liturgical calendar of the prince: religious ceremonies were celebrated at his birthday, his accession to the throne (*adventus divi*), his departure to fight Licinus and, finally, his death. Even today we read in the Byzantine missal for 21st May: "Feast of the Holy Great Sovereigns Constantine and Helen, Equal to the Apostles."

derstood.[41] Following the Eastern monarchs, the Roman emperors took this title, and it passed to the Christian emperors. Constantine was designated *basileus cosmou*. This cosmic dimension of imperial royalty, which comes from its sacred origin, found a means of privileged expression in the solar symbolism governing many aspects of imperial ritual and representations of the prince, but at the same time determined by the representation of Christ Pantocrator, the true King of the world, of which the earthly king is the reflection.

The importance by the end of classical antiquity of the *Sol invictus*, "the invincible Sun", which originated in the near East, is well known. The expression was introduced by Commodus into the imperial Titulary: the emperor "was" the "lord sun of the empire" (*sol dominus imperii*). The title of the *Sol invictus* is inscribed on the Arch of Constantine and on coins, where the prince is represented with the features of Apollo and Hercules. He had a colossal statue erected which represented him with the features of Helios Apollo with a lance in one hand and, in the other, the globe with the cross on top, sign of universal royalty. The dedication of the monument was drawn up as follows: "To Constantine, who is resplendent like the sun" (*Constantino lamponti heliou diken*).[42] We have already pointed out another statue,[43] made of porphyry, which was raised in the Circus in Constantinople; the head of the emperor on it was adorned with solar rays which were none other than the nails from the cross of Christ arranged in the form of a halo.[44]

Solar symbolism, as we know from the chroniclers and the poets, also appears precisely in the Circus, which was just mentioned, and in the Hippodrome; owing to their round or oval form, these were conceived as representing the course of the sun and the circuit of the year. But the solar symbology was more intimately associated with the imperial Shield, which played a

---

41. See Chapter II, p. 52.

42. Nicephorus Callistus 7.49.

43. See this Chapter, p. 161.

44. Zosimus, op. cit. 2; Zonaras, op. cit. 15.3.

part of the highest importance in the accession to power. In this case as well the origin must be sought in the East. In Iran, the shield, owing to its round form, was assimilated to the winged solar disk we spoke of earlier;[45] the ceremonial shield was the equivalent of an image of the world, evoking the cosmic cycle. Seals from the Achaemenid Empire show shields that represent the universe in motion: the shield turns around an axis moved by three oxen. The king was the reflection of the solar god, and there is a relief in which Ahuramazda can be seen within the circular ring of the world and, below him, the king, also within a circle; the king at the middle of the circle expresses the same belief as the king at the centre of the circular city or on the throne of the mobile rotunda[46] (see plate p. 165). The West also knew the *clipeus coelestis*, the "heavenly shield", sometimes bordered with the zodiac; thus, the terracotta shields discovered in the tomb of Eretria (Museum of Fine Arts, Boston), in which Helios radiating appears in the centre surrounded by stars, this being the *sol in clipeo*.[47] In the Albani villa, Jupiter is represented in the middle of a ring in the form of the zodiac. A dyptich from the sixth century represents Christ as Pantocrator in a *clipeus coelestis* with the sun, the moon and a planet around him, and the inscription reads: "All power hath been given me in heaven and on earth."

This is the symbolic context in which the rite of "Raising on the shield" in Constantinople was situated. Raised over this *imago mundi*, the emperor was promoted to the rank of cosmocrator through this symbolic ascension towards the celestial dome and the stars.[48] The poet Corippus sang the ceremony in his Panegy-

---

45. See Chapter II, p. 57.

46. See Chapter II, pp. 56-57.

47. See Tertullian, *Apol.* 16.

48. The raising on the shield, which, as is known, was also practiced by the Germanic peoples, is one of a number modalities, found universally, of the ritual ascension: ascension of shamans by tree, post, cord; in India, ascension of the sacrificer along the length of the sacrificial post, etc. The ritual ascension is frequently a rite of initiation, for example in Orphism

Christ the King, Cosmocrator, at the centre of the Zodiac wheel, his head crowned with solar rays. At the corners, the four winds (*Scholium de XII zodiaci signis et de ventis*, 10 cent. ms. in Paris).

ric to Justinian II; he shows us the emperor surrounded by light, illumined by his own light: "Upon this shield a most valiant sun-like prince hath been raised: a second light of the day shineth from the city; one and the same day, astonished, saw two suns rising at once."⁴⁹ Also in the thirteenth century, Manuel Holobolos evoked the rite of the shield as an elevation, an ascension to the stars, and he saluted the emperor with the title of "great sun".⁵⁰ Finally, it is the same sentiment that inspired the annual ceremony of the *Prokypsis*; on the day of Christmas Eve, the solsticial festival, the court gathered in the Palace, in a prepared hall as for a spectacle; the curtain was drawn and the imperial family appeared on a podium with the background entirely dark, and a choir chanted the invocation to the solar god, here assimilated to the emperor:

> Sun, giant, king, tireless light-bearer,
> Eye of the world and torch of the Romans,
> Arise, Arise, what dost thou await?⁵¹

The persistence of this ancient solar cult within Christian realms encountered no difficulty, because very early the *Sol invictus* of the ancient religion was assimilated to the *Sol Justitiae*, the "Sun of Righteousness", a Hebrew title that from the beginning was applied to Christ, and more especially to Christ in his relationship to royalty, to Christ king, to Christ *cosmocrator*. And the emperor, in his turn, was assimilated to this solar Christ. When

---

and Mithraism. In the light of these facts, the raising of the prince on the shield appears as a royal initiation.

49. *Panegyr. Justin* 2.148ff. Another passage in this work, describes an abode, "in the depths of the palace", which on the upper part of the ceiling shines with its own light as if it were freely open to the sky, resplendent with a notable metallic brilliance (*ibid.* 1, pp. 97-101).

50. Very characteristic is a miniature representing the anointing of David by the prophet Nathan: David, dressed as a Byzantine emperor, is carried on a shield.

51. Text in O. Treitinger, *Die oströmische Kaiser—und Reichsidee nach ihrer Gestaltung im höfischen Zeremoniell.*, 1938, p. 116.

he is seated on the throne, dressed in the purple tunic, with the omophorion decorated with gold and draped over his entire body, enveloping it, the cruciform sceptre in his right hand, the globe of the world in his left hand, his feet resting on the foot-stool of porphyry decorated with precious stones, like the divine throne in the Apocalypse, his head under the baldaquin, symbol of heaven, the *basileus* truly seems like the image on earth of Christ Pantocrator, such as he was represented in so many works of art from church apses to miniatures. That is the idea which appears in concrete form in the Barberini dyptich (Louvre Museum, see plate p. 168): the emperor wears the imperial costume; above him appears Christ on the cosmic disk, surrounded by the heavenly bodies, with the standard of the cross in his hand; there we see together and presented in their intimate relationship the heavenly emperor and the earthly emperor who, in the words of Pope Celestine addressed to Theodosius II, is "co-ruler (*symbasileuon*) with Christ our God".[52]

Christ being at once priest and king *in divinis*, the prince necessarily had conferred upon him a priestly character, the reflection of Christ-priest. In fact, he certainly was, in a certain manner at least, a king-priest, and this conception was taken very seriously. The title of priest-king (*hieros basileus*) was officially given to him by the ecclesiastic hierarchy: he was acclaimed thus by the bishops gathered at the Council of Chalcedon ("to the priest-king, master of the faith", *to hierei to basilei ... didascale pisteos*).[53]

On certain feasts he was even acclaimed with the title of "king and great priest" (*archiereus basileus*). Speaking of Constantius, in order to oppose him to Julian, St. Gregory Nazianzen exlaimed: "How hast thou been able, in such short time, to abandon this *royal priesthood* which you exercised here below, to give thyself over to this evil and this fury?"[54] The popes themselves thought no differently, at least during the first part of the medi-

---

52. *Act. Concil. oecum.* (Schwartz) I¹7, p. 129ff.

53. Mansi, *Concil. coll.* 7, 170 & 177 A.

54. St. Greg. Nazianzen, *Invectiva prior.*

The emperor as a human embodiment of Christ the Pantocrator (on top), flanked by the sun and the moon (Barberini ivory, 6th cent., Louvre).

eval age. The Pope St. Leo addressed Theodosius II thus: "The Church rejoices to see in thee the royal character and the priestly character joined together"; and he also said: "Thy soul of priest and apostle must become indignant at the evils from which the Church of Constantinople groans";[55] he praises in Marcian "a royal authority and a priestly zeal", and requested Emperor Leo I that the "most Christian prince bear always a priestly and apostolic heart."[56]

All these affirmations have to be compared with the theme of Melchizedek, very frequently treated in Christian art of the first centuries and which served as the scriptural basis for the imperial idea. Thus, in St. Vitalis, in the south window of the presbytery, Melchizedek is represented, his head covered and surrounded by a halo, dressed in a purple mantle and wearing the royal diadem. The importance of this fact cannot be exaggerated, when one recalls what we have said of the role of Melchizedek in the Judeo-Christian tradition, as representing the "King of the World" and invested with the double function of priest and king.[57] Thus the *basileus* appears as invested with a royalty connected to the primordial forms of sacred royalty, which is easily explained if we recall that a new era of history, like the Christian era, reproduces analogically, at its level, the primordial era. The Byzantine emperor, at least in a certain sense, was truly a representative of the "King of the World", which, let it be said in passing, explains the attitude taken by him regarding the ecclesiatical hierarchy. Let us point out—and this is very interesting—that in certain religious ceremonies the emperor wore the tiara of three crowns. Generally, it is related that the tiara was adopted by the popes, first with one crown, and later, Boniface VIII added a crown, and finally Urban V added the third crown. But in reality, the tiara of three crowns has an Eastern origin and had already long existed in Constantinople, as can be seen from

---

55. Letter annexed to the text of Chalcedon.

56. PL 54.1031; 1131 C.

57. See Chapter IV, p. 128ff.

the *ceremonial* of the Palace.[58] Now, the tiara of three crowns is related on the one hand to the triple dignity of prophet, priest and king, and on the other hand to the authority over the three worlds.[59]

---

58. *De Caeremoniis,* Constantin Porphyrogenete 1,7.

59. See pp. 133-34. The "three worlds" in traditional doctrines are heaven, earth and the hells; the expression also designates a closely related triple division: earth, the sublunary heaven and the superior heaven. Of course, there is no need to heed the opinion of profane scholars for whom this triple division pertains to "primitive" cosmology; in reality what is entailed is the expression of a doctrine making use of cosmological symbolism to designate realities of a metaphysical order, or in other words, a synthetic exposition of the "multiple states of Being": the earth corresponds to the world of corporeal manifestation, including man in his present state, heaven to the spiritual world, the hells to inferior states (in relation to man). In the other triple division, things are considered solely in relation to man and to the states superior to the corporeal state: earth always corresponds to this corporeal state, the sublunary to the psychic world or the world of the soul, and the superior heaven to the spirit; in summary, a division of the superior place of the first formula. This last triple division also corresponds to the ternary of prophet, priest and king. The triple crown of the tiara expresses both triple divisions, and this explains why it is an attribute of the "King of the World", who possesses these three functions and rules all the planes of creation. Some persons will be surprised to know that the tiara was not originally part of the head-dress of the pope; during the first centuries he, like the other bishops, wore only a mitre. Historians say that it was towards the 8th or 9th century that the pope adopted the tiara, at the time that the Roman pontificate possessed its first States, thereby becoming a temporal leader, and consider the tiara as the insignia of the temporal power of the pope. But this latter statement is difficult to reconcile with the existence of *three* crowns; the statement is true in a certain sense, above all as regards the first crown, but it does not take into account the essential significance of the tiara, which is much vaster, as we have said, and as it results from the prayer pronounced by the first Deacon when he places the tiara on the head of the one elected: "Receive the tiara adorned with three crowns, and know that thou art the father of the princes and the kings, the one who rules the world (*rectorem orbis*), the vicar on earth of the Saviour Jesus Christ." Once again we are led to the doctrine of the King of the World, that is, of the intimate union of the priesthood and royalty. There is another fact, taken from the history of the Hebrews, that is significant in this connection. We know that the Jewish high priest wore a simple tiara, without a crown, and with a diadem in front (Exod. 28:36 ff.; 39:30 ff.); later, this diadem gave way to a triple crown, as Flavius Josephus tells us (3.7.6), probably starting

How is the ecclesiastic character of the emperor manifested?

Let us first recall that his status, from the strictly canonical point of view, is that of a subdeacon or a deacon, as so serious an author as Simeon of Thessalonica says. In view of this title, if the child is destined to succeed his father, he is tonsured by the patriarch; this took place with the young son of Porphyry and for the young Leo, son of Basil the Macedonian. During the Divine Liturgy, the emperor receives the censer and censes the icon of the Crucified. In conformity to the rite established for ecclesiastics and the priest, he receives communion by himself, that is, he receives the bread in his hand to give the communion to himself, and he drinks the wine directly from the chalice, whereas the laity receives from the hand of the priest a piece of bread dipped in wine. In processions he is always preceded by flags and torches, followed by the images of the pontiffs, the

---

from the post-exile era or that of the Maccabees, or in other words, the epoch in which the high priest exercised the royal functions. The problem that arises is that of knowing why the pope adopted the tiara at the time we mentioned and not before. In general, the reply is that it was during this time that the Roman pontiff recovered and adopted the imperial titles and insignia, the purple, the title of "Supreme Pontiff", etc., and the tiara that the emperor of Byzantium already wore. And that is true; the pontiffs at that time dedicated themselves to transform the papacy, which was characterised solely by the primacy of being the seat of Peter in the pontifical monarchy. But this only pushes the problem further back, for why, precisely, this transformation in which the pope becomes in effect a priest-king? It is futile to put forth ambition and desire for power as the cause on the part of the pontiffs; this reason could indeed move some of them, but it is no less true that this pontifical monarchy was desired, accepted and defended by numerous popes who were saintly people. The true reasons for the facts pertain to an order other than that of the visible reasons of positivist history. It may be asked whether the establishment of the pontifical monarchy was not the sign that at this time the exterior representation, on Christian soil, foreseeing the times that followed, passed from the emperor to the bishop of Rome. This question deserves to be studied in connection with the problem of Prester John, but it is not possible for us to treat this theme here. Let us recall finally that the last three popes have renounced wearing the tiara: and a new question could be asked regarding the profound meaning of this gesture, independently of outward reasons that have been given; and the answer that can be surmised is perhaps not very reassuring.

banners of the four great martyrs, the passage of St. George slaying the dragon, and finally the equestrian effigy of the *basileus*.[60]

During the course of the public liturgy, the emperor is taken to speak to the people and, as a depositary of the word of God, to give a true sermon, at the end of which he blesses those present with a triple sign of the cross, as a priest does.[61] In his private chapel in the palace, he celebrates some liturgies, which the documents do not define clearly, is crowned with the tiara, as we have said, and dressed with the omophorion and the humeral, insignia of the ancient Roman pontificate preserved during the Christian era. The religious and even liturgical character can be met with even in official actions that could be termed civil but which in essence were not so in Byzantium, where they took on a sacral character. Thus, not only do we see Constantine prescribe the prayers that all soldiers had to recite morning and evening, but an act so little religious as the investiture of a palace functionary takes on the air of a priestly investiture; the ceremonial, in effect, establishes that the candidate must prostrate before the emperor and that he in turn confers his rank, saying, "In the name of the Father, the Son and the Holy spirit, the Imperial Majesty, which comes from God, raises thee to the dignity of patrician, of *syncellus*..."[62]

PONTIFEX MAXIMUS · Such are the principal functions of the emperor in the properly liturgical or paraliturgical domain. But his ecclesiastic prerogatives do not end there in the least. And to tell the truth, we are tempted to smile when we are told that he enjoys canonically the status of a deacon, because, on the other hand, he bears the title of *Pontifex Maximus*, "supreme pontiff", a title inherited from the pagan emperor and which all the Christian emperors kept for a long time—Theodosius still claimed it, as can been seen from a passage of Servius[63]—and whose prerogatives were in any case conserved until the end. To

---

60. Codinus Curopalata, *De officialibus palatii Constantinopolitani*, 6.

61. *De Caerem.* (Const. Porphyr.) 2, 10.

62. *Ibid.* 2, 4 & 5.

63. Servius 3.268.

gauge the extension of these, the role of the *Pontifex Maximus* in ancient Rome should be briefly recalled. As head of the College of Pontiffs instituted by Numa, he had the highest authority in all the priesthoods, named the titularies and was in charge of overseeing them. He was also in charge of overseeing the cults; he himself was in charge of the cult of the city Hearth, the importance of which we spoke earlier, also that of the public Penates and that of Jupiter Capitolinus, the patron of the city. As the leader of the cult, he with his colleagues was responsible for the liturgical calendar. Finally, he established and maintained the pontifical law, namely, the ensemble of religious obligations, and at the same time he determined the rites. In other words, he was the head of the official cult.

Now, the Christian emperor continued to fulfil the role of leader in the new cult, except, of course, for that which related to the administration of sacraments. At the juncture of the two worlds, Constantine exercised his pontificate for the Christians until the end of his life, ordering, for example, rest on Friday and Sunday and fixing the date of Easter.[64] This role as administrator of the religion was never disputed at all by the ecclesiastic hierarchy. In a text, which we have already cited in part, the archbishop Demetrios Chomatenos, comparing the Christian emperor to pagan emperors, writes: "Our emperor is the Christ (the Anointed) of the Lord because of of his royal anointing; he is our Christ and our god, as in the example of his predecessors; *he is also our great pontiff; he has been so and he still keeps this title. Thus he rightly enjoys pontifical privileges.*"[65]

And it was not as a deacon that he was considered the emperor, but in truth as bishop. Eusebius writes: "Constantine sat in the counsel of the ministers of God and did not disdain to mingle in their midst, as if he were one of them." And the prince himself defined the statute attributed to him: "I am also a bishop, but ye are the bishops charged with the inner affairs of the Church; and I have been constituted bishop by God for

---

64. *Code Theod.* 2.7.1.

65. D. Chometenos, *Respons. II ad Const. Cabasilam* in *Jus graeco-romanum Leunclavius*, lib. V.

the outward affairs of the Church (*ton ectos tes ecclesias hypo theou cathestamenos episcopos*)."[66] For this reason, the emperor was assimilated to the Apostles, and was named *isapostolos*, "equal to the Apostles".

The emperors who succeeded Constantine did not lose this episcopal and apostolic dignity. It suffices to read in this connection what Constantine Porphyrogenitus wrote about himself: "God has given in us proof of His munificence and His goodness *by entrusting to us, as to Peter,* the first Apostle, the guardianship of his faithful flock."[67] A similar text seems to situate the emperor at the same rank as the bishop of Rome.

Moreover, it is rather as one such that he exercised his authority in the Church. He is its all-powerful administrator; it is he who elects the bishops and, in this domain, his authority extends even to the pope; in fact, although the pope was elected by the clergy and the people, his election had to be approved and confirmed by the emperor.[68] In the domain of jurisdiction, all ecclesiastical suits depend on him, and for the same reason the civil suits. And likewise with legislation, for the emperor knows the canon law as well as the civil law, and his concern is with with both. The decisions of the ecclesiastic canon have neither worth nor the force of law unless he approves and promulgates them, which moreover assures their execution. Synods and councils have only a deliberative and consultative role, so that the bishops, in fact, constitute no more than the "Ecclesiastic Council" of the prince, along with his "Political Council". Thus, it is Emperor Basil I who promulgated the decree that turns the canons of the seven Councils into law; the *Theodosian Code* is full of articles of religious legislation, and the same is true for the *Code of Justinian* and the *Basilica*.[69] Thus the religious law, like

---

66. Eusebius *V. Constant.* 1.37; 4.24.

67. Preface to *Laws of Constantine Porphyrogenitus*.

68. A remnant of this prerogative remained with the Western Roman Emperor, and then with the Holy Roman Empire even until the beginning of the 20th century. The last emperor who exercised his right of veto over the election of a Pope was Franz Joseph I (1848-1916).

69. Juridical compilation made at the instigation of Basil I.

the civil law, falls within the competence of the prince, for "religion is part of law," according to Pomponius, reproduced in the *Basilica* and in Justinian.

But there is more. Demetrios Comatenos writes: "The emperor is the supreme master of the beliefs for the churches." Even conceding that there is some exaggeration in this statement, coming from the pen of an administrative prelate, that does not negate the fact that the emperor always was aware that his duty was to guard the religion and to protect the faith; and this duty can be said to have been assumed by him as a real theologian. For the emperors of Byzantium were theologians, as they were canonists, and it can even be said that they were at least as deeply interested in theology as in politics, since, moreover, for them both things could not be dissociated. In this domain, a major activity was to organise councils. These, in fact, depended almost entirely on the emperor. He alone can convoke a council, fix the venue, the date and the program. It is Constantine who took the initiative of having Arius condemned and exiled him, and who then, as guarantor of his faith, pardoned him;[70] Marcianus called the council in Chalcedon to fix the doctrine of Nicea; Constantius called the synod that had to establish the consubstantiality of the Persons in the Trinity;[71] Constantine Pogonatos convoked the ecumenical council for the purpose of condemning the monothelites. It was the emperor who presided over the council and directed it; the bishops deliberated under the gaze of the prince, who took part in the discussion as Constantine had done at first at Nicea, as Eusebius recounts: "He would intervene in the deliberation inasmuch as he was the bishop instituted by God."[72] Once again we meet with the title mentioned a moment ago. And also, as "bishop" he anathematises the heretics: "We hurl anathema against all heresy," says Basil I in the decree mentioned earlier; and we meet with similar formulas in other laws against heresies, those promulgated by

---

70. See Socrates 1,22.

71. Symacchus, *Ep.* 10, 54.

72. Eusebius, *V. Const.* 1, 37 & 38.

Gratian or Justinian.[73] Demetrios Comenatos defines very well the status of the "archbishop of the exterior" in the text from which we previously cited a few lines. Here is what he writes: "It pertains to the emperor to change or innovate in canonical and ecclesiastic matters; because for the churches he is the supreme master of the beliefs. He presides over the synods and gives to his sentences the force which he draws from within himself; he maintains the different ranks of the religious hierarchy; he regulates through his laws the life and discipline of those who serve the altar; he intervenes in the judgment of the bishops and of the clergy, and in the elections of churches without pastors."[74] If the list of these attributions be compared with those of the ancient *Pontifex Maximus*, it will be noted that the prerogatives of the Christian emperor cover most of those enjoyed by the pagan sovereigns in religious matters. For, with the exception of the administration of the sacraments, the Christian emperor possessed, in an eminent manner, the rest of the attributions of the ecclesiastic hierarchy, all the administrative and judiciary power, on the one hand, and at the same time, in large measure, its doctrinal and teaching function. Thus, it can rightly be said that he was the true head of the Church.

It is not for us to say here whether the role played by the emperors in Constantinople in this domain went beyond the necessary limits separating each domain, the priestly and the royal. Let us simply say that in a normal society it is completely natural that the possessor of the political power, by the very fact that this has a sacred character, also participates to some degree in the priestly function, for the dissociation of the original unity of the two powers cannot be total without provoking the appearance of that infirmity which is precisely that of present-day societies of the Western type. We shall have occasion to speak again on this point.

Yet, whatever may be the importance of this "ecclesiastic" function of the prince, it must be understood that the sacred character of the royal function is not initially attached to his at-

---

73. *Cod. Theod.* 16.5.5; 16.6.3; Evagrius 4.9.
74. D. Chomeanto, loc. cit.

tributions in the domain of worship, but to his specific attributions that relate to the properly royal principle, the source of which lies in Christ-king; if royalty is sacred, it is so as possessor of this power on earth, and as such the emperor bore the title of "vicar of god" or, if a different translation be preferred, of "lieutenant of God", a title that was recognised by the papacy itself.[75]

HOLY ROMAN EMPIRE

We have dwelt rather extensively on the chapter of the Eastern Empire given its importance for our subject; it was in fact the first realisation of a sacred royalty of Christian type, and upon it were modelled in large measure those that were to be created afterward. And the first would be the Holy Western Empire.

Desired by the papacy in order to return Rome—the vital centre of Christianity—its luster and power, the Western Holy Roman Empire to some extent inherited uses and customs from German royalty; but in its general conception, in the majority of its practices, and even in many material details, it was a replica of the Eastern Empire. From the German tradition came the manner of designating the sovereign, elected by the princes, who represented the people, and not by the Army and the Senate. But the consecration and coronation by the Pope were practiced according to a ritual that differed little from that of Byzantium.[76] And the same can be said for the imperial dress and insignia: we encounter once again in the West the long tunic girded at the waist, the purple chlamyde clasped on the left shoulder with a fibula and which leaves the right shoulder free, the red leather shoes and the *cappa magna*, the short sceptre topped with an eagle, the large sceptre, much like the episcopal staff, the golden globe with the cross on top, the "venerable Lance" or "The Lance of St. Maurice", containing a nail from the True Cross

---

75. *Ep.* 2 of the Pope Anastasius to the emperor of the same name: "As it were, the vicar of God, who commands on earth".

76. We shall not speak of this here. This ritual, aside from a few details, is in fact the one employed for the kings, and will be analysed in the next chapter.

and carried before the emperor like a standard (see plate p. 179). The Western crown, however, differed markedly from that of the East, as we shall see shortly. The greater part of the terms of the imperial titulary in the diverse documents are the same as those we have set forth above: the empire is *sacrum, sacratissimum*; it is the *respublica divina*; the emperor is *sacer, sanctissimus domi-nus*; deceased, he becomes a *divus*; he speaks of the *perennitas nostra* ("our eternity"). This vocabulary naturally harks back to an identical conception to that of Byzantium; the empire is an almost divine royalty, and the Western Emperor also appears as a "priest-king".

Moreover, Charlemagne, before being crowned by the pope in the year 800, was acclaimed *rex et sacerdos* "priest and king"; king for power, priest for the teaching *magisterium*, Alcuin ex-plained. The rite of consecration of the emperor was the same as that for the bishops, that is, an initial anointing on the head with holy chrism, followed by others on the arms, between the shoul-ders, on the breast, on the hands, and accessorily on the eyes and on the nasal wings. The anointing in Byzantium was already like that and it continued to be that way for the Czar in Russia. In the West until the eighteenth century, the imperial consecration was considered a true sacrament, even by the Vatican, who at that time had not fixed the number at the seven present sacra-ments; and a completely official representative of the papacy, St. Peter Damian, wrote: "The kings and priests are called gods and christs because of the function joined to the sacrament they have received."[77] For this reason the emperor was called *Vicarius Dei* and *Vicarius Christi*, as well as *Caput christianae plebis* (head of the Christian people) and *Episcopus episcoporum* ("bishop of bishops"). Thereafter, the papacy, wishing to lessen imperial power for his own advantage, decided to no longer anoint the emperor—nor the kings—with the holy chrism on the head, as done with bishops, but simply with the oil of the catechumens between the shoulders and on the arms. But what interests us here is to see the religious status of the emperor when it was truly at the full strength of its intrinsic truth. What then appears

---

77. *Liber gratissimus* in *Mon. Germ. litt.* I.31.

Emperor Charles the Bald (miniature from the Codex Aureus of St. Emmeram, 9th cent., Munich, Bayerische Staatsbibliothek).

"Crown of Charlemagne," the of the Holy Empire
(Kunsthistorisches Museum, Vienna).

Consecration mantle of EHenry II, decorated with
of the Zand constellations (Bamberg Cathedral
Museum).

Consecration mantle of EHenry II (Bamberg Cathedral.Museum).

180

clearly to all is its divine character. "God hath transformed thee today into another man," says Archbishop Herbert to Conrad II, upon the occasion of his coronation, "and He hath made thee participate in His divinity."[78] Thanks to the consecration, we read, what the king—"Christ of the Lord"—does, he does not do as man, but as "God and Christ of the Lord".[79] Let us point out that in all these texts the word king designates the emperor. "The king is the image of Christ and, as such, is totally deified and sanctified (*totus deificatus et sanctificatus*)."[80] And naturally, they make reference to the biblical archetype, to Melchizedek; thus V. Fortunato does not hesitate to say of Childebert: "He is by rights our Melchisedek, at once priest and king."[81] Universal king, king of the world—such is the ideal image that the emperor incarnated when seated on the throne, with the heavenly ciborium above, the globe in his hand, the crown on his head and the great mantle on his shoulders (see plate p. 180). We should like to insist somewhat on these last two insignia owing to their profound significance in this respect, for they symbolise marvellously the very concept of the Holy Empire.

CROWN & MANTLE · The imperial crown that we know, kept in the treasure of Vienna (see plate p. 180), does not go back to the time of Charlemagne, contrary to what some people have thought. If we refer to one of the inscriptions, it is very probable that what is in question is the crown of Conrad III Hohenstaufen (1138-1152); but it matters little, for its composition corresponds perfectly to the ideas that were united to the Empire from beginning to end of its history. It is an octagonal crown; eight plates of inlaid gold make-up the diadem; four are simply adorned with jewels, and the other four bear enamels representing Christ Pantocrator and the kings David, Solomon and Ezechias. The symbolical intention is obvious, which is to attach the empire, firstly to its divine source, and also to the royal Israelite lineage

---

78. *Mon. germ.* 1878 edition, Breslau, pp. 17-19.

79. *Mon. germ. Lib. litt.* III, 662f.

80. Anonymous of York.

81. *Mon. germ. Auct. Ant.* IV, 40.

to which Christ himself belonged in His earthly life. On the plaque placed in front the cross is fixed the sign of victory of the *christianissimus princeps*, "the most Christian prince". The cross bears a white opal, unique of its kind, the *orphanus der Weise*, or *der Waise* of the German poets, the symbol of the preeminence of the emperor over all the kings. Also symbolic is the octagonal form of the crown. The importance of the number eight in Christian arithmetology is known to us: it is the number of eternal life. In the imperial crown, the eight symbolises the union of the *Roma quadrata* and the *Hierosolyma quadrata*, the Rome of the emperors and the popes, centre of earthly Christianity, earthly image and reflection of the heavenly Jerusalem. The union of the two cities prefigures the universal reign of Christ, the realisation of which is at the very heart of the imperial mystique and which justifies the title of universal king conceded to the emperor.

Another aspect of this universal royalty appears in the famous choir mantle of Emperor Henry II (St. Henry), held in the treasure of Bamberg Cathedral (see plates p. 180). This magnificent garment of purple and blue silk represents in its semi-circle the synthetic image of the universe. At the centre of the starry sky, which extends over the entire mantle and thus over whoever wears it, is Christ cosmocrator surrounded with the four evangelical symbols. To the right of this central point, there are the sun and the moon, the angelic choirs and the twenty-four elders of the Apocalypse. All the rest is filled with the constellations, the signs of the zodiac, the planets and Pythagorean numbers indicating the proportions of the cosmos. Here is summarised all the astrology of the year 1000, centred on the Omnipotent. From Him the emperor draws all his power; the forces of the cosmos radiate within the emperor, and conversely, they irradiate from him to his surroundings; his empire is inserted within the laws of the universe; the prince remains in the light that comes from Above and from the creation; he incarnates and summarises in himself the Whole by participation in the virtue of the Pantocrator.

Once again, we encounter here, in Christian formulation, a conception that is well known, because it is found wherever there is a sacred royalty. Let us note in addition that the mantle at Bamberg is the heir of a type of mantle that was used by

certain Roman emperors,[82] and which in the last analysis comes
from Babylon, where the "heavenly mantle", the "starry mantle",
was the dress of the gods. It also passed on to the iconography
of the Virgin.[83]

DANTE · Thus, to organise the earthly city in the image of
celestial harmony, so that it would reflect the heavenly Jerusalem toward which it must lead men, was the final ideal of the
Empire, an end which was to be attained through the conjoined
action of the emperor and the pope, as Dante expounded well at
the end of his *De Monarchia*:

> Ineffable providence has proposed to man two ends: be-
> atitude in this life, which consists in the exercise of virtue and
> which is represented by the earthly Paradise; and beatitude in
> eternal life, which consists in enjoying the vision of God, to
> which human virtue cannot be raised without the help of the
> divine light, and which is represented by the celestial Paradise.
> These two beatitudes are attained to by different means, as if to
> different conclusions; for we arrive at the first by philosophical
> teachings, providing we follow them by acting according to the
> moral and intellectual virtues; and to the second by spiritual
> teachings, which transcend human reason, provided we follow
> them by acting according to the theological virtues, Faith, Hope
> and Charity. These conclusions, and these means, even though
> they are taught to us, the former by human reason, which is man-
> ifest to us entirely by the philosophers, and the latter by the Holy
> Spirit, which has revealed to us the supernatural truth that we
> need, through the prophets and the holy authors, through the
> Son of God, Jesus Christ, coeternal with the Spirit, and through
> his disciples, these conclusions and these means human concu-
> piscence would cause them to be abandoned if men, like horses
> who wander in their animality, were not restrained in their path
> by a brake. That is why man has need of a double direction in

---

82. Suetonius, *Nero* 25; Plutarch, *Alex.*32; Athenaeus 12.50.535; Apianus, *Punica* 66; Dio Cassius 44,4 & 6; 53.26; 67.3.

83. On this point, see, R. Eisler, *Sternenmantel u. Himmelszelt*, Munich, 1910.

accordance with this double end, that is to say of the Supreme Pontiff, who, according to Revelation, leads mankind to eternal life, and the Emperor, who, according to philosophical teachings, leads him to temporal felicity. And since to that port no one could arrive, or very few would arrive and at the cost of the worst difficulties, if mankind could not rest free in the tranquility of peace, after having stilled the waves of insinuating concupiscence, to this end must all tend, above all he that rules the earth, the Roman prince: that in this small abode of mortals men may live freely and in peace.[84]

This passage requires an explanation if an error is to be avoided regarding the meaning that must be given to the "philosophy" and the "philosophical teachings" Dante speaks of. Obviously, it cannot be a question of philosophy in the profane sense in which it is understood today; "philosophy" has to be understood in the sense that it had in Antiquity and in the Middle Ages, a sense corresponding quite well to its etymology: "the love of wisdom". The word embraces the set of human knowledge developed by reason, but always in conformity with the transcendent truth, without which human knowledge can only fall into error and drag men with them. Once this is clear, we can see what Dante's view was of the role of the Empire, which, in addition to its purely political scope, consisted in creating the indispensable conditions of a traditional culture, that is to say, in promoting all the sciences and all the arts which, under the supervision of the spiritual authority, should allow man to realise in the best possible way his earthly destiny, which is, as it were, the basis of his spiritual destiny.

The great emperors were very conscious of this role and took great care to be faithful to it, beginning with the first, Charlemagne, who was and remained the model of the best of his successors. Representative of Christ, protector of the Church, he took charge of the interests of Christianity, defending it outwardly with arms, and inwardly by the diffusion of the faith and of culture. The foundation of the Empire was the religion: the

---

84. *De Monarchia* 3.16.

emperor took charge of the salvation of the people of God; the State was conceived as the kingdom of wisdom, to use Dante's terminology, penetrated by the spiritual, preparing the City of God. Church and Empire were strongly united in a single Christendom. With Ludwig the Pious, the empire is barely distinguishable from the Church; it is the body of Christ. This synthesis was realised in the most harmonious and complete way during the reign of Otto III. Beginning in the year 1000, a Europe unified on the basis of Roman law and the spiritual authority of the Church might have seen the light of day. If this union had been realised by the joint action of Pope Gerbert (Silvester II) and Emperor Otto III, his disciple, today we would no doubt be far from the upheavals that trouble our old continent. Otto III, imaginative but realistic, was an impassioned mystic, nourished by a culture in which Rome, Byzantium and Carolingian Germany converged. Above all he had inherited the universalist imperial ideal, which quickened all his politics: his goal was to reunite the different countries in order to constitute a universal empire founded on the Christian order. Rome, proud of its ancient past, reinforced by its role as capital of the Apostle, had to be the capital of the world for Otto. Whereas Charlemagne sought to apply the Roman concept only within his conquests, and whereas Otto I sought above all by these to assure German domination—a temptation that unfortunately would dominate later—Otto III, through the influence of Gerbert, desired a universal empire by right and in fact, in which all people would be equal: the dream of Alexander, but become Christian. Thus, the year 1000 sees the birth of a world in equilibrium which was going to be able to develop full of energy and confidence, contrary to the legends that certain chroniclers have spread regarding the "terrors of the year 1000". Unfortunately, Otto III was to die very young, and he did not have the time to see all his projects through to a firm footing, so that his work would be capable of lasting.[85]

If his successor Henry II (St. Henry) was animated by the same spirit, the following emperors too often had far less gran-

---

85. See the very interesting book by E. Huant, *Othon III, la merveille du monde*, Paris, 1972.

diose goals in view. Nonetheless, the imperial mystique had not died: it was seen during the reign of Frederick II, immersed in an atmosphere of messianism recalling the era of Augustus; to his followers, Frederick appears as the one who would inaugurate, like a saviour, a new "golden age". The "myth" of Frederick II was dominated by two figures: that of the Emperor Augustus, particularly, who precisely believed he inaugurated a new "golden age", and that of Adam, who had been truly a cosmocrator. This reference to Adam reflected the desire to recover the "lost Paradise" by means of the universal Christian Empire. The reign of Frederick II ended in catastrophe, and the imperial institution was left badly damaged in consequence; nevertheless, the imperial mystique and its messianism did not disappear; both developed in two directions corresponding to the two factions which then took birth: the Guelphs and the Ghibellines, giving rise to a certain number of prophecies, all of which reflected nostalgia for the Great Christian Empire. On the side of the Ghibellines, it was believed that Frederick II remained alive, a belief to which we have already alluded; and it was hoped that he himself, or one of his descendents, would renew the imperial institution. On the side of the Guelphs, in Joaquinite surroundings, who lived in an atmosphere of eschatological awaiting, the end of the world and the purification of the Church were predicted, and the coming of the emperor descending from Charlemagne, who would bring down the enemies of Christ and would prepare His second coming.

Both prophecies end equally with the victory of the emperor over the enemies of Christ and his journey to Jerusalem, where he would deliver the Empire to God. An oracle, originating among Minorites at the end of the fourteenth century, announced the coming of an angelic pope, who, with the emperor, would reform the world. A hermit of the fifteenth century, Telesphorus of Corenza, took up this oracle in which the role of a reformer was no long held by the emperor, but by a king of France by the name of Charles.

All this literature obviously attests to the failure of the great imperial idea. We must analyse, at least briefly, the causes, for these are directly related to the very foundations of the temporal power and its relation to the spiritual authority, which is the proper subject of this book. These causes were of two orders: political and intellectual.

The political causes were the different vicissitudes in the conflict that opposed a certain number of emperors to the papacy. The "investiture controversy", and the "struggle between the priesthood and the empire" are episodes of mediaeval history too well known for it to be necessary to recall the details here. What has to be seen is the profound root of this conflict, which has to be sought in the sentiments of the actors. There were great errors on both sides, for a good number of both emperors and popes did not display the conduct that could legitimately be expected of them. To summarise the issue in a word, both sides let themselves be carried away by the desire for power. It is certain that some emperors wanted to be totally independent of the spiritual authority and to act solely according to their own will, claiming, in order to justify their attitude, that their power came to them directly from God and they did not have to render account to anyone else. The Church could not tolerate this plainly heterodox claim, which moreover was an obstacle to its mission. But on the other hand, the papacy itself was not irreproachable, to say the least. Very early it had the ambition of being the effective agent of the Empire's renovation and of practically confiscating the imperial power for its own advantage. This tendency became clear above all after the rupture with Byzantium (1054). Gregory VII claimed for the pope alone the imperial insignia, a claim it was attempted to justify by the famous *Donation of Constantine*; this document stated that Constantine, upon leaving Rome, had given Pope Sylvester, in addition to the Lateran Palace, the insignia of empire: the diadem, the sceptre, the purple chlamyde, the scarlet tunic, the eagle and the globe. Of these insignia, the pope has kept until now the red *cappa*. However, this *Donation of Constantine* was certainly a forgery, and anyone who believed it was very naive: how could anyone suppose that Constantine, so imbued with imperial dignity, would strip himself of it in order to enrobe the pope? Be that as it may, the papacy attempted, and often succeeded, in augmenting its temporal power and effectively playing the part pertaining to the emperor. In so doing, it stepped outside its domain: for if it is true that the high priest possesses the two keys, the gold and the silver, he has to keep only the first and to give the second to the prince. The error of the papacy at certain moments was to wish to exercise effective temporal power, whereas it is only its principle. Thus, in the West there were two ideas of Empire, which completely falsified the role of the institution and necessarily led to the conflicts that ultimately ruined it.

ARISTOTLE · To the political causes of its decline were added causes of an intellectual order. The very idea of Empire decayed upon contact with the new religious philosophy that became dominant in the thirteenth century. The Aristotelianism that imposed itself henceforth in Western intellectual circles presented a conception of political power contrary to that of the Empire and, moreover, to all the previous royalties of the Middle Ages, a conception based on the notion of the *State* as opposed to the notion of Empire and Royalty. The Empire had God as its foundation; the State, according to Aristotle, was founded on the natural human order, given that man is by nature the *zoon politikon*; the Empire tended to be the antechamber of the City of God; the State, in turn, tries above all to realise well being here below. Whereas the Empire sought to reflect the heavenly order in the world and realise unity in the direction of the life of man, with Aristotelianism and the political movement that issued from it there appear a diversity of sovereignties and administrative centralisation in each nationality. Aristotelianism and scholastic philosophy are at the origin of the progressive laicisation of temporal power; it is not the sole cause of this laicisation, for, of course, there has to be added the growing influence of Roman Law, which would lead to the phenomenon of the Legalists of the Ancien Regime. Roman Law could have been understood in a very different sense—as is shown by what occurred in Byzantium—if its study had not developed in an atmosphere of political Aristotelianism. We believe that St. Thomas Aquinas himself did not foresee that his politics, inspired by Aristotle, opened a breach in the completely orthodox doctrine that he himself had defined as a theologian.[86] The Church in the West gained very little by basing its teaching almost solely on scholasticism and throwing aside the other previous philosophies and theologies of both the East and the West. For Aristotelianism represented a great laicisation of ancient philosophy and of conceptions referring to man and society; the work of Aristotle is certainly responsible for the partial failure of the effort at the traditional re-establishment that his master Plato had attempted. The Christian East and the first part of the Middle Ages in the West had had the wisdom to refer to Plato. If that had been maintained perhaps we would have been able to avoid rationalism in philosophy and pragmatism and empiricism in politics.

In a word, beginning in the thirteenth century and above all in the fourteenth, the combined play of these different causes was to open a breach in the orthodox conception of temporal power in Europe and the idea of an undivided Christendom. Nevertheless, neither the one nor the other disappeared suddenly; the erosion was slow, at least for royalty, which, in its national forms, for a long time still maintained its sacral character; above all in France, which seems to have recollected the profound ideal of the Empire, enabling it to survive, and earning the king of France the title, borne previously by Charlemagne, of "most Christian king".

---

86. See Chapter III, p. 96-97 and Chapter IV, p. 138-139.

CHAPTER VI

THE MOST CHRISTIAN KING

Among the authentic Christian royalties—that is, prior to the great Revolution—the French royalty has always been considered to be the one that best incarnated the true conception of royalty. And this is because to the very end it remained closely united to the religion; whereas in other Western countries the princes loosened this bond and their governments tended increasingly to laicise themselves in fact, if not in theory, the king of France perpetuated the most consummate type of sacred monarchy, so that "from the pharaoh to the most Christian king", as we wrote in the subtitle of this book, there can be traced a line of astonishing continuity of the institution of royalty, although independently of the specific characteristics of the Christian prince that we have analysed in previous chapters.

This Frankish, and later French, royalty was the heir to several venerable traditions which converged in it and became amalgamated into a harmonious synthesis, and in a kind of condensation intended to preserve them on the eve of the well-known destruction. Aside from the Germanic element that has already been pointed out, and which was at the origin of the idea of "royal companionage" to which we shall return, one has to recall the importance of the Roman and Celtic elements in its genesis and development, as well as, of course, the Judeo-Christian element that integrated the others.

The legacy of Rome passed to France, both through the papacy and the bishops, and through Byzantium, the prestige of which never ceased to fascinate the Western princes. After the victory of Vouille over the Goths in 507, Clovis entered as victor in Tours, then the holy city of the Gauls. There, Gregory of Tours tells us, "he received the diploma of Consul from the Emperor Anastasius, and in the suburb of Saint-Martin he put on the purple tunic, the chlamyde, and thereafter he was called consul and augustus." Now, let us recall that, some thirty years earlier, Odoacer, the conqueror of Rome, had sent all the insignia of Roman power to the Emperor of Byzantium, refusing to attribute them to himself. And lo and behold, in 507 they returned to Clovis, and thus, and by the official initiative of the Basileus himself, he rejoined the imperial tradition, with which French royalty was thereby invested, in a certain manner; in effect, in the House of France an imperial renovation was sown, the architect of which would be Charlemagne, "king of the Franks". And it is with the crown called "of Charlemagne" that the king of France was crowned at the moment of the coronation, and with this insignia the king inherited—as the papacy recognised—the particularly imperial mission of defending all of Christendom.

The Celtic heritage manifests above all after the twelfth century. It is the time in which there appear, or rather reappear, legends that are furnished by material from Breton written works and, in particular, those of the Grail Cycle. This is not the place to enlarge on the prime importance of the mystical current which developed around the myths of the Grail, a current with which there were also mingled influences from the Near East; but the influence that it exercised in the conception of royalty cannot be ignored. King Arthur, the archetype of the perfect king, and Merlin, the true representative of the spiritual authority, were figures then considered to represent the Two Powers which tried to establish, or re-establish, order in the world by means of chivalry, in full flower at that time, and above all by the "heavenly chivalry" of which stories of the Grail spoke, and which was realised concretely with the Order of the Templars. That at this time there was a special activity of the spiritual authority at the loftiest level is proved by the fact that it was then that the famous Prester John manifested himself through letters sent jointly to Manuel Comnene and Frederick II.

But, of course, the fundamental element that entered into the composition of the French monarchy is that of Christianity, and with it the Hebraic element from which it is inseparable, for Christian royalty generally, as we have seen, prolongs that of the

Hebrews. This is especially true of Frankish and French royalty. On the facade of the cathedral at Reims, the coronation cathedral—there are symmetrically sculpted scenes of the baptism of Clovis, the coronation of David by Samuel, and the history of Solomon. Moreover, the facades of almost all the great cathedrals offer the "gallery of kings", showing the Davidic ancestry of the kings of France. We are not unaware that certain historians, although they are Catholics and monarchists, refuse to recognise this Hebraic ancestry in the name of historical criticism. It goes without saying that in taking this position they miss the point entirely, for it is not a question of claiming a physical ancestry but a *spiritual filiation*, precisely, which, as we shall see, is irrecusable. But the persons of whom we speak do not seem to know the exact significance of the "symbolic genealogies" and their role in the rituals.[1] Again, that is just one of their least serious errors which, indeed, sometimes affect directly the very nature of the royalty they claim to defend and promote. For it is to be completely unaware of its true nature to see in the institution of royalty merely one kind of political regime among others, even if it is deemed to be the best or even the only good one, or if the role of the prince were reduced to that of promoting an intelligent government and a rational, positive and realistic administration, as opposed to regimes that are based on nebulous ideologies. The royalty of the princes of the House of France, above all in the Middle Ages, but also even in the period known as the Ancien Regime, was distinguished from all straightforward political regimes, however humanly excellent, by its suprahuman dimension, which gave its spirit and its activity a radically different orientation and an infinitely vaster scope. And as we have already mentioned, this supra-human dimension in turn attaches it, with all its specific features, to the traditional and sacred conception of royalty.

And the principal feature of this royalty is its divine character. The prince exercises his power solely by heavenly mandate. The

---

1. Another aspect of the Hebrew legacy passed to France is constituted by the fact that the Angel of this country is St. Michael, which precisely was the Angel of Israel.

most significant text in this respect is the celebrated passage in the discourse of Joan of Arc to the Dauphin: "Noble Dauphin, I have come sent by God to help thee, to help thee and thy kingdom. The *King of Heaven* informs thee through me that thou art to be consecrated and crowned in the city of Reims, and that thou shalt be His lieutenant, that He is the true King of France" (17th July, 1429). A more explicit statement cannot be imagined; but, let us hasten to add, Joan did no more than to recall, at a moment when all seemed to forget it, the mission with which all previous kings had been invested. That is why Charles V said, praying on his deathbed, "My sweet Savior and Redeemer... Thou who hast instituted me as thy *vicar* in the government of France..." *Vicarius Dei*, the title already appears in Suger, and we have also seen that it goes back to the origins of Christian royalty, for it pertained to the emperor of Byzantium. Moreover, it is made official, so to speak, by the ritual of coronation, which employs this title several times. The "mandate of Heaven" makes it possible to understand what the "divine right" of the king really signified, namely, none other than the divine origin of his power. The Estates-General of 1614 proposed, supported unanimously by the Third Estate, that the "divine right" of the king be a "fundamental law of the realm".[2] But it had already always been one.

The "mandate of heaven" confers upon the very person of the king a sacred, even divine, character. It is again Suger who says, in his *Life of Louis VI*, that the king, "vicar of God, realized the image of God in his person and gave it life.... The king bears within himself the living image of God." This was echoed by Bodin in the sixteenth century: "The king is the image of God on earth,"[3] an assertion accepted by the Sorbonne and by Parliament. The king would even come to be told: "The seat of

---

2. Although it is true that this was with the refusal to recognise the superior right of the spiritual authority, which was a grave deviation. In contrast, in the 12th century Vincent de Beauvais specified that the "divine right" was transmitted by the Church, (*Speculum doctrinale*, 7, 31-32), which meant that the Church retained control in principle.

3. Bodin, *Les six Livres*, (1583).

Thy Majesty represents the throne of the living God to us...The orders of the kingdom render you honor and respect as to a *visible divinity*."[4] This expression is close to that of *theos epiphanes*, by which the Hellenistic kings were greeted. Hyperbole of the flatterer, some will say; but that is in no wise the case, for these words, rightly considered, say nothing different than those of Hugues de Fleury in the Middle Ages: "The king symbolizes in the kingdom the image of the Father." But the "image of the Father" is Christ, and the ritual of coronation does not hesitate to tell the prince that he "bears the name and occupies the place of Jesus Christ Saviour".[5] This is echoed by Peter of Blois in the twelfth century: "The king is holy, he is the Christ of the Lord."

These affirmations may be astonishing today; they are nonetheless in the direct line of the universal monarchic tradition as we have seen, and moreover, they are absolutely not incompatible with Christian and Catholic theology, for they do not intend to designate a total and substantial incarnation of the divinity in the royal person, but what could be termed a *functional incarnation*; it is the function of the King of the World, the Christ, who, in order to act, incarnates in the human person, who, in turn, serves as an instrument.

And since Christ is also the Priest *in divinis*, the king will also be in a certain manner a king-priest. "The kings of France," writes A. Duchesne "were never considered lay persons, but rather adorned with the priesthood and royalty conjointly."[6] And it is also said, in the *Remonstrance au Roy Charles VII pour la Réformation du Royaume*: "To us, my sovereign Lord, thou art not a mere lay person, but an ecclesiastic prelate." This is echoed by Juvenal des Ursins in his *Epistle* to the same prince: "The king is a prelate." In France we meet again with the imperial conception of the era of Constantine: the prince is a bishop, "the bishop of the exterior". He is "the common bishop of France", said La Roche-Flavin in the seventeenth century, and a decision of the

---

4. Speech of the Solicitor-General Omer Talon to Parliament (18th May, 1643).

5. Prayer of the placing of the crown (*Ordo of Mainz*).

6. André Duchesne, *Antiquitez*, (1609).

Council of 1766 speaks of the "right that gives the sovereign the quality of bishop of the exterior, a right that the Church itself has often invoked." "The king is at once monarch and priest," said Nicholas de Camanges in 1613, in perfect conformity with mediaeval tradition: "All power comes from God," wrote Gerson, "and this occurs more especially in the royal power of the King of France than in any other thing...for, when St. Remigius baptised Clovis as the first Christian king, he anointed him with the Holy Ampulla, sent by miracle, and consecrated him with the sign of royal power and as a priestly or pontifical dignity.[7] The same language is met with in the Estates-General of 1484. Finally, the coronation ritual speaks in the same sense; in placing the crown on the king, the archbishop utters a prayer during the course of which is said: "Thou must know that thanks to it (the crown) *thou sharest in our ministry.* In the inward affairs, we are the pastors and the directors of souls; thou, in the outward affairs, art the true servant of God, the intrepid defender of the Church of Christ against all its enemies and of the kingdom which God hath entrusted to thee." To tell the truth, in many circumstances the priestly character of the king was not limited to that. Robert the Pious, for example, celebrated councils at the head of his clergy—as did Charlemagne and the emperor of Byzantium—and argued against heretics; the first Capets blessed their subjects and gave them absolution, if we are to believe the *Song of Roland* (v. 337-345); and Philip Augustus did the same at Bouvines.

Let us also recall certain ecclesiastic privileges that were granted to the king: to sit in the choir, to have direct access to the altar, to receive the kiss of peace, to be censed by the deacon, to take communion with the two species, and to participate in the service of the altar during the offertory. But that was not what was most important: the more decisive signs of the priestly character of royalty are the coronation vestments and, above all, the anointing on the head with Holy Chrism, which is the rite of consecration of a bishop. We shall study these two points when

---

7. Gerson, *Harangue faite au nom de l'Université de Paris devant le roy Charles VI*, (1405).

we come to speak of the coronation ceremony. From this it can be seen that the priestly character is proper to the royal function itself, for it is conferred by an *episcopal* anointing. Consequently, the royal function is priestly in and of itself in a certain manner, which is easy to understand since, once again, the two functions, the priestly and the royal, are unified in the King of the World, as we have explained previously. This is the reason, we repeat, that at the beginning of our humanity the earthly king also exercised, in addition to the royal function, all the priestly functions. Subsequently both functions were distinguished and entrusted to different persons, but the distinction was never a separation, which moreover is impossible; there has always be a trace, more or less important according to case, of royalty in the priest and of priesthood in the king, as always occurs when a bi-unity divides to give rise to a duality; thus, in the human person, the man always has something of the woman, and conversely, so that in both there exists the reflection of the primordial androgyne. Hence, the temporal power of the king is by nature partly priestly, simply because it is inherently sacred and, as such, it cannot be alien to the priesthood, which is none other than the function of "giving" the "sacred", for that is the very etymology of the word: *sacer* and *dos*.[8] Therefore, the priesthood of the king is not an element superadded or conceded to his proper role, but rather is inherent to royalty itself, which is easily understood, since the Christian king receives his power from Christ the King who is inseparable from Christ the Priest. The modern mind may perhaps have difficulty in grasping this state of things, because the man of today tends to imagine that political power is a purely lay matter. Such is not the case, and is quite the contrary. This is a point that must never be lost sight of.

The sacredness inherent in the royal function is manifested in the enunciation of its very object, which is essentially to secure justice, peace and abundance for men. Now, who would seriously claim that these goods can be granted to men without their obtaining them from God's benevolence? True justice, true

---

8. Likewise, in Greek, the priest is termed *hiereus*, that is to say, "maker of the sacred" (*hieros*).

peace, and an abundance of goods that is not artificial, are realized solely by conformity with the divine Law. There is no difficulty in acknowledging this truth; except that for the most part this divine Law is considered only in its *moral* aspect, which is very important, certainly, but is not the only one. The tendency to consider only the moral aspect in the behavior of men and societies is a characteristic tendency of the modern mentality, which is narrowly dominated by the *individualism* that has created a split, not only between the individual and his fellows, but also between men and the world, the universe, nature. Now, the divine Law, as we have already said, but bears repeating, encompasses all that is created, and if in consequence human action is to be truly correct and beneficial, it must be included in the total mechanism of nature so as to conform fully to the divine Law in all its aspects. That is why, in traditional societies all aspects of life, however humble, are in a sense placed "in resonance" with the universe by the mediation of symbols.[9] The same occurs *a fortiori* for the most important acts, which are divine worship and the governing of men.

COSMIC ASPECT · The only way, therefore, to understand Western royalty, and the French royalty that is our present subject, is to consider it in its cosmic aspect, which is fundamental to it, exactly as was the case with the other varieties of Christian monarchy that were the Byzantine Empire and the Holy Roman Empire.

Constantine Porphyrogenitus was perfectly aware of the planetary harmony that the imperial government had to offer when he said: "The imperial realm must resemble the harmony and motion that the Creator hath given to this universe"; and this is something that Giles of Rome repeats exactly, as regards its basis: "What we see in the order and governing of the universe, we must realize in the government of the State."

In and by the sacred king the heavenly government is incarnate, is rendered present on earth. Social structure imitates the structure of heaven; it offers itself as a series of concentric circles

---

9. We have made a first approximation to this in our *Métiers de Dieu*, Paris, 1975.

around the central point, the king, from the most outward circles constituted by the least specified levels of the population,
passing through the qualified groups, the guilds, up to the superior groups, the knights and clergy and the Royal Court. It
is a static structure that is enlivened in accordance with a dynamism similar to that of heavens: everything revolves around the
king, like the planets around the sun—and what comes to mind
is the passage from Plato that shows us the celestial choir revolving around the gods[10]—the dynamism of the cycle of the zodiac
marking time, the "moving image of eternity".[11] If we evoke the
zodiac it is because its symbolism, as will be seen, plays a part in
the ritual of coronation. It has in any case a direct relationship
with a function of the king, which is to hallow time through the
observing of the liturgical cycle and of the feasts which, as is
known, correspond to the movement of the sun in the zodiac.
From this point of view human society is modelled on the order
of the world, which is circular in relation to space, and cyclical in
relation to time. Much could be said concerning the role of the
liturgy in the structuring of mediaeval society, of which it was,
as it were, the "respiration", and in which the prince participated
actively. And in this everyone imitated him: it suffices to recall
the extensive use in all social classes of the breviary, the *Book of
Hours*, which is basically structured according to the daily and
annual cycles. In a word, thanks to the influence of the king,
united, moreover, to that of the clergy, the community placed
itself in harmony with the cosmic order and reflected the divine
order. It should be well understood, in fact, that the order of the
visible world is the "mediator" which must be passed through—
above all in the domain of action—in order to grasp the divine
order, of which it is the first and most magnificent reflection:
"The heavens shew forth the glory of God," sings the Psalmist.

In sacred royalty, a royalty of evident cosmic nature, the sovereign is a "universal king"—in the sense that we have already
defined several times, that is to say, as "God's lieutenant"—the
manifestation of He who is truly the universal King, the King

---

10. Plato, *Phaedrus* 246 E; 147 A; 248 A & C; 249 C.

11. Plato, *Timaeus* 37 D.

of the World. In the Middle Ages the king of France was a "universal king" to the extent, precisely, that he makes prevail in his kingdom the order that the heavenly King of kings makes prevail in the Universe. Thus, he can realize the *righteousness* and the *peace* which, as will now be better understood, are rooted in a total *wisdom*, embracing all creation. A magnificent prayer, pronounced by the archbishop prior to the anointing of the king, asks God to enrich the prince with the "the gift of piety" and "the grace of the truth"; to give him "wisdom together with the rule of discipline"; that he may be seen directing the ways of the people in peace and wisdom united"; that henceforth he may nourish, teach, safeguard and instruct the Church of the entire realm and the peoples who depend on it; that through faith and peace he may "establish and govern in communion with the summit of the Fatherly glory". The king is master of wisdom, for he incarnates the celestial truth that regulates the world and realizes the "summit of the Fatherly glory"; an astonishing formula which places him at God's level; his act is an imitation of God the Father because, *like* God the Father, he governs in accordance with His Law.

By his wisdom the king knows the Law, the harmony of creation; by his power—issuing by virtue of the coronation from that of God—his wisdom acts in its application to society, thereby realizing *justice* in the broadest sense, which is a reflection of *justness*, a fundamental attribute of the Creator. Thus, he also realizes *peace*, which is not merely the absence of war, but also and above all the *harmony* of the social body. Hallowing this body by his action, inspired by God's action, he establishes, or re-establishes, the right hierarchic relationships between things and beings, that is to say *order* in the deepest sense; for peace, St. Augustine tells us, is the "tranquility of order", the reflection of the tranquil splendor of the celestial spheres.

If in this manner the king is he who maintains the harmony of the community, integrating it with cosmic life, and who maintains an order established on justice against attacks from the forces of chaos, assuring the equilibrium of the community by its inclusion in nature, it will not surprise us to know that the sovereign also assures the right functioning of nature itself, from which ensue several aspects of his function that modern minds, once again, have certain difficulties in understanding or even acknowledging; we refer to the role pertaining to the king in the maintaining of abundance and the health of the people.

We have seen, from examples cited during the course of our exposition, that in all sacred monarchies the sovereign was considered responsible for the harvests, for the fertility of the soil, and that in some places it was considered that it was he himself who, according to need, "made rain and good weather", thanks to the appropriate rites. The Christian king no longer executes such rites, but it is certain that, as regulator and distributor of the goods of nature, he exercises a beneficent influence on the fertility of the earth. A canon attributed to St. Patrick describes in this way the blessings that a good king offers his people: "Good weather, calm seas, abundant harvests and trees laden with fruit" (conversely, during the reign of a bad king, there is only scarcity, sterile cows, rotting fruit, lack of grain).[12] This role of the prince is also confirmed by the ritual of coronation—which, as we have seen, attributes great importance to him—if we are to judge by the extension of the prayer pronounced by the archbishop and is expressed thus:

> May Almighty God give the dew of heaven and the fatness of the earth, as well as abundance of wheat, wine and oil.... May Almighty God bless thee with the blessings of high heaven, of mountains and hills, and with the blessings of the lower abyss, of the breasts, of grapes and apples.... May the blessings of the Ancient Father, Abraham, Isaac and Jacob be the strength of the prince; receive the works of his hands; may his land, by Thy blessing, be filled with apples, with the fruit of heaven, with dew, and may the inner abyss be filled with the fruit of the sun and the moon, and may the peak of the ancient mountains be filled with the apples of the eternal hills, with the wheats of the earth and its fullness.

---

12. Cited by Frazer in *The Golden Bough*, abridged ed., pp. 83 & 84.

In this prayer one will have recognized the Biblical expressions drawn from Psalm 72 that we cited when we spoke of the Hebraic king.[13] Let us add once more that in the course of the coronation mass, at the time of the offertory, the king takes a cup of wine, a loaf of silver, a loaf of gold, and a bag containing thirteen gold coins to the altar; that is to say, symbols of the fruits of the earth—bread and wine—and the riches of abundance in general—the gold coins, by which it is shown that he is responsible for prosperity.[14]

This dominion of the king over the forces of nature appeared also in his power of healing. This special gift was sufficiently spectacular to foster a multitude of studies of the kings of France by the most diverse historians and to give rise to impassioned controversies between those who accepted the reality of the cures brought about and those who denied them. The cures, in fact, were quite real, something which for us is not at all extraordinary, given the nature of sacred royalty. "The king is holy (as possessor of royalty, not necessarily as an individual); he is the Christ of the Lord. Not in vain has he received the sacrament of anointing, the efficacy of which, if by chance someone were unaware of it or would doubt it, would be amply demonstrated by the disappearance of that plague which attacks the grain and by the curing of scrofula,"[15] says Peter of Blois, and he is quite right in relating the gift of healing to the royal anointing and in speaking of the "Christ of the Lord". In fact, it is the participation in the prerogatives of Christ which is the necessary explanation for this gift. We know to what extent Christ appears in the Gospels as the divine physician and the immense number of healings that he performed during his earthly life.[16] Let us point out in this connection that Jesus accomplished the healings by a

---

13. See Chapter IV, p. 109.

14. Gold and silver—from which the two breads are made—relate respectively to the sun and the moon, and are the two "emitters" of the fertilising powers of the sun.

15. Letter of P. de Blois (PL 207-440 D).

16. See the chapter dedicated to "Christ physician" in our book previously mentioned, *Les Métiers de Dieu*.

force that emanated from Him; thus, touched by surprise by the woman having a flow of blood, He said: "Someone has touched me, for I perceive that power has gone out from me" (Luke: 45-46). This passage from the New Testament can be related to the story by St. Gelasisus, who tells that in all the places where the king passed, the people would crowd together, and when they managed to touch his mule or his clothing or something of his, they lowered their hands to their faces with such devotion as if they had touched a reliquary. It is important to note that the cures brought about by the king of France were not what are called "miracles" as the saints perform, but a common and regular activity, for the king did not cure only the day after the coronation, but in an habitual manner during his entire reign. That is the proof that the gift of healing in him pertained simply to the royal function. However, the exercise of this gift was accomplished *ritually*: the king wore a dalmatic under the royal mantle and kept his head bare; he traced the figure of the cross on the face of the infirm from the forehead to the chin and from cheek to cheek, then touched the wounds saying: "God heals thee, the king touches thee." Did he secretly utter other formulae? The question has to be asked once we know through Yves de Saint Denis that, on his deathbed, Philip the Fair *secretly* taught his son how to touch the sick and the holy words that he should utter. For if it were a question only of the words and gestures we have just mentioned, then why did he *secretly* teach the way to proceed? Be that as it may, let us say, to bring this matter to a conclusion, that the gift of healing, like the gift of bringing fertility to the soil, is a totally privileged characteristic of sacred royalties, and that it is easy to explain these gifts, showing that they are merely particular aspects of that more general power, conferred upon the prince by the coronation, of harnessing spiritual forces and, at the same time, the cosmic forces that act in nature, so as to direct them for the greater good of men; for, in the perspective of a traditional society, material goods, food or health, are always considered as means of influencing, through the body, the total harmony of the being. And, to be sure, these particular gifts did not exempt the sovereign from promoting agriculture by ordinary means, nor of overseeing the health of his subjects by favoring medicine and creating hospitals, but they were visible signs of all of the blessings that descend through the king to the country, and which are necessary for the full efficacy of normal means of action.

SOLAR SYMBOLISM · For—and this has to be emphasised—the king is not *above all* an administrator, nor even a politician, but rather a man *functionally* elevated to the level of a cosmic and spiritual being, who spreads over his surroundings the vivifying energies proceeding from heaven. For this reason, the king is almost everywhere compared to the sun, the light and heat of which are the indispensable agents of life. In the same way, the king, filled by the rite of coronation with the divine Light and the creative Fire, projects on his kingdom an illuminating solar gaze, which is the true source and principle of his rule. It was said that the pharaoh possessed the fourteen *kaou* (subtle bodies) of the solar system, that is to say, the total *ka* of the sun, and that he was the image of the solar god, Ra, in his kingdom. In Assyria, the king Adad was entitled *shamsi*, that is to say "the solar". The sun was always considered to be the symbol of divinity, as one of its most impressive manifestations; the sun, writes Plato, "the image of the Supreme Good (= God) manifesting in the sphere of visible things".[17] The sun is the source of light and of life; its rays represent the heavenly spiritual influences received by the earth; it is at the centre of the sky as the heart is at the centre of the being; in India, it is the Heart of the world, the abode of Purusha and of Brahma. The Orpheans, for their part, saw in it, and rightly so, the Intelligence of the world, and a Latin author, Firmicus Maternus, addresses the sun in these terms: "Supremely good, supremely great sun, who occupieth the centre of heaven, intellect and regulator of the world, supreme head and master of all things, who maketh the fires of the other stars last forever, pouring upon them, in the right proportion, the flame of thy own light..."; and after having invoked the other luminaries, says this prayer:

---

17. Plato, *Republic* 508 B-C. See *supra* p. 163ff. concerning the solar symbolism in the case of the emperor of Byzantium.

By the harmony of thy rule, by thy obedience to the judgment of the Supreme God who concedes a perpetual empire to our sovereign Lord Constantine and his sons ... may they reign over our children and the children of our children without interruption throughout an infinity of centuries, so that, having spurned all evil and all affliction, mankind might acquire the benefit of an eternal peace and an eternal felicity.

This text is interesting because it develops exactly the traditional idea that the sun has a relationship with the king in the measure that its vivifying energy and the regularity of its movements are a model for royal activity. The king is at the centre of his reign as the sun is at the centre of the world and is its regulator through the *justice* and *justness* of its acts. The idea, which was already ancient, found no difficulty in being applied to the Christian prince with reference to Christ, who called Himself *sol justitiae* and *sol veritatis*, "sun of righteousness" and "sun of truth".

VERSAILLES · In France there is a last and splendid illustration of this symbolism in the conception and realisation of the Palace at Versailles, the palace of the "Sun King", a title which, in this perspective, takes on a precise and significant meaning quite distinct from that usually attributed to it, in which nothing more is seen than the sign of a trivial desire for glory and power. In reality, something quite different is involved. It has been demonstrated that the Palace of Versailles, with its gardens, is a highly symbolical construction, a palace of the sun and, better yet, a *temple* of the sun.[18]

The entire complex at Versailles is structured in terms of a strict orientation along the North-South and East-West axes, a cross aligned with the cardinal directions, so as to order it in accordance with the passage of time. The axes cross at the centre of the palace at the chamber of the king who, like the sun, is the motionless mover around which all time and space turn.

---

18. A first approach to this is the book of E. Guillou, *Versailles, le Palais du Soleil*, Paris, 1963; but the true explanation is to be found in the film of P. Barba-Nègra, *Versailles, le palais temple du Roi–Soleil*, with dialogue written by J. Phaure.

All the details of the palace itself, as well as of the gardens, are symbols either of time or space. At the Western face of the castle, for example, there are the four seasons and the four stages of life represented by Silenus (Winter), Antinous (Spring), Apollo (Summer), and Bacchus (Autumn). In the rooms of the Grand Appartement, which have paintings on the ceilings, there appear the planets around the sun, the entire park is dominated by Apollo, particularly by the chariot of Apollo, at the beginning of the great Canal, emerging from the waters of the night and looking towards the East. In turn, on the North side, the place of midnight and of the original darkness, we meet with monsters surrounding Neptune. At the centre of this group there is the king in the midst of Time and Space; he maintains the harmonic movement of the elements from the time of creation: directions, elements, stages of life and seasons. On the West side, next to the gardens, the centre is also marked by the presence of the statues of the four great rivers of France, which represent the kingdom and, analogically, the four great rivers of Paradise.

The palace and gardens are constituted in a manner analogous to the circular cities and palaces of the ancient Near East that we have described[19] and which were images of the world, and also recall the *ming-tang*.[20] For the kings, the whole assemblage played the part of a *mandala*, of a model of the world and the kingdom in miniature serving as a support of meditation, so as to place and maintain themselves in harmony with the cosmos. This *mandala* continually structured the royal psyche, putting it in harmony with the forms and the rhythms of the world, themselves symbols of the invisible, capable of linking us to higher realities. To repeat, the visible world serves as mediator for approaching the invisible, as St. Paul declares (*Romans* 1:18).

---

19. See Chapter II, p. 43ff.

20. Let us also mention the palace of the king of Connaught, Ailill, in Ireland; circular like the sky, with seven compartments arranged around a central hearth, and covered by a domed roof, image of the heavenly vault. This palace was a microcosm, a reflection of heaven on earth and a way of communication of the centre with Heaven.

We shall not leave Versailles without saying a word about the splendor and luxury which are—or rather, were—displayed there, since it is an opportunity for an important reflection. We recall statements that still appear in certain books and manuals of history intended for schools, concerning the supposedly enormous cost required to build Versailles and which it is claimed contributed to ruining the country, notwithstanding those serious historians who long ago corrected these gross and not always involuntary errors. But what is important for our subject is not this, but the very existence of this luxury, which some may question regarding its opportuneness or even its legitimacy. We have no hesitation in declaring that it is perfectly legitimate. It is even necessary, and we have already touched on this in Chapter II. In reality, the court of princes must reflect the particular quality that is attached to the "centre" and the "summit", and nothing more appropriately manifests this quality than magnificence. Royal pomp is legitimate because it is the outward sign of the loftiness, grandeur and fruitfulness of this function inasmuch as it emanates from the divine world, the beauty of which must be reflected in the life of the prince, in his palace, his dress, etc., which, incidentally, explains why all princes worthy of the name have promoted the fine arts and literature and have surrounded themselves with poets and artists. Everything about them must be splendid, and like the sun evoked previously, everything must, so to speak, exude a radiant beauty that pours over others like solar light, which Plutarch said, "adorns all things and over all of them pours that potent enchantment that comes from itself".[21]

Pageantry is like the liturgy of sacred authority and a reflection on earth of the heavenly glory of God. Of course, the prince can always practice ascesis and renounce luxury in his private life; pomp is not intended for his private person, but for the *royal personality*, the transcendent personality with which he is covered and which is manifested in his *public life*.

---

21. Plutarch, *Discourse to an Unlearned Prince*, 3-780 A.

Now, the existence of this somewhat dual personality in the king, leads us directly to address the subject of the coronation, which is its source.

CONSECRATION AND CORONATION

To properly situate the matter, it is worth recalling with precision the different elements that enter into play for the accession to the throne. There are three elements: election, inheritance and coronation. The question of the relationships between these three elements would be very simple had it not been complicated by controversies that arose over the basis of power. The normal functioning of these three constitutive elements is clear: the election or inheritance, according to the case, gives the right to power, but its regular transmission, the investiture, is brought about through the coronation. But starting from a certain date, at approximately the beginning of the Renaissance, there appeared in the kings of France the tendency to assert that their power was transmitted by election in the full sense, according to the constitutive law of the kingdom, and by inheritance, so that the prince could reign normally without being crowned, as occurred in cases where the coronation was deferred. Thus, if this opinion were true, it would mean that the coronation was not absolutely necessary, as it would not be that which confers the investiture; its role would be limited to recognising and confirming that all power, including the power to rule, comes from God; the public renewal of the social pact with the nation—that is, the election in the broad sense; and assuring the blessing of heaven on the king.

This thesis is that of the legalists, and it is certain that it increasingly gained ground starting from the date we mention, to the extent of being adopted by a great number of monarchists, including ecclesiastics. We have encountered it in a relatively recent work written by a religious who, moreover, is a fierce defender of royalty. But this thesis is not admissible. In the end, if it is upheld, the power is completely laicized, which is what happened. If, in fact, the coronation is merely a confirmation accompanied by useful benedictions, then little by little it will be discarded. Louis XVI, in order to be crowned, had finally to act with authority to impose his will on his entourage, which insisted on dissuading him.

Let us look at this closely: there is no doubt that a non-sacred ruler, if he recognizes that power in itself belongs only to God, and if he commits himself to follow the religious law, can be accepted and can govern *legally*. But in that case, we are in the presence of a political regime that has nothing to do with sacred royalty, which is something completely distinct from a *legal* government that is more or less accompanied by an ecclesiastic government; and this is because the coronation is something very distinct from a confirmation and a simple benediction. It has not merely a *declarative* value, but a truly *constitutive* one, and it is that, and that alone, that invests regularity and makes a government not merely *legal* but *legitimate,* for it "makes" a sovereign radically different from the one we have just evoked, as will be understood, we trust, from all that has been said since the beginning of this book. Therefore, royalty is not legitimate and is not fully itself except through the coronation. Such is the universal sacred tradition of humanity and such is the official doctrine of Christianity, independently, moreover, of what certain of its ministers may think. We have amply demonstrated this in the preceding.[22] In addition, during the first eight centuries of royalty in France, the princes were recognized and proclaimed kings only after the day of the coronation; until that moment, as the ancient chronicles used to say, "the king was asleep," an expression charged with meaning which we will examine further ahead. Charles VII, before being crowned, ruled as the *dauphin*, and the entire mission of Joan of Arc demonstrates marvelously the prime importance of the coronation. Louis VII, for his part, considered that the coronation was constitutive of the monar-

---

22. See Chapter IV, p. 137ff. For example, it is what archbishop Hincmar recalled to Charles the Bald in his *De regis persona*, and to Carloman in his *De ordine palatii*; royalty is a religious institution; the king holds his power from God; to have possession of it, it must be delegated to him by the bishops through the coronation.

chy, in accordance with the doctrine of the Church, and set his ceremonial by means of a charter.[23]

The legitimacy of the kings of France takes on a special quality in the sense that it is based on a tradition going back to an extraordinary manifestation and a true celestial investiture historically verifiable: we refer, of course, to the coronation of Clovis and to the miracle of the Holy Ampulla, for both things are indissolubly tied together. These facts must be insisted upon, for they put us in the presence of a particularly impressive and tangible example of the "heavenly mandate", since the Divine Power intervened here in a miraculous and visible fashion. Following his baptism, Clovis was crowned, and crowned with an oil that came from heaven. The facts are indisputable; they were solemnly affirmed in the *Testimony of Saint Remigius* by the archbishop himself, and supported by an impressive series of authorities: St. Avit, a contemporary of St. Remigius, Gregory of Tours, the Archbishop Hincmar of Reims, St. Thomas Aquinas, Gerson, Popes Sylvester II, Urban II and Innocent II, as well as by the continued attitude of all the popes who consider the king of France superior to all the other kings, precisely because of his heavenly privilege; this, in particular, is affirmed by a decree of 1558 from the Republic of Venice. It is only in the seventeenth century that there began to appear fault-finders doubting the authenticity of the *Testament*, the coronation of Clovis and the miracle of the Holy Ampulla; among them, a Calvinist, Jean de Serre, the Spaniard Chifflet, and unfortunately it was assumed by the Jesuits, whose behavior was to be so odious until the reign of Louis XV.[24] But from the seventeenth century, Dom Mabillon, who is recognized by all for his unfailing historical knowledge, defended the authenticity of the *Testament*, which had been dem-

---

23. *Gallia christiana*, v. 10, p. 48 ff.

24. To support their polemic, the Jesuits did not hesitate to employ the most dishonest procedures. One of them defended his position basing himself on an incomplete text of the Testament of St. Remigius, and they even went so far as to suppress the pages where the Holy Ampulla is spoken of in books dealing with French history. Thus, in the volume of *De Gallorum imperio et philosophia* by Forcadel (1580), possessed by the Jesuits, pages 370-371 were removed for that reason.

onstrated in a definitive and indisputable fashion by the canon Dessailly.[25] Nevertheless, the detractors of the seventeenth century have a posterity that continues to live in numerous historians who view history exclusively from a positivist standpoint and who out of principle deny the reality of higher supernatural phenomena. This critical attitude often hides one that is political in nature: they deny the testimonies we are speaking of because supernatural facts are denied, and at the same time the supernatural facts are denied because sacred royalty is denied. The same reason makes the same people deny the reality—which is duly established nonetheless—of the healing of scrofulas. Such conduct is only surprising when "believers", and especially ecclesiastics, adopt it; for if we deny the celestial intervention that took place with Clovis, why not also deny the one that marked the career of Joan of Arc, the miracles of the saints and, in the last analysis, those of Christ Himself? And what is more, this is what has taken place, for the supernatural has become indiscernible.

It is no play on words to say that the consecration of kings is a sacrament,[26] the "eighth sacrament", as Renan used to say. In reality it is not the eighth, because when the ritual of consecration was instituted, the official number of sacraments was not determined; it was much later, during the Middle Ages, when the Western Church fixed the number at seven; approximately at the same time, moreover, that it decided no longer to crown the kings with the Holy Chrism, but only with the oil of the catechumens.[27] Nonetheless, the privilege of the Holy Chrism

---

25. Chan. Desailly, *L'authenticité du grand testament de Saint Rémy*, Paris. In this book are to be found all the desirable documents and references pertaining to this subject. The work of Dom Mabillon is found in the *Annales Bénédictines*, v. I.

26. The apparent play on words is made between the word *sacrement* (in English, "sacrament") and *sacre*, which in English is "coronation". (Translator's note)

27. The Eastern Church, in turn, never abandoned the Holy Chrism for the consecration of the kings. Here there is an important question, for it is correct to ask whether a coronation made with the oil of the Catechumens is still a coronation. We do not believe it is. In any case, what is certain and indisputable is that if it is still a coronation, it no longer has anything to do

was not removed from the king of France, and that is a major reason for considering the French coronation a sacrament; for the anointing of the Holy Chrism, which is its fundamental rite, inherited from the Hebraic liturgy, makes it resemble, as a sister, the episcopal coronation. Moreover, it is the reason why the papacy, in wishing to strongly mark off the priesthood from the royalty, transformed the rite of anointing.

Hence the royal coronation is indeed a sacrament, as had always been affirmed previously by the religious authority. One of the greatest popes, for example, St. Gregory, writes concerning the anointing of Saul by Samuel: "Without any doubt, what that anointing signifies is that which we now see in the Holy Church; for he who is raised to the summit of power is anointed outwardly in order that, inwardly, he be fortified by the virtue of the sacrament...Thus, let the head of the king be anointed, for the soul of the ruler needs to be filled with spiritual grace."[28] And this same doctrine is recalled by St. Peter Damian and Rome in a bull for the coronation of Henry III.[29]

In reality, the authentic royal consecration is a development of the sacrament of baptism, the fundamental rite of Christian initiation, which in fact comprises, after immersion in water, a *chrismation*, an anointing on the forehead with the Holy Chrism that consecrates the recipient, and confers upon him the "royal priesthood", in accordance with the words of St. Peter, who tells us that the entire Church is a "kingdom of priests", because the disciples of Christ receive "a royal priesthood" (1 Peter 2:9). This royal priesthood in the faithful "christified" by baptism, is a reflection of Christ Priest and King. Thus this priesthood is the patrimony of all those who have been baptised; except that for the simple faithful, as we have said, it is solely for personal realisation. Royal priesthood has to be specified in view of the particular necessities of the community, considered firstly as a spiritual society and secondly as a civil society; he who receives a

---

with the true coronation which conforms to the Judeo-Christian tradition.

28. St. Gregory the Great, *In prim. Reg. expositiones*, 4,5 (PL 79, 278).

29. St. Peter Damian, *Sermo de dedic. eccl.*

ministerial function in view of the spiritual society, also receives the priestly ordination in order to exercise it; the designated head of the civil society receives the royal consecration. What both consecrations do is to validate, so to speak, and reinforce in the recipient one of the two attributes represented by "royal priesthood".

This resemblance between baptism and coronation makes us understand a very important aspect of the latter: its sacrificial aspect. The consecration is based on the *sacrifice*, which must be understood according to the two meanings of the word, namely, immolation and making holy (*sacer facere*). In baptism, the sacrificial aspect is evident: the "old man" dies with Christ in order to be reborn as a "new man" with Christ, as in the teaching of St. Paul:

> Know ye not, that so many of us as were baptised into Jesus Christ were baptised into his death? Therefore we are buried with him by baptism into death: that like as Christ was raised up from the dead by the glory of the Father, even so we also should walk in newness of life. For if we have been planted together in the likeness of his death, we shall be also in the likeness of his resurrection (Rom. 6:3-5).

And also, "Buried with him in baptism, wherein also ye are risen with him through the faith of the operation of God, who hath raised him from the dead" (Col. 2:12). It is the triple immersion of the baptised which symbolizes this death by reference to the three days in the tomb and the descent into hell; and the Chrismation corresponds to the resurrection with the gift of the Holy Spirit.

Many readers will have already recognized in baptism the fundamental pattern of all initiation, which is articulated in accordance with the binomial death and resurrection. And this is what we find in the ritual of the royal coronation, which has the aim of making the prince "another man", as Samuel said to Saul: "And the Spirit of the Lord will come upon thee, and thou... shalt be turned into another man" (Sam. 10:6); of transforming the individual man into "true man" in the image of Christ—in

213

this case, that of Christ the King—the prince dies as an individual and is reborn as transcendent Personality endowed with divine attributes, as the *functional incarnation* of Christ in His function as "King of the World". A prayer of the ceremony expressly asks God that the king might obtain "the purity of the New Man descended from heaven", that is, of Christ, who is the "New Adam", so that he might apply on earth the law of creation re-established in its purity. Thus the coronation realises the incarnation of the governing principle of the world, which is in the Divine Word, in order to bring it to human society, to organise it and make it live according to heavenly laws. Human society can, in reality, organise itself and live in that way through the king, for once crowned, he is turned into the *collective soul of his people*; as such, he includes the entire social body in the image of Christ, who includes all men and the universe in the *Corpus mysticum*, so that the social body reflects the mystical body and models itself upon it.

The royal coronation, one of the oldest institutions of humanity, always and everywhere has developed in accordance with a process that is almost identical in its essential elements, for everywhere it can be reduced to the basic paradigm of "death and resurrection". These elements are, in the first place, a purification in the widest sense, that is, a symbolic "death" of the "old man", and realised according to diverse procedures: lustration with water, immersion, seclusion in an isolated place, and so on; the second element, corresponding to "resurrection" or the creation of the "new man", consists frequently in an anointing with oil or any other substance that serves as a vehicle for the celestial influence that descends on the recipient. An anointing with oil was general in all the ancient Middle East; in India, it is done with a mixture of butter, honey and water; in Mexico, an oil extracted from the juice of Indian rubber was used. Around these two essential acts, there developed in different cultures more or less secondary rites, some of which had the same function as the first, and others that constituted new elements, yet important enough to be met with almost everywhere; these would be the collation of the insignia of power—that is, the crown and the enthronement—the homage of the great and of the people, and the bestowing of the new name.

The ceremonial is developed like a liturgy—which it is in fact—and in the manner of a sacred representation, the personages of which are, as with all liturgies, the priest and the prince, and men of high rank who represent all of the people.

In the ritual practiced in France, since in principle the coronation takes place on a Sunday, there is a "vigil" of a liturgical type on the Saturday, with a vigil on the part of the prince. The ceremony itself, on the Sunday, includes successively: the taking of the oath, the divesting of clothing, the anointing, the taking of the royal apparel, the collation of the insignia of power, the coronation, the enthronement, and the homage.[30]

The importance of the vigil must not be underestimated, for it is an integral part of the coronation. After Complines on Saturday, the Cathedral at Reims is closed and the king arrives to make his vigil. It is a rite taken from knighthood, which is normal, since the king is first among the knights. It is above all the question of an important preliminary phase of the consecration; it is a first form—there will be others—of the rite of "death", the first phase of the royal initiation. It is a form of return to the origin, necessary in order to bring about the rebirth of the "new man". The framework concurs, for it is night and the cathedral is in semi-darkness. The ambiance corresponds to this stage of the process, the return to the origin. The king, says the ritual, "comes to pray there"; not ordinary prayer, but in the sense of the spiritual treatises, that is, meditation. The future king—alone, in silence, at night, ensconced in the temple, the beneficent emanations of which penetrate him—is faced with himself and, in this propitious ambiance, can begin to "strip" himself.[31]

---

30. Here we follow the ritual used with Louis VII in the French version of Jean du Tillet. This ritual was published by Christian Jacq and Patrice de la Perriere with the title *Les origines sacrées de la royauté française*, Paris, 1982, with a rich commentary extracted from the best sources, which we have consulted.

31. Much could be said concerning the significance of the Cathedral of Reims, especially conceived for the coronation, to which almost all of its symbolism refers. This appears magnificently in the film of P. Barba Nègra,

After the vigil, the prince enters the episcopal palace, where a cell has been prepared for him to spend the night, for the *sleep* of the king is also part of the ritual. Let us first consider the name of the palace, the *Palace of Tau*: its plan and name evoke the sacrificial cross of the coronation rite. Next, let us consider this *sleep*, which more than any other sleep is the image of death. We have proof of this in the scene that takes place Sunday morning. At dawn, after the chanting of the *Prime*, the Bishop of Laon and the Bishop Count de Beauvais go in procession to fetch the king. The first chamber of the king is found closed. The cantor knocks at the door with his staff. A voice behind the door says, "What do you ask for?" "The king," replies the Bishop of Laon. "The king is asleep," says the voice. They knock once again, ask the same question, and get the same response. The third time, the bishop says, "We ask for (So-and-So) ... whom God hath given us as king." Then the doors open. The prelates read a prayer, and then *raise* the king and conduct him in procession to the church.

We are faced here with a rite that certainly does not have a liturgical origin. The triple knocking at the door and the three series of responses led some to relate this to the rite of the procession on Palm Sunday, during the course of which the celebrant, who has left the church and has shut its doors, returns to it and calls three times before they are re-opened to him. But the meaning of the two rites is totally different. That of Palm Sunday evokes the entry of Jesus into Jerusalem, and symbolically the entry into the heavenly Jerusalem, that is, Paradise. The rite of raising the king, consequently, has nothing to do with that ceremony. One has rather to think of settings met with in certain stories originating in initiatory rituals, in the course of which a question is asked and repeated three times, for example in the tale of *Sleeping Beauty*, which is not without relationship with our text. And perhaps, even more, one has to think of the passage in the Grail stories—we spoke earlier of their influence on the conception of French monarchy—where the wounded King Arthur embarks for the Isle of Avalon, "where the king still lives,

---

Reims cathédrale des sacres, texts by J.P. Bayard, G. de La Place, P. de La Perrière and J. Phaure.

lying on a golden bed". In light of this text the meaning can be grasped not only of the sleep of the king at the Palace of Tau, but also of the scene of his being raised. "The king is asleep," as we have said before, so long as he has not been crowned. The previous king has died, and the dauphin is not yet king; he is asleep, but is "awakened". And it is the bishop, the spiritual authority, who does this, who "calls" him to make him king, to have "Arthur awaken within him", that is, the archetypal king, the royal Personality. And once again we meet with a form of the rite of death parallel to that of the vigil: the sleep of the king is the sleep in the course of which he leaves his individuality to awaken to a new life and a new personality.

The procession coming from the Palace of Tau enters the cathedral; the king goes to the place reserved for him in the choir and the archbishop goes up to the altar. The role of the altar in the ceremony must be emphasised; and it is understood when the symbolism of the altar is recalled: it is the sacrosanct centre of the temple and centre of the world, the lower pole of the *Axis mundi*, by which the earth communicates with heaven.[32] The cathedral altar is really the centre from which descend the divine energies that will bring about the royal consecration; at the same time it is the sign of the sacrificial character of this august rite.

The first act is the taking of the *oath*. At the request of the archbishop, the king, on the Holy Book, swears to ensure justice and defend the Church (for that is the duty of the "kshatriya" in relation to the "brahmin"), maintain the peace and practice mercy. To all this the people respond: *Amen*, as occurred in the assembly of the Hebrew people.[33] The oath is the counterpart of the coronation and, since it includes the participation of the people, what is involved is a real exchange of oaths, because through the *amen*, the people promise fidelity to the king, a promise having a religious character, because in the last analysis it is a promise made to God. The oath is an integral part of the royal consecration, and we also find it more or less in one or another form in

---

32. We have developed this subject at length in our *Symbolisme du temple chrétien* and *Divine Liturgie* (Edit. de la Maisnie).

33. See our *Divine Liturgie*, p. 54 and II Kings, 23.

the other traditions; thus, in ancient Mexico, at the beginning of the ceremony, a high ranking personage would give a speech on the duties of the king, after which the high priest had the king swear that he would maintain the religion, and would be good and mild towards the people. The priest would then proceed to anoint him.

After the oath, the king is taken to the altar, before which he prostrates completely, while the *Te Deum* is sung. This prostration, practiced by the recipient of the priestly and episcopal ordinations, as well as during the reception into a religious order, is a fresh symbol of the "death" of the "old man", the death that precedes his "resurrection" in another personality. In Sweden there existed a much more significant and realistic rite in this respect: the king, after his coronation in Uppsala, would return to enter the cathedral, wearing a mantle of mourning filled with images of death, and before the altar he would lie down in a stone coffin; afterward, he would emerge, in a symbolic resurrection, and take possession of his throne.

Once he had arisen from his prostration, the king undertook another rite of "death": the stripping of his clothing; he would leave his lay clothing, except for a silk shirt, in which openings had been left with a view to the anointing. Over the shirt he would then wear the royal robes. This signifies, says Jean Golein in his *Traité du sacre*, dedicated to Charles V of France, that the king "leaves the worldly state to take up that of the royal Religion".

He receives not only new clothing, but also, as we have said, the other *insignia of power*, also termed the *regalia*: the crown, the sword, the golden spurs, the golden sceptre, the hand of justice, the chausses. But the giving of these insignia is done on two occasions: before and after the anointing. This is due to the fact that, among these insignia some are properly royal, and thus their collation must not be effected until the king has been consecrated, while the others pertain to the knighthood, and can be given before the consecration. At any rate, these *regalia* are all *instruments of the royal office*, which explains that, in all traditions, they are indissolubly linked to the royal consecration, to such a point that in certain countries they can serve as the consecration itself, as we have seen in the case of the emperor of Japan.[34] For that reason as well, they are sometimes considered *talismans* of the prince, for these objects have been turned into "condensers" of beneficent forces. Something of the kind occurred in France, judging by the care with which all the *regalia* were kept in the abbey of St. Denis, mystical centre of French royalty, from where they were taken to Reims with a ceremonial analogous to that which surrounded the arrival of the Holy Ampulla from the church of St. Remigius. Also, at the beginning of the coronation ceremony, the *regalia* were left on the altar to indicate that that is where the power comes from, as Jean Golein also says, and afterward they were blessed separately by the archbishop: a blessing the aim of which was at one and the same time to empty them of all evil influence and to fill them with beneficent forces.

The first insignia given to the king were the chausses, the spurs and the sword, that is, the insignia of the knight. In general, the king had already received the initiation into knighthood; but here it was repeated to reinforce it, in a certain manner, and to show clearly that he had to be the "perfect knight". The Great Chamberlain put special boots on the king, and the Duke of Bourgogne put on his spurs of gold and lapis lazuli, which, moreover, were withdrawn right away; then the archbishop girded the sword about him, then took it off, drew it from its scabbard, and left it on the altar. During the continuation of the ceremony, it was carried, naked and held upright, before the king. These insignia, naturally, have a symbolic meaning: the chausses are the sign of an active personality ready, the commentators tell us, to spread the gospel of peace in accordance with St. Paul's command (Ephes, 6:15). The spurs underscore this symbolism: they are the sign of quickness to accomplish duty; the knight was told that the spurs mean: "thou hast set thy heart on serving God thy whole age (life)."[35] The symbolism of the sword is much richer and polyvalent; it is a military attribute, of

---

34. Cf. Chapter I, p. 17.

35. *Ordine de chevalerie* (13th century).

course, but with a double meaning: both destroyer and builder; destroyer of injustice and builder of justice. *Gladius legis custos.* Of human *justice*, for the sword is above all the sign of divine *righteousness*, the principle of human justice. The sword is the instrument of interior warfare; Christ brought it (Matt. 10:34) to conquer with knowledge and destroy ignorance, on the one hand, and to separate imperfections from qualities, on the other hand: for as St. Paul says, "The word of God is living and powerful, and sharper than any two-edged sword, piercing even to the division of soul and spirit, and of joints and marrow, and is a discerner of the thoughts and intents of the heart" (Heb. 4:12). The sword is Speech, the lightning of the Word, which in effect appears in the Apocalypse, a two-edged sword in the mouth (= organ of speech) (Rev. 1:16, 19:15). It shines like lightning and at the same time it "thunders". The sword also symbolises the *Axis* of the world: its two edges signify the universal polarity, which is resolved in equilibrium in the axis which it itself constitutes. That is why the gesture of the Constable who carries the naked sword before the king is enormously significant: the king, like the sword, is situated at the centre of the world, at the axis which joins the earth to heaven and by which he communicates with the power above, of which he is the possessor here below.[36] It is a particularly eloquent symbol of his mission: by his axial position, the king commands the diverse or contradictory elements of his kingdom to make them into a harmony that accords with universal order, which is fundamentally the operation which produces *justice* and *peace*, the two attributes that define the royal mission.

The return of the sword ends the first, and in a sense, preparatory, part of the ceremony. And here we come to its very heart, which is the rite of anointing. The archbishop prepares by mixing some miraculous and heavenly oil of the Holy Ampulla with the Holy Chrism, the significance of which is thus modified.[37]

---

36. The reader will be able to relate what we say here with that we have said concerning the emperor of China (*supra*, Chapter II, p. 47ff.).

37. The Holy Ampulla has been brought in the morning from the Church of St. Remigius, carried by the Abbot and escorted by barons.

Then, after three long prayers, he anoints the king in *seven* places on the body: first on the head, and then on the breast, between the shoulders, on the shoulders, and on the joints of the arms; in certain forms of the ritual there was added an anointing on the palms of the hands, which brought the total number to *nine*. While anointing, he pronounces the formula: "I anoint thee with holy oil to make thee king, in the name of the Father, of the Son, and of the Holy Spirit." The terms of the prayers that accompany the anointing very clearly express their meaning; in particular, the words of Samuel to Saul: "Thou shalt be turned into another man," specifying the following idea: "Lord, enclose the hands of Thy servant with the purity of the new Man descended from heaven."

The Holy Chrism is the vehicle of the spiritual influence that descends on the recipient, and it is the very power of the Holy Spirit. "The Chrism," says Hugh of St. Victor, "is made of oil and balsam; the oil designates the infusion of grace; the balsam, the odour of good reputation...[the anointing of the Chrism] is the principal anointing, for it is principally that which gives the Paraclete."[38] The explanation of the role of Holy Chrism is further deepened by St. Cyril of Jerusalem, who compares the Chrism to the Eucharist and assures that it operates by means of the presence of the Divinity: "Just as, after the epiclesis of the Holy Spirit, the bread of the Eucharist is no longer ordinary bread, but the body of Jesus Christ, so too, the holy balsam is no longer something simple or, if you prefer, profane, but a gift of Jesus Christ and the Holy Spirit, a gift made efficacious by the presence of the Divinity."[39]

Oil is the element that is perfectly adapted to signify the descent of grace into man. It is a "solar" element that illumines and warms, so that it symbolises the spiritual Fire and the spiritual Light that is the Holy Spirit.

It is important, moreover, to consider the places of the body on which the royal anointing is performed. These places correspond most certainly to "points" of the subtle organism; at any

---

38. Hugh of St. Victor, *De Sacramentis*, 2.7.1; 2.15.1.

39. St. Cyril of Jerusalem, *Catecheses mystagogicae.*

rate, as regards the two main anointings: on the top of the head
and on the breast; anointings, moreover, that are also done at
baptism. The anointing on the head is the most important, in a
certain sense, if we refer back to the Hebrew tradition, in which,
moreover, it is the sole anointing, just as in Assyria and Canaan;[40]
but it is inseparable from the second one, on the breast. In fact,
if we recall the plan of the subtle organism, we note that the
anointing on the head is made on the crown *chakra* or fontanelle, called in India the *sahasrara padma* or "thousand-petalled
lotus", the place which on a child is marked by the fontanelle,
and which is the passage by which the soul "descends" into the
body and from where it "leaves" to escape bodily limitations and
rise to the higher states. The *tonsure* of clerics outwardly marks
this "crown of the head", and it is the reason for which, in the
Byzantine rite of baptism, after the anointing of Holy Chrism
on this place, the priest makes a small tonsure, since each of
the faithful also participates in the priesthood. It is evident that
both rites, the anointing and the tonsure, have the aim of "opening" this place on the head to the spiritual influence that descends on the baptised or, in the case at hand, on the king. But
this "point" on the head has an intimate relationship with that
of the breast, which is the *chakra* of the *heart* (*chakra anahata*),
for the heart is the spiritual centre of man, just as it is his physical centre. Also, the vertical that descends from the head to the
heart, from the crown chakra to the chakra of the heart, is the
trajectory of contemplation, in the Hindu tradition as well as in
Byzantine Hesychasm. What is involved is to "make the mind
descend into the heart" in order to unite the mind to the heart;
when the union is realised, the crown of the head is "illumined",
which iconography translates by the halo of the saints. That the
royal anointing realises this descent, at least at a certain level, is

---

40. In Assyria, a golden cup filled with oil, from which the high priest
took the oil to anoint the king, was put on the altar in the temple. In the
case of Syria, we have a very interesting document, which is a letter of a
monarch named Addu Nirari, who writes to the pharaoh to remind him
of the day on which he was consecrated, when they poured oil *on his head*
(Knudtzon, *Die El-Amarna Tafeln*, I, 51).

what is clearly said in a certain passage of the prayer uttered by the archbishop: "Thy most holy anointing flows over his head, *descends to the inward, penetrates the depth of his heart*." And we say, "at least at a certain level", for it goes without saying that the crowned king has not, by that fact alone, become a "great saint"; the descent of grace works above all for the benefit of the royal Personality, and it is insofar as he holds the royal *function* of Christ that the king is holy, and not necessarily insofar as he is an individual. In this there is something altogether comparable to the priesthood: the priest is always "holy" inasmuch as he takes on the priesthood of Christ, the priestly *function* of Christ, whatever may be his degree, or even total lack, of personal sanctity. To put things another way, it may be said that anointing aims at giving the king his "immortal body", distinct from his "mortal body", to use the terms of the Middle Ages, which is a way of distinguishing the individual from the transcendent Personality with which he is endowed.

We will encounter this *corpus immortale* in the part of the ceremony that follows the anointing, namely the dressing of the king. The Great Chamberlain dresses the king with the tunic, the dalmatic and the mantle. The significance of this vestiture is quite remarkable for, contrary to the proverb that says that "clothes do not make the man", it is obvious that clothing has a close relationship with the personality, above all with the new personality that can be acquired. We know that in certain cases the spiritual investiture can be accomplished by means of a garment; thus Elijah, before being raised to heaven, transmits his powers to his disciple Elisha, giving him his robe. Upon giving up his lay clothing, the king has "stripped himself of the old man"; upon taking the royal robes, he receives his new personality, the same as the one baptised with his white tunic, the "nuptial robe" of the "heavenly supper"; or even as Enoch, to whom God orders that his earthly clothing be removed at the moment of ascending to heaven and that the clothing of glory be put on him.[41]

---

41. II Enoch 22, 8 ff. The mantle is a chasuble in its ancient form.

The symbolism of the three articles of clothing is very rich. In the first place, they stand in direct relation with the priestly character conferred on the king by the anointing; in effect, they are the attributes of the three degrees of the priesthood: the tunic of the subdeacon, the dalmatic of the deacon, and the mantle of the priesthood.[42] These three items can be seen in a statue of Charles the Bald at St. Denis. The most important of the three is indisputably the mantle, of which we have already spoken in connection with the emperor.

At present, there is no doubt, according to the works of scholars, that the imperial and royal mantle derives from that of the high priest of Israel, which was hyacinth, violet or blue in colour, bordered with pomegranates and bell-flowers. This "ephod" reached almost to the ground and possessed a cosmic symbolism, since it says in the Book of Wisdom, "Upon His long robe the whole world was depicted" (Wisdom 18:24). We have already seen that the mantle of Emperor Henry II had the same significance,[43] likewise that of Otto III, and also that of the King of France. An author of the seventeenth century, Claude Villette, cites the statement of a Parisian canon who says textually, "Formerly the royal cape was cut on the pattern of the heavenly cape, wide and extended in circular fashion like the sky, of azure colour like the sky, brilliant with golden fleur de lis, like the sky covered with lights…[44] The Merovingian Clotaire I wore a dalmatic adorned with silver half moons and a mantle bordered with golden flowers with six petals with circles, that is, the symbols of the moon (silver) and the sun (gold), as a summary of the sky. The mantle given to St. Denis by the wife of Hugo Capet was called *orbis terrarum*, "orb of the universe", the same words, as we have seen, inscribed in the cape of Henry II preserved in

---

42. See, for example, Menin, *Cérémonial d'Alletz* (the coronations of Louis XV and Louis XVI and the regulation of Louis XVII). In England, the king put on the alb with short sleeves, dalmatic, stole and *pallium regale* or chasuble in the form of a cape, which corresponds to the mantle in France.

43. See Chapter V, p. 182.

44. C. Villette, *Les raisons de l'office … des cérémonies du sacre de nos roys de France*, and other works (Rouen, 1638), p. 199.

Bamberg. Quite soon, *fleurs de lis* substituted the signs of the luminaries, which were more explicit, but the blue background was kept, and the flowers continued to symbolize the luminaries in the sky, as can be seen in particular from the text we have just cited.

This cosmic symbolism, as we have said, has a close relationship with the royal function; the mantle is the dome of the sky, the universe in movement, emitter of creative forces in which the king participates and of which he makes use to organize the kingdom in the image of the order of the world. In addition, dressed with this mantle, the king no longer appears as an individual, but is transformed into cosmic man and universal man; or, to express things otherwise, and to use the terms of the Middle Ages, the royal mantle is the visible sign of the *corpus immortale*, which the human entity of the prince has taken on by the holy anointing.

The bestowal of these royal insignias is followed by that of the ring, the sceptre and the hand of justice.

The archbishop places a gold ring on the right ring finger of the king. The ring has multiple meanings; but what is made explicit in the royal consecration is the most obvious one: the ring which serves to unite, to link, is here the sign of a faithful attachment, of a covenant, of a double covenant of the prince and of a veritable hierogamy of the king, realized by the Church with the divinity on the one hand, and with his people considered as a mystical community on the other.[45]

THE SCEPTRE · There is no need to recall extensively that the sceptre is an absolutely universal insignia of power. Inspired by the royal Psalm 110, which sings: "The Lord shall send the rod of thy strength out of Zion: rule thou in the midst of thine enemies," the formula that accompanies the placing of the sceptre in the right hand of the kings is this: "Take the sceptre, insignia

---

45. By its circular form, the ring also symbolises the circle of the universe. In this sense it possessed great value in China, where it was considered that the "jade ring" had its central opening in the vertical axis of Ursa Major and the Pole Star, that is to say, the World Axis. It was an emblem of the emperor, "son of heaven", identified with the Axis.

of royal power, namely the straight rod of the kingdom, rod of virtue, by which thou rulest thyself truly, and, by royal power, defendest from evildoers the holy Church, which is the Christian people entrusted to thee by God, chastisest the evil, and giveth peace to those who act in accordance with righteousness..."
This formula expresses perfectly the symbolism of the sceptre, which is essentially the materialisation of a vertical line. Now, it is worth pointing out that the straight line in almost all countries is taken as the sign of that which is conformed to order: the Latin words *rectus* and *di-rectus*, that are at the origin of the word *rectitude* and *direct*, are applied firstly to the straight line.[46] If to this we add that the sceptre is *vertically* straight, it will be seen that the idea of ascension, of elevation, is superimposed on that of rectitude, so that it has very properly been said: "The sceptre is the sociological incarnation of the processes of elevation".[47] Here are joined the ideas of power, justice and law, which come from Above, along with the idea of the axis: like the sword, it is a new image of that Axis of the World which is the "geometric place", so to speak, of the royal function, since it is the reflection of the supreme Principle, in relation to which the whole universe is ordered.[48] Further, at its tip, the sceptre ends in a fleur de lis (formerly a lotus), which turns it into a "flowered staff" and a symbol of fertility, a reduction of that other symbol of fertility,

---

46. The reader will find other examples taken from the liturgy, and rather extensive developments on the symbolism of the sceptre, in our study, "La pensée mythique dans le symbolisme du bâton épiscopal," *Actes du Colloque de Liège: Le Mythe, son langage et son message*, published in *Homo religiosus*, v. 8, 1984, (Publications du Centre d'histoire des religions de l'université de Louvain la Neuve).

47. G. Durand, *Les structures anthropologiques de l'imaginaire*, Paris, 1969, p. 138.

48. Another aspect of the axial symbolism of the sceptre is that which refers to the bodily structure of man, in whom the vertebral column constitutes the governing axis of the entire body and the principle of vertical posture, the physical privilege of man among all the animals. See in this respect our recently cited study.

the tree, which is also an axial symbol, a reflection of the Axis of the World assimilated to the Cosmic Tree.[49]

The king of France, and only he, received in his left hand another sceptre called the "hand of justice". It is a staff of half an arm's length, having on its tip an ivory hand with three fingers raised (thumb, index and middle), and wearing a gold ring adorned with a sapphire on the ring finger. The ritual terms it the "staff of virtue and justice", by means of which the prince "gives safety to the good and gives fear to the evil", "shows the way to those that have strayed" and "raises the humble". These formulae largely coincide with those that accompany the bestowal of the sceptre, so that it is somewhat difficult to distinguish the specific symbolism of each of the two objects. An interesting exegesis puts them into relationship with the two columns of the Tree of the Sephiroth, all the more so in that this tree, in one of its meanings, describes the corporeal planimetrical makeup of man; thus, the sceptre in the right hand of the king would correspond to the right hand column of the Sephiroth, designated by reference to man, the "Hand of Mercy (*Hesed*)", and the left column, called the "Hand of Rigour (*Din*)", which may be translated also by the "Hand of Justice". Still, this relationship is not without difficulty owing to the fact that the "hand of justice" of the king looks much like the "hand of blessing" of the Latin Church—which would obviously lead one to relate it to the "Hand of Mercy". No doubt, research is required regarding this, which we cannot undertake to do here. Let us point out, to conclude, that the sapphire on the ring finger is not without relationship with justice; thus, according to the mediaeval authors Marbodius and Konrad of Haim, the sapphire has the beauty of the heavenly throne which, in fact, in apocalyptic literature, is adorned with sapphires; now, the heavenly Throne is directly related to divine Justice.

---

49. Some sceptres, such as that of Dagobert, that of Edward the Confessor, those of the emperors Otto III and Conrad III, had on their tips the figure of a bird: it is a way of remembering that the axis, in its higher part, touches the celestial, for it is deemed that the bird is symbolically an intermediary between earth and heaven.

And now we come to the solemn act of coronation properly so-called. From the altar, the archbishop takes the great crown called the "Crown of Charlemagne", and accompanied by the Twelve Peers in a circle, holds it over the King's head, saying: "God crown thee with the crown of glory and righteousness."

The official institution of the "Peers of the Kingdom" goes back to the eleventh or twelfth centuries, but in reality it is an ancient idea of Germanic inheritance, that of the brothers of the king, or the "Brothers of the kingdom", his immediate counselors. Their role in the ceremony of royal consecration is to confirm the election of the king as representatives of the entire people, twelve being the number of totality. Through them the coronation is the reflection of the collective character of the coronation. Also, it is known that there were six ecclesiastic Peers and six lay Peers; from this point of view, the Peers represent the uniting of the spiritual and temporal authorities for the "creation" of the king.

It is certain that the institution of the Peers is inherited from the tradition that gave birth to the myths of the Round Table, around which were twelve knights; there we have yet another element of the Celtic tradition integrated into French royalty. Moreover, the Round Table founded by Merlin, with its knights, comprised a cosmological symbolism that is expressly affirmed in the story of the Quest for the Holy Grail—it represents the zodiac with its twelve signs, that is to say, the summary of the celestial universe which the ideal king must reproduce on earth. This cosmological symbolism applies in a striking way when the coronation with the circle of the Twelve Peers surrounding the king is considered from this point of view; it is the very image of the cosmic Great Wheel, of which the king is the hub, the motionless centre; he then appears as the *chakravartin*, "He who turns the Wheel", the universal monarch.[50]

THE CROWN · The importance of the crown in the royal institution is largely proved by the fact that the word has become, by metonymy, the synonym of royalty. This stems from the symbolism of the crown, which is formed of two parts: the diadem,

---

50. See Chapter II, p. 64.

that is, the circle of gold that surrounds the head, and the coif, formed generally by small arches that cover the head. The essential element is the diadem. In effect, it rests on the part of the head that is rightly termed the "crown", and is found above the coronary artery. Now, the coronary artery corresponds, in the subtle anatomy, to the chakra termed *sahasrara padma* or the "thousand-petalled Lotus", which we mentioned earlier in connection with the anointing, saying that this *chakra* is "illuminated" when the man has attained the highest degree of spirituality. This amounts to saying, as regards our present subject, that the crown is the symbolic materialisation of this spiritual efflorescence, which moreover appears in the ornaments surmounting the diadem: fleur de lis (the Western substitute for the lotus) or points of gold representing the solar radiance. The crown is a "sign of glory" because it proclaims that the prince is henceforth endowed with the royal Personality, which is of divine nature and luminous. Let us recall that, in the Tree of the Sephiroth, the superior Sephira corresponds to the Divinity, which is rightly termed *Kether*, "Crown". Thus, the crowning is the act by which the new royal man is perfected; it completes or proclaims the new reality brought about by the anointing. The crown is in actuality the tangible sign of "royalty by divine right".

Until now we have spoken of the king alone, and have said nothing concerning the queen, whose role is much more effaced, above all in France. But it must not be forgotten that she was crowned and received an anointing, generally at the same time as her husband. It is true that for her the anointing was not accomplished with the chrism mixed with the oil from the Holy Ampulla, for it is true that she did not personally receive the royal power, but was associated with it in close union with her husband. No doubt there needs to be a study undertaken of the relationship that exists between the royal consecration and matrimony, not only in France but everywhere. In India, in any case, this relationship is so important that a king cannot be consecrated without the queen. In China, the empress played a great part in the rites of government referring to the fertility of the Empire, which is not at all surprising given the well-known correspondences between the female and the Earth. There is another symbolic correspondence that unites woman to the moon, the luminary of fertility, and in royal symbolism the pair king-queen tends to be assimilated to the pair sun-moon; that is why, in Byzantium, during the Prokypsis ceremony, which we spoke of earlier, the emperor was revered as the sun and the empress as the moon.

A relationship at a much higher level, in the case of France, is the one pointed out by Jean Golein in his work on the coronation cited previously: according to him, the royal anointing recalls the descent of the Holy Spirit at Pentecost over the Apostles and the Virgin, and adds that, in the coronation, "the queen represents the Virgin Mary." This is a very interesting statement when we relate it to the scene of the coronation of the Virgin by Christ sculpted on the central portal at Reims, the cathedral of the coronation. The presence of this scene may be fortuitous, as everything in this edifice is related to the coronation of the king. One has to deduce that the links, according to Jean Golein, that unite the queen to the Virgin constitute something of capital importance in the royal ceremony. We cannot undertake a study of such a difficult question within the framework of the present work, but it was necessary at least to mention it, before coming to the last act of the consecration of the king.

THE THRONE · This last act is his enthronement. After the scene of the coronation, the archbishop, with the Peers holding the crown, conducts the king to the throne which has been prepared for him, and seats him in a way such that, as says the ritual, he can be seen by all.

The importance of the enthronement will not escape anyone when it is known that, among the insignia of power, the throne has an eminent value, equal to the crown, and with good reason, since it, like the crown, designates royalty itself. This eminent value comes to it always from its symbolic "charge"; we deliberately employ the word "charge", for the throne is an object of which the value is determined by its symbolical context.

The initial necessary and universally verifiable idea is that the throne is simply a divine object, since "heaven grants it". Among the Assyro-Baylonians this is said expressly, and the throne was so sacrosanct that it received worship. Among the Ashantis of

Africa it is said that the golden throne "descended from the heavens". In India, the sovereign receives the throne from the hands of the priests, who then proclaim his divinity,[51] because the throne "makes the king". It will not have escaped the reader that the same occurs in the French coronation, since it is the archbishop who conducts the king to the throne and seats him upon it.

The fundamental element in the symbolism that confers upon the throne such a value and such a role is, once again, the central and axial element. The throne is assimilated to the centre of the world, to the Axis Mundi, in the form of the cosmic Tree, the cosmic Pillar; it is this that ensues from the study of the royal thrones in the different traditions. At the same time, the throne is assimilated to the cosmos itself; it constitutes a microcosm, a "scale-model of the universe". The ornamentation of the throne emphasises this fundamental symbolism, for we must recall that in traditional art there is no "gratuitous" or purely decorative ornamentation; to decorate an object, only those details are ad-mitted that relate to the symbolism pertaining to the intended use of the object.

The most instructive examples are given to us once again by India, where the royal throne has the extremely important role we have already pointed out.[52] Among the different types en-countered there we will take into account the two that are deco-rated with animals, for they are the ones that allow the establish-ing of a relationship between the thrones of the Near East and those of the Western Middle Ages. In the first place, we have the "lion throne", in which we see the figures of animals raised along the length of the upright supports or joining the armrests at the backrest, so that the legs of the throne are formed by the feet of wild beasts or bovids. Another type of throne displays primar-ily a decoration on the back, constituted by a series of royal or fantastic animals; from the top to the bottom there successively

---

51. *Shatapatha Brahmana*, 12.8.3.4 ff.

52. We have taken the documentation referring to the Indian thrones from the excellent study of J. Auboyer, *Le trône et son symbolisme dans l'Inde ancienne*, Paris, 1949.

appear *nagas* and *makaras* with different birds, in the centre a
lion and a ram, and below an elephant. These animals symbolize
respectively water, air, fire and earth, that is, the four constitutive elements of the universe, of which the throne thus becomes
a reduction. The "lion throne" does not differ from this in its
symbolism, for along with the lions on the uprights, lions are
found arranged in small niches, the ensemble of which evokes
the cosmic Mountain, Mount Meru, to which the throne is then
assimilated. Other secondary decorative elements complete the
symbolism, so that the throne is divided into three zones and
summarizes the four elements, as it is said in the *Atharva Veda*
15, 3 and in the *Kaushitaki Upanishad* 1, 5. In passing, let us note
that the throne is the symbol of the cosmic Mountain independently of the ornamental details, for this symbolism is inherent
in its very structure, since it is always placed on a more or less
elevated pedestal, but always comprising several levels, which in
themselves evoke elevation.

Analogous thrones have been employed in the ancient Near
East. These are seats supported by the feet of four "animals": the
stag, lion, serpent and man. They symbolize the four gates of the
zodiac, the four cardinal directions, and the four seasons of the
year. All this represents the totality of the cosmos subject to both
the temporal and universal power of the king.

Among the animals, the lion, a solar animal, is eminently the
royal animal. It is abundantly represented in the famous throne
of Solomon, made of ivory, covered with fine gold, placed above
six levels, with the back adorned with the heads of bulls, and the
arms constituted by two lions and another twelve lions on the
steps (I Kings 10:18-20).

These six levels, which lead to the seventh, occupied by the
seat of the king, have been related to the *ziggurat*, and this takes
us back to the cosmic Mountain, the divine abode with which
the throne of Solomon, image of the throne of God, is identified:
"This high mountain," we read in the Book of Enoch, "whose
summit is like the throne of God, is where the Holy Great One,
the Lord of Glory, the Eternal King, will sit, when He shall come
down to visit the earth with goodness" (Enoch 25:3). And also,
in the Gospel we read these words of Christ: "But I say unto you,

Swear not at all; neither by heaven; for it is God's throne: nor by the earth; for it is his footstool" (Matt. 5:34-35).[53]

Another expression of the divine throne, of the throne of Yahweh, is the famous Tetramorph, so often sculpted in the tympanum of the Romanesque cathedrals, which presents images of man, the lion, the bull and the eagle, and which is a summary of the universe. Its Mesopotamian origin is certain; it is a variant of the type which we have already pointed out.[54] Now, what is interesting is that the studies of the royal thrones of the Middle Ages lead to the conclusion that they derive, with variations, from the Tetramorph of the vision of Ezekiel reproduced in the tympana of the cathedrals. The more or less constant decoration of these thrones is formed of four beasts, or rather, of the four heads and four feet of beasts—generally, lions, dogs and wolves. A miniature of Charles V shows the king on a throne formed by two lions at the feet and two dragons on the upper part. In any case, the animal that we always meet with is the lion, the solar and royal symbol. An interesting derivation can be seen in the counter-seal of John II the Good; it is a disc bearing the shield of France with the crown on top and at the sides the sceptre and the hand of justice. The shield represents the king, as is well-known. The disc is surrounded by the four figures of the Tetramorph, which means that the king is carried on the divine throne.

The cosmic symbolism of the royal throne is emphasised by the almost constant presence of the canopy or ciborium which is above it, and the interior of the canopy is often blue and scattered with golden stars, or with golden *fleur de lis*, which are the equivalent, in order to show that it symbolizes the heavens. In the *Grandes chroniques de France*, Charles V is represented in this way, and dressed in a blue mantle. This ensemble of the throne with its levels and its canopy constitute a symbolic complex representing the universe, with the earth below, the sky above, and the king seated in the middle, identified with the Axis of the cosmos: he is the universal king presented within the same decor

---

53. See in this respect: Widengren, "A propos du Psaume 109," *Upsala Universitetes Arskrift*, 1941.

54. See this Chapter, p. 232.

we have encountered in imperial China, in particular the chariot of the emperor with its canopy, similar, moreover, to the chariot of the Assyrian king.[55]

Further, the throne covered with the ciborium is similar to the altar, over which is normally raised a ciborium with the form of a cupola: the symbolism here is the same as that of the throne.[56] And this connection is not fortuitous, for there is an undoubted relationship between the throne and the altar. This is so even archaeologically, so to speak, for in India there exist altar-thrones, whose seat is constituted by a slab, and which also serve as altars for offerings. But above all, what has to be understood clearly in the connection we are establishing is that the throne plays a part analogous to that of the altar, the place of sacrifice, in the sense that the throne "sacrifices" the one who sits upon it, by making the individual disappear in order to make the new man appear, as we have said before. For when the king is seated on the throne, covered with the mantle of blue and gold, with the sceptres in hand, the dazzling crown on the forehead, feet on the "footstool of the earth", as the Psalm says, and his head covered by the celestial dome of the canopy, he has been turned into a superhuman being, and the image he presents, for his people, is a true theophany: the joy and veneration that this spectacle arouses arise from the fact that all the sensible signs that constitute it intuitively reveal that the one seated on the throne is truly, by the grace of the rite, the earthly image of Divinity.

And it is this sentiment of the divine presence in the king that was really the bond that united society. Through the coronation, the king became the visible expression, at the same time as the instrument, of the union of God with his people; and it is thus that he accomplished the integration of the community. It has been said that the king formed a "corporation" with his people, that is, a truly organic community. With the coronation, the king "died" as an individual to be reborn as a communitarian Man, integrating in himself each one of the members of the community. This must be understood in the light of the theological doc-

---

55. See Chap I, p. 23 and plate p. 34.

56. See our book, *Le Symbolisme du Temple chrétien*, p. 120.

trine of the Mystical Body: just as on the spiritual plane all the faithful are one in Christ and form a single Body with Him, so too on the temporal plane they are one in the king, the "image of Christ" on earth. The king, the first-born son of the Church, integrates in himself the whole community, recapitulated in his people, just as Christ, "First-born of Creation", recapitulates the entire universe (Ephesians 1:10). Besides, between these two planes there is no separation; on the contrary, as a coronation prayer proclaims: "Almighty and eternal God, Thou hast judged it good to raise Thy servant to the height of royalty, grant him, we pray Thee, that in the course of this age he dispose of the welfare of the community as a whole, in the measure that he not separate himself from Thy truth by a crooked path." In this essential sacral political conception, the temporal welfare in the last analysis is no more than an aspect of the spiritual salvation to which it ought to lead. Thus, in the oaths exchanged in 853-854 AD between Lothair I and Charles the Bald, oaths in which they commended to Heaven their children and their kingdoms, both princes expressed themselves as follows: "We wish to unite ourselves indissolubly by faith and by works, so as to be united in Christ and that ye be one with us."[57]

By integrating society into the cosmic order as a reflection of the heavenly order, the crowned king effects this union and bestows peace upon it. The temporal power, intimately united to the spiritual authority, realizes with it a harmony capable of creating a collective conscience ultimately ruled by the heavenly King. This is the most general end sought by sacred royalty; and only a sacred royalty can arrive as this result. This point has to be emphasised, for it is crucially important in judging the forms of society. The consecrated king unites society by transforming the individuals into members of a mystical Body that raises them above themselves. Laicized political regimes act in the opposite direction, atomising the community, leaving individuals increasingly alone and isolated; and thus isolated, a viable society cannot be constituted. All that remains is to try to *group* them, hence form a *collectivity*, which is something quite different from

---

57. *Mon. Germ. Capit. Reg. Franc.*, II.73.

a *body*, because it lacks a principle of *union*; from then on it is a rule by *parties*, with *division* and interminable struggles ensuing. The temptation is great, therefore, in order to avoid anarchy, to proceed towards *unification*, which is the very negation of *union*, and which is necessarily produced by force. This possibility is all the more to be feared when it is required by a deviation of the collective psychism. In fact, it is certain that the human group aspires to be ruled by sovereignty which, as the psychologists say, is an archetype in virtue of which the group is hypostasized in the chief, as we have described at length above. But this archetype of sovereignty, as it tends to occur in the constitutive elements of the psychism, is of a double nature, both beneficent and malefic.[58] The danger is that the entire being of the chief can be absorbed by the mass, which, as such, is moved by the pulsations of the unconscious; and this occurs almost inevitably if the chief is merely a man like any other, if he is not *aspired upwards*, so to speak, by a transcendent Power which saves him, and at the same time saves the people, from the quicksand of the dark and anonymous forces into which they would sink; for from such cases dictatorships are born, whose examples unfortunately abound before our eyes, since besides dictatorships which are nominally declared to be such, the phenomenon to which we allude can be confirmed in many political regimes whose deceptive appearances conceal a mass totalitarianism.

On the contrary, in a community of sacral type, each member, far from being annihilated, has the means to realize himself fully, for the king, by integrating in himself each subject, promotes him to royal rank. Here the archetype of sovereignty works in the authentic sense: the man is aspired upwards, to employ the terms we have just used above.

This participation of all in the royal function is particularly marked in the French monarchic tradition, as we shall see, but it does not belong to it exclusively. We encounter the idea clearly expressed in India, where it is said that Vishnu—one of the royal

---

58. To this ambivalence of the sovereign on the microcosmic plane there corresponds on the macrocosmic plane the opposition between the "King of the World" and the one whom the Gospel calls the "Prince of this world".

gods—is in the people as he is in the king.[59] Of course, this must not be understood in a "democratic" sense that would have sovereignty reside in the people as its source in the same sense as in the divinity. What is meant is that royalty, the source of which is Vishnu *in divinis*, is infused in the people through the channel of the prince which operates as a "condenser" of *mana*, if the expression be allowed. And that is how the words of St. Louis to his army at Damietta must be understood: "My friends and my faithful, we shall be invincible if we are inseparable in our love.... I am not the king of France, I am not the Holy Church, it is you, inasmuch as you are all the king who are the Holy Church."[60] Astonishing words; but they must be understood in the light of theology, as we shall see shortly. Firstly, in support of what we said about India, let us also recall the thought of ancient Egypt, which has the same meaning. We have previously seen that the essential end of the royal function in Egypt was to maintain the *Maat* in the kingdom, that is to say, justice in the broadest sense, which comprises divine peace and harmony.[61] And so how is this obtained? The answer is the following way: in the first place, the king is nourished on the *Maat*: "I have offered to Amon," says the queen Hatshepsut, "the *Maat* that he loves, for I know that he lives from it. She also is my bread, and I drink her dew. Am I not one with him?"[62] Hence, through the king the *Maat* passes into all of his subjects, who live from it, as is proved by many declarations which have been preserved.[63] The pharaoh was something completely different from the species of the absolutist tyrant who reigned over a nation of slaves, which is the image that for long some have tried to foist upon us. In the eyes of all, the pharaoh symbolized the end which every mortal must attain: the realized man, the true Man. He was the living

---

59. Rangawivami Aiyangar, *Raja dharma*, p. 108.

60. Mathieu Paris, *Chronica maiora*, cited in Michaud, *Histoire des Croisades*, v.3, pp. 44-465.

61. See Chapter II, p. 47.

62. Inscription of Speos Artemidos (*Urk*, IV, 384).

63. See in this respect S. Morenz, *La religion égyptienne*, p. 162 ff.

image and model of the realisation of the perfect man, which is the goal of existence.

These reflections allow us to better understand the bearing of the words of St. Louis at Damietta, words which are nothing other than the application of the New Testament doctrine that we have mentioned and which teaches that the Christian people constitutes a "*royal* priesthood". The Christian is called upon to be "king", that is to say, realized man, perfect man. The Perfect Man is Christ, the archetype of our spiritual realisation; but this is accomplished on the temporal plane and within the framework of the visible society. To this society the King is given, the first man of the realm, who incarnates and symbolises the way of spiritualisation in the midst of temporal life, not as an individual, but as an incarnate principle, as the image of Christ, the model that must be attained through the king. Contemplating the king, the subject contemplates the idealized image of that which he must become, namely, a "son of God"; he contemplates this and admires the image of his own person virtually glorified and become like Christ. Thereafter he has but to keep within himself the remembrance of this image so as to make of it the guide and end of his life.

Such, in the last analysis, is the reason for being of the royal function, and all its other tasks have no purpose other than to contribute to this realisation.

EPILOGUE

At the conclusion of this examination of sacred royalties throughout the ancient world, the question could legitimately be asked why an institution that maintained itself everywhere without essential changes for millennia collapsed suddenly, and also everywhere, in the space of an extremely short time compared to its previous duration—for the traditional monarchies have disappeared over a very short interval during the course of the last two centuries.[1]

The explanations that historians and sociologists—we mean serious authors, not doctrinaires or partisans blinded by their ideologies or prejudices—give for this phenomenon are not completely satisfactory, for they do not go back to the profound source of the events and ideas that have provoked the disappearance of which we speak. In fact, the political philosophy that inspired the revolutions, starting in the eighteenth century, which drove out the ancient royalties, is merely the culmination of a transformation in ideas and institutions that comes from afar, not only in time, but also in the spiritual order.

To understand such an upheaval, which has altogether changed the way of living of mankind from top to bottom, one has to consider closely the conception of traditional society—a conception that we have outlined in the third chapter—to discover the true reason for its historical developments up until the moment of its disappearance.

---

1. The only sacred royalty that subsists to this day that we know of is that of the emperor of Japan. It is true that there, as well, are prophets armed with ideals of the new age imposed by decree of the "Abolition of the divinity of the emperor". The decree is ridiculous, and without real effect, for a decree does not change what is in the nature of things; after the decree, as well as before it, the Nippon empire remains a sacred monarchy, for it is the inheritor of a tradition that has never been interrupted.

Traditional society and political power rest on a triple foundation: a metaphysical and religious foundation, a specifically sociological and structural foundation, and finally, a cosmological foundation that conditions its evolution.

The first is constituted by the doctrine of the two swords that we have expounded in detail. Let us only recall the essential, in order that the rest of our explanations may be perfectly clear. All social and political thought ought to be attached to a metaphysical principle; if this principle is denied, then the entire structure is destroyed. This metaphysical principle is none other than the affirmation of the superiority of the spiritual over the material in general, and of the spiritual over the temporal at the social and political level, which is to say, in the final analysis, the superiority of the divine and universal over the human and individual. The temporal or political power depends on the spiritual authority, which is its guarantor. This dependence is manifested by the coronation of kings, who are legitimated when they have received the investiture and the consecration implying their submission to the divine law and the transmission of a spiritual influence necessary for the regular exercise of their function.

When one passes from considering the metaphysical principle of power to considering its application, two other factors come into play: the sociological element and the cosmological element. Human society, in which and over which government is exercised, has a proper, natural structure, which consists in a hierarchical coordination of functions: this is the doctrine of castes, which we have explained above according to the Hindu model, clearly specifying that the Hindu system is to be found, in analogous forms, in the majority of traditional societies. Hence, the "Three Orders" of the Western Middle Ages. Let us briefly recall that, in the Hindu system, there exist four castes: the Brahmins, the Kshatriyas, the Vaishyas and the Shudras; the first two correspond to the functions of spiritual authority and temporal power, priesthood and royalty; the Vaishyas, to the economic function; the Shudras, the manual workers, to the most material functions. These castes are obviously hierarchical; the Kshatriyas, warriors and rulers, are subject to the Brahmins; the Shudras are subject to the Vaishyas, and these last two groups remain under the authority of the Kshatriyas. The same occurs in the normal political and social order, in which case, since the spiritual element vivifies the entire social body from above and harmonises it in accordance with the divine laws, the society and the civil government comply with their final end, as it has been defined by St. Thomas Aquinas in the passage of his book that we have reproduced in chapter III.

Such is the traditional social structure viewed from a static point of view and, as it were, outside time. But an existing society undergoes the influence of time, which rules its dynamics. As with all manifested reality, society, together with the individuals that comprise it, is subject to the law of the evolution of the cosmos. That is why we see the intervention of the third fundamental element of the social and political constitution: cyclical evolution. Time, in fact, does not unfold, as the moderns believe, in a linear fashion, connected with the affirmation of indefinite progress. Human and cosmic becoming unfold in a cyclical manner, as it has been taught everywhere and always. A humanity such as ours unfolds throughout a great period called, according to Hindu terminology, a *manvantara*, covering 64,800 years.[2] This long period is divided into four sub-periods, called *yugas* or "ages": the *Krita Yuga*, *Dwapara Yuga*, *Treta Yuga* and the *Kali Yuga*, which correspond to those of the Greco-Latin tradition: the golden age, silver age, bronze age and iron age. The succession of these four ages constitutes the process of cyclic descent. This process is the descent of manifestation from its essential pole to its substantial pole; it is a process of progressive materialisation. In the first era, the longest one, humanity lives in a state of sanctity and happiness; it is the earthly Paradise. Then, little by little, this state becomes degraded, and the last stage, the shortest—6,480 years—and which is our age, constitutes its lowest phase: its Hindu name, *Kali yuga*, signifies "dark age", because it is that of the obscuration of principial truths. And its Greco-Latin name, "iron age",[3] signifies nothing differ-

---

2. The very basis of the doctrine of cycles, as well as of the numbers we cite, rests on astronomical and astrological observations.

3. Let us specify that the expression "Iron Age" has little to do with that

ent, but adds the note of hardness that necessarily accompanies all materialisation. However, this decadence is neither total nor homogeneous. The profile of this dark Age is the result of two forces, the descending force and the ascending force, which always act concomitantly in the world, with the predominance of the descending force in the Iron Age, it is true, but also with the possibility of more or less durable rectifications due to the ascending force. Moreover, the Fourth Age, like the others moreover, is also subdivided into four sub-periods that correspond analogically to the four ages of the *manvantara*; and the analogical subdivisions are repeated in much shorter fractions; here we have the dynamic scheme that conditions the evolution of all historic periods of manifestation. This descending evolution of humanity is defined by a progressive loss of intellectuality and spirituality, which are substituted by a human philosophy, that is to say, limited to the individual reason and to a state of mind that confines itself to the empirical study of sensible facts and to the search for a purely material progress, in short, an ideal, if one may say so, limited exclusively to man and his lowest necessities. Such is the general trend of the evolution of the Dark Age; but taking into account what we have said concerning the two antagonist concomitant forces, this descent has been interrupted by rectifications, the most spectacular being that which Christianity brought about, which however, does not check the general evolution.

The conception of society and of the political regimen follows this cyclic evolution of humanity, for at all levels there is a correspondence between the four ages of the cycle and the four castes, so that to the cyclic descent there corresponds a social degradation marked by the predominance of the corresponding caste with its manner of seeing and its particular qualities—or defects. The normal hierarchy of the castes is in equilibrium during the golden age; the equilibrium is perfect in the primordial golden age, and it is more or less re-established in the analogous "golden age" of a given particular cycle within a particular society. This equilibrium of the normal hierarchy of the castes is

---

of the "Iron Age" employed by the specialists of prehistory.

broken by the phenomenon that has been termed the *Revolt of the kshatriyas*: that is, the possessors of the temporal power in revolt against the spiritual authority of the brahmins—to whom they ought to be subject—and they declare themselves independent, and henceforth independent of the divine Law, in the final analysis, or even try to reduce the priesthood to servitude.

It is the Dark Age that has seen the true usurpation of the kshatriyas come about, above all in its last part, which begins in the sixth century before Christ, and continues to the present. But the first manifestations of this revolt certainly began in a previous epoch, for we have echoes of it in narratives of a mythic character. It is these intense struggles between the two castes that are referred to in the story of Parashurama, the incarnation of Vishnu, who warred against the rebellious kshatriyas and vanquished them, which corresponds to a rectification. And no doubt the same occurs in the story of the competition between the Brahmin Vasishta, the priest of the Purohita family, a solar family, and the Kshatriya Vishvamitra, prince of the lunar dynasty, who was overcome by the Brahmin. Curiously, but understandably, in the last analysis, is that the Celtic tradition has a totally parallel description inscribed in a Gallo-Roman sculpted stone found in Neumagen: in it can be seen a bear overthrowing a boar. Now, it is well known that these animals are symbols of the two functions, above all in the Celtic zone; the bear of the kshatriya, and the boar of the priesthood.[4] In ancient Tibet, King Grigum died in combat as a consequence of the rivalry between him and the "priesthood"; and there are other echoes of the hostility of the kings towards Lamaism, which finally triumphed and established a theocracy. In China, the events took place above all in the Age of the Tyrannies: a struggle against the Confucians and Taoists. The "legalists" tried to install an autocratic state in which the king would be totally free to make the laws, which would be based on nothing other than his will; a conception totally opposed to that of the "son of Heaven", who is bound to observe custom as the expression of the higher Law, and excluding all whim.

---

4. See *Espérandieu*, v. 11, no. 5206.

In the cycle of the Christian civilisation in the West, the revolt began rather early in the Middle Ages. Firstly, there was the
"Investiture Struggle", which opposed Henry IV and Henry V
to the Papacy in the 11th and 12th centuries. More serious, later,
was the "Struggle between the Priesthood and the Empire", with
Frederick I Barbarossa.

Frederick was not a tyrant, as has sometimes been said; he
tried to restore the Empire to the form Charlemagne and Otto III
had given it, to be able to oppose the excesses of the authority of
the Pope, a fact which must also not be forgotten or minimised.
But however legitimate the opposition to these excesses may be,
up to a point, these did not at all justify the conduct adopted by
Frederick, who instigated the election of an anti-pope against
the recognised pope, Alexander III, thus making himself guilty
of an attempt at schism. And no less guilty was his claim, supported by bishops and theologians devoted to him, to establish
that *power came to him directly from God*, and hence there was no
reason to heed any order coming from the ecclesiastic authority;
a claim that other princes, progressively more numerous as time
went on, expressed with increasing forcefulness.

The best known case of the second part of the Middle Ages,
and also the one which perhaps had the most influence on the
subsequent evolution of the political conceptions in Europe, is
that of Philip the Fair. No doubt, in the quarrel that opposed
the king to Boniface VIII, the pope could be blamed for having been clumsy and for having fallen somewhat into a desire
for power; but again, as in the hostilities between the emperor
Frederick Barbarossa and Alexander III, there is no common
measure between the errors of the Pope and the rebellion of the
king. In reality, when the pope published the bulls *Ausculta fili*
and *Unam sanctam*, in connection with the matter of the Archbishop of Pamiers, he did no more than recall the traditional
doctrine of the two swords and the supremacy of the spiritual
authority. And it is against this, precisely, that Philip the Fair
rebelled, and the matter of Saisset simply furnished an occasion.
In dealing with his affairs with Rome, he made the mistake of
sending the sinister Nogaret, a legalist, a descendant of a heretic
and perhaps a heretic himself. What followed is well known, as

well as the sad events of Anagni in 1303, in the course of which Boniface VIII was insulted by the representative of France, and perhaps struck.

All this was in accordance with the evolution of political thought; increasingly, then, it was sought to erect the power of the State and the total independence of the prince. Philip the Fair had an anonymous pamphlet circulated in the kingdom in which he proclaimed in particular: "The direction of the temporality of the kingdom pertains to the king alone and no one else; and he neither has nor does he recognise any superior and has no intention of submitting or subjecting himself to anyone in all that concerns the temporal in his kingdom."[5] The royal legalists, appealing to Roman Law, inspired other pamphlets and treatises in the same vein.

This difference, born from the matter with Saisset, is inseparable from the matter of the Templars, their trial and their suppression, for it is the other and complementary side of the struggle against the spiritual authority. Indeed, the Templars, by their dual character as monks and knights, incarnated an important aspect of the spiritual authority, different from that of the papacy, but perfectly allowed by it, and which, in the thought of their founder, St. Bernard, was to assure—thanks precisely to their original character pertaining both to the "brahmin" and the "kshatriya"—the maintenance of a harmonious equilibrium of the civil society within the orthodox traditional perspective. Now, it is just this that constituted an obstacle to the new burgeoning political conception in which governments wished to make themselves totally independent, thus opening the way to political absolutism.

---

5. In P. Dupuy, *Histoire du différand entre le pape Boniface VIII et Philippe le Bel*, Paris, 1655. The reader will have noticed that this text, commenting on the Gospel text "My kingdom is not of this world," commits the nonsensical heretical error that we have denounced in chapter IV. As for "Render unto Caesar that which is Caesar's," it alludes to the *distinction* between the two powers, but most definitely does not imply their *independence*.

As we have said, this new conception was the work of the legalists who had their seat in the parliaments, aided at times by some theologians, it must be said, who followed in their steps. Thus, little by little, "gallicism" was born in France, which was only one of the forms of a general movement of political philosophy. And this, in the seventeenth century, led to the abrupt formulation of the "Declaration of 1682" of the French bishops, inspired by Louis XIV, and which is the clear echo of the text previously cited of the time of Philip the Fair. Here is the essential passage:

> God gave to the blessed Peter, to his successors, the vicars of Christ, and to the Church itself, authority over the spiritual matters and concerning eternal salvation, and not over that which pertains to the civil order and temporal order, according to these words of the Lord: *My kingdom is not of this world*, and these others: *Render unto Caesar the things which are Caesar's, and unto God the things that are God's.*

This teaching of the Apostle: *Let every soul be subject unto the higher powers. For there is no power but of God: the powers that be are ordained of God. Whosoever therefore resisteth the power, resisteth the ordinance of God*, must be understood as follows: the kings and the princes have not been placed under the authority of the ecclesiastic power by God's disposition for the things of the temporal government; they cannot be deposed either directly or indirectly in virtue of the power of the keys possessed by the Church; their subjects cannot be freed from the obedience which they owe, nor from the oaths of fealty they have sworn. This doctrine, necessary for the peace of the Catholic people and as useful for the Church as for the State, must be respected, for it is fully in conformity with the word of God, with the tradition of the Fathers and with the examples of the saints.

It is not surprising that some bishops could have come to this. They were led to this less by their servility towards the princes, as it is usually claimed, than by the strayings of those theologians to whom we alluded just before, and who since the end of the Middle Ages developed theses of political theology that were completely heterodox. Thus, in 1324, Marcilius of Padua, rector of the University of Paris, and Jean de Jandum published a writing titled *Defensor pacis*, in which they affirm *the pure natural character of the State without any metaphysical reference*; all authority is constituted, they said, by the legislator; spiritual life is totally distinct from material life, that is to say, from the temporal, so that the *Divine Law cannot subject the state*. In 1338, William of Occam published his treatise *De potestate et juribus Romani imperii*, in which he lowered the papacy, seeing in it merely a strictly spiritual power, and exalted the empire by affirming that the emperor derived his power from God alone and, consequently, did not have to render account to anyone.

That was the justification of the "revolt of the kshatriyas" against the spiritual authority on the part of the very ones who should have recalled the orthodox doctrine, but who no doubt preferred to serve the desire for power of the rebellious princes. We hasten to say, however, that the majority of the theologians did not fall into this heterodoxy, and also, that the spiritual authority at its highest level never ceased to defend against all odds the traditional orthodox doctrine. If any reproach can be levelled at it, it is to have committed an error that in the end turned against it, when it decided, as we said previously, to no longer confer upon royalty the anointing of the Holy Chrism on the head, but solely with the oil of the catechumens on the arms (with the exception of the king of France), specifying that through this it wished to distinguish clearly the royalty from the priesthood, as Innocent III, in 1204, and Alexander IV, in 1260, proclaimed. Parallel to this it valorised the coronation, and no longer the anointing, as constitutive of royalty. As a consequence of this, force was given to the principle which says, "The person does not make the king, but the Law," a principle which in itself is not false, but which only has an authentic value within the perspective of sacred, integral royalty, and not in royalty that has been diminished in relation to its archetype. Having done this, the Church opened the way to a distinction from the temporal power that became increasingly pronounced, and which led in a manner that should have been easy to foresee, to its desire for independence.

This desire for independence on the part of the temporal power goes hand in hand with individualism, that is to say, the reduction of the entire civilisation to human elements alone; and also with naturalism, which is the rejection, in practice at least, of the supernatural. This is what is clearly seen in the heterodox theologians cited above. Individualism and nationalism make their appearance with the usurpation of the "kshatriyas". To be sure, not all the Christian princes behaved as rebels against the Church; nevertheless, although the framework of government kept on being traditional and theoretically submitted to the spiritual authority, in practice politics tended to become increasingly independent of it and to laicise itself; and the sciences of government, particularly law, tended to become secularised, and in so doing, moreover, followed the general movement of the whole culture since the age of the Renaissance. Thus in minimising, or in neglecting in fact, and in varying degrees according to the case, the stable principle constituted by the spiritual authority, the "kshatriyas" gave themselves—and the temporal power—over to change and to upheaval, so that their rebellion against the supremacy of the spiritual brought in its train a cascade of upheavals. The lower castes asked themselves why they remained subject to the "kshatriyas", for as soon as the superior principle of the hierarchy is denied, there no longer remains any foundation for the hierarchy, and any caste believes it is authorised to rule. Besides, if there is no principle based on *wisdom*, what prevails is *force*, and force is greater with those who are most numerous.

In the following stage of cyclical evolution, the "kshatriya" has been dispossessed by the "vaishya", the merchants in the broadest sense, and in the West, by the bourgeoisie. And it noteworthy how, in revolting, the "kshatriyas" were led to put themselves at the level of the "vaishyas", and to place them increasingly in the most important posts. This was a phenomenon that would be determinative for the subsequent evolution: thus, it is well known that it was the bourgeoisie who in all of Europe made the revolutions which either ushered in the constitutional monarchies or purely and simply suppressed the kings. To justify their action, the bourgeoisie based themselves on a theory that inspired the Declaration of 1789, namely, that sovereignty resides in the nation as a whole. They did not invent this theory, for it had appeared several centuries earlier in the heterodox theologians cited a moment ago: Marsilius of Padua, William of Occam, and even, somewhat earlier, John of Salisbury, all of whom in their writings held that the political power belongs to the people as a whole and that the people delegate it to the king. This theory made incessant headway in the minds of the bourgeoisie, the nobles of the robe, and even the high nobility, aided, in the seventeenth and eighteenth centuries, by the Jesuits, who had adopted it, following their celebrated doctor Suarez, and they spread it ceaselessly among the alumni of their numerous colleges. It was the complete inversion of the traditional doctrine, and it was already political laicism, from which the following generations were to extract all the logical consequences. The bourgeois revolution soon got left behind, and the "shudras", also in the name of the new proclaimed principle of sovereignty, made haste to secure power.

Following these upheavals, the entire social mentality was changed. In reality, the "kshatriyas", even the rebels, still have a conception of things in which real knowledge and true principles of conduct subsist, and also a certain greatness, the sense of honour and heroism. With the lower castes, on the contrary, everything is reduced to the profane; the "vaishyas" by their mental nature, as we have already said, give preponderance to the *economic*; as for the "shudras", what is most important for them are more or less material realities, and so the last stage of descent is arrived at, in which a completely materialist society arises, in which the power has no other concern than to assure the greatest productivity of material goods so as to satisfy the greatest number possible of the lower desires. This is the state of things that we have before our eyes. Let us hasten to add that in saying this we are not driven by any feeling of contempt regarding the lower castes; these have their qualities, which pertain to their corresponding role, and these qualities give what they are supposed to give when the social hierarchy is respected and each is in his place, for then the influence of the spiritual principle that quickens the social body regulates the functioning of the lower activities and allows both the community and the individuals to rise above them in order to realise a spiritual destiny. But the disorder turns fatal and catastrophic the moment that the characteristic tendencies of the inferior castes becomes the motor and inspiration of the entire life of the social group.

We say that this is a catastrophic disorder because it brings in its train a fall of the society that is increasingly rapid. This is the characteristic trait of cyclic evolution in its last phase; we are witnesses to a continual acceleration of events, in virtue of a cosmic law comparable to that which is applied, in physics, to the fall of bodies, in that the velocity of this fall accelerates as the distance of the moving object from its starting point increases. In addition it is noteworthy that many people, although they have no knowledge of the doctrine of the temporal cycles or of its laws, are completely aware of this acceleration of history and this shrinking of the duration of time that afflicts our age. As we have said, this is in fact the last phase of the great cycle of our humanity, that "end of days" (let us point out that it is not the "end of the world") of which the Scriptures speak.

This acceleration and shrinking of time enables us to answer the question we posed at the beginning of this epilogue, regarding the swift and almost simultaneous disappearance of sacred royalties. The reason for this will be readily understood: the period which began approximately two centuries ago corresponds to the very latest phase of the cycle. The acceleration of the fall explains the swiftness in the disappearance of traditional social and political forms. The fact that the ends of the particular cycles of various civilisations are coinciding with the end of the universal cycle explains the universality of the phenomenon.

But then a new question arises, which many will have asked themselves: what can we expect in the near future? We cannot enlarge on the answer, for it would be the object of an exposition that would take us away from our subject. We shall content ourselves with saying what is essential, namely, that in the wake of the great upheavals inherent in this end of the cycle, when all the most inferior possibilities of this cycle have been exhausted and have been "judged", a new cycle will begin, for the end of one cycle necessarily coincides with the beginning of a new one. It is then that the re-establishment of all things in order will come about. And this re-establishment—to return to our subject—will be the work of the one who certain mediaeval texts that we have cited call the "Great Monarch"—the incarnation of integral sacred royalty, who will sweep away the last vestiges of the dark powers. For prior to this, these dark forces, which act in the entire world at the present time, will engage in still many more struggles, to the very point of perhaps causing a false universal "great monarch to arise",[6] for it is in the nature of these dark powers, at these moments, to produce "prodigies" and to parody by anticipation the manifestation of the forces of the powers of light.[7] Christ has warned us; we have only to follow his counsel: "Watch and pray."

---

6. The Hitlerian adventure—the occult and dark roots of which are certain—may be considered to be the first foreshadowing of the false universal monarch. Hitler wished to re-establish the Roman-Germanic Holy Empire with a universal reach, and with this perspective in mind he ordered the imperial insignia—among which was the crown said to be that of Charlemagne—to be sent from Vienna to Nuremberg, where they had been during the Middle Ages. This first parody resulted in failure, and very naive were those who believed in it. That which possibly will come about will be capable of deceiving many more by taking on the appearance of the authentic sacred royalty, for it has been said that the "Angels of darkness" can disguise themselves as "Angels of light".

7. Concerning one of these parodies, which at present deceive so many modern scientists, one may benefit from reading the excellent work of J. Robin, *Les Objets volants non identifiés ou la Grande Parodie*, Ed. de la Maisnie, 1979.

INDEX

activity of the ruler, 61-2, 97-8; *see also* non-action

administrative function, 62, 63, 71, 96, 204

agrarian rites, 69-70, 112, 201, 203

Ahuramazda, 30, 32, 57, 164

Alexander, 14, 146, 185

Alexander III, 244

Alexander IV, 247

Amenophis III, 10, 11

Amon, 10, 47, 237

anointing, 27, 106-107, 155-6, 173, 178, 196, 202, 212, 214, 220-3, 230, 247

Anthesteria, 89

apotheosis, 14, 29, 39, 158-9; *see also* death

Aquinas, St Thomas, 96-7, 136, 139, 188, 210, 241

architecture, 52-8, 60-1, 64, 67n, 205-7

Aristotle, 5, 36, 88-9, 99, 188-9

Arthur, 39, 192, 216-7

Ashanti, 7

ashvamedha, 45, 73-4

astrology, 55, 56, 60, 67, 81, 128, 165, 182, 199, 228, 241n

Athens, 14, 36, 82, 89, 90

augury, 37, 83, 89

Augustine, St, 137, 200

Augustus, 147, 150, 157, 186, 192

Aurelian, 14

Australia, 50n

Avalon, 216

Axis Mundi, 16n, 21-3, 27-8, 36, 48, 56, 61, 66, 67, 97, 164, 217, 220, 225n, 226, 231, 233

Babylonia, 33-5

body politic, 101, 235-6

Boniface VIII, 139-40, 169, 244-5

Buddha, 28-9, 64

Caligula, 14

cardinal points, 12, 26, 36n, 49, 52, 56, 66-8, 70, 72, 126, 205, 232

castes, 26, 41, 59-60, 91-3, 95-6, 120, 132, 240-3, 248-50; *see also* revolt of the *kshatriyas*

chakra, 222, 229

chakravartin, 56, 64, 68, 128, 228

Charlemagne, 39, 178, 180, 181, 184, 185, 186, 189, 192, 196, 228, 244, 251n

Chesterton, G.K., 2, 3, 4

China, 19-25, 65-8

Chrism, 155, 211-2, 220-2, 229

Christ as king, *see* temporal power

Chuang-Tzu, 63

clothes, 223

Clovis, 191-3, 196, 210

collectivity, 101, 235

consecration, 99-100, 208-38

Constantine, 84n, 141, 145, 151-2, 157-8, 160, 162-4, 172, 173-5, 187

contemplation, 97-8, 222, 238

cord, 15-16, 164n

coronation, 208-38

corpus immortale, 223, 225

cosmic symbolism, 162-72, 198-207

Crete, 35

crown, 8, 11, 12, 34, 38, 45, 64, 76, 106, 108n, 123, 126-8, 133, 156, 157, 165, 169-70, 170n, 172, 178, 181-2, 192, 195, 196, 208, 209-10, 214, 217, 222-3, 228-30, 233, 234;

Three Orders, 240
Three Treasures (*Shansu no Shinki*), 17-18
Three Worlds (*tribhuvana*), 27, 132-3, 170n
throne, 8, 11, 12n, 18, 27, 29, 56, 64, 107, 126, 230-4; *see also* hetimasia
Thucydides, xi, 84
tiara, 31, 34, 133, 169-72
Tibet, 15-16
Tradition, ix, xi, xiii, 3, 6, 49, 50, 51, 77, 120, 138, 144, 146, 209
Transcendent Man, 23
transmission of authority, 137-9
triumph, 38, 84, 122, 152, 155,
True Man, 21-3, 61, 64, 66, 81, 117n, 213
Turkic people, 15
tyranny, 2, 139, 243

vajra, 45, 220

vermillion, 38
Versailles, 205-7
vicar, 138, 177, 194,
Virgil, 147-9, 158
virtues of the ruler, 8, 17, 62, 64, 65, 66, 68, 78-80, 81, 183
Vishnu, 26, 28, 45, 74, 86, 236-7, 243
Voltaire. F., 2

war, 82-6, 96, 118n
Western Roman Empire *see* Holy Roman Empire
whip, 12
wilder Jaeger, 39

xvarnah, 31

Yahweh, 107-9, 113-6, 119, 131
Yudhishthira, 31

Zen, 17

TITLES IN THE MATHESON MONOGRAPHS

Ascent to Heaven in Islamic and Jewish Mysticism,
by Algis Uždavinys, 2011

Christianity & Islam: Essays on Ontology and Archetype,
by Samuel Zinner, 2010

*The Gospel of Thomas: In the Light of Early Jewish, Christian and Islamic
Esoteric Trajectories*, by Samuel Zinner, 2011

*The Living Palm Tree: Parables, Stories and Teachings from the
Kabbalah*, by Mario Satz, translated by Juan Acevedo, 2010

Louis Massignon: The Vow and the Oath,
by Patrick Laude, translated by Edin Q. Lohja, 2011

Orpheus and the Roots of Platonism,
by Algis Uždavinys, 2011

Sacred Royalty: From The Paraoh to The Most Christian King,
by Jean Hani, tanslated by Gustavo Polit, 2011